WITCHCRAFT
Goes
Mainstream

BROOKS
ALEXANDER

HARVEST HOUSE PUBLISHERS

EUGENE, OREGON

Cover by Koechel Peterson & Associates, Inc., Minneapolis, Minnesota

WITCHCRAFT GOES MAINSTREAM
Copyright © 2004 by Brooks Alexander
Published by Harvest House Publishers
Eugene, Oregon 97402
www.harvesthousepublishers.com

Library of Congress Cataloging-in-Publication Data
Alexander, Brooks, 1936–
  Witchcraft goes mainstream / Brooks Alexander.
    p. cm.
  Includes bibliographical references (p.   ).
  ISBN 0-7369-1221-5 (pbk.)
  1. Witchcraft. I. Title.
  BF1566.A44 2004
  261.2'994--dc22   2004013663

Printed in the United States of America

04 05 06 07 08 09 10 11 12 /VP-KB/ 10 9 8 7 6 5 4 3 2 1

For those who helped

Contents

My Encounters with Modern Witchcraft 7

1. "Witchcraft". . . "Neopaganism". . . What Exactly
   Are We Talking About? 27

2. The Halloween Witch Is Dead: The Changing
   Face of Modern Witchcraft 45

3. Teens and the Media: Witchcraft in
   Popular Entertainment. 73

4. Witchcraft in Popular Entertainment:
   The Craft, Buffy, and Beyond 91

5. Three Myths About Modern Witchcraft. 121

6. Witchcraft for Real: Was There,
   or Wasn't There? 143

7. From Witchcraft to Wicca: 1700–2000 177

   Conclusion: Witchcraft, Christianity,
   and Cultural Change 217

   A Final Word from the Author: What Now? 251

   Appendix A: Witchcraft in the Military 259

   Appendix B: "Getting Ready":
   Suggested Reading. 271

   Bibliography 279

My Encounters
with Modern Witchcraft

✢ ✢ ✢

"Nonsense draws evil after it."
—C.S. LEWIS

I FIRST HEARD THE RUMORS OF modern-day "witchcraft" in the summer of 1968, back when I was still a denizen of the counterculture.

I had "turned on, tuned in, and dropped out" of law school at the University of Texas in 1965 to follow the psychedelic/occult/Eastern religious promises of experience and enlightenment. The currents of cultural change washed me westward, and I eventually landed in California—first in Los Angeles, then in San Diego, and finally in San Francisco and the Haight–Ashbury district for the grand psychedelic carnival they called "the Summer of Love" in 1967.

By the following summer, I had left "the City" behind and was living among the redwood trees in the coastal rain forest of Northern California—one of many refugees from the corruption and exploitation that had overtaken the counterculture with dizzying rapidity. One balmy evening I gathered with a group of friends to share some food, companionship, and conversation. Among those assembled was a traveler, recently arrived from a visit to several communes on the East Coast, including one in New York state. The pilgrim held our attention as he told of meeting a group of people who actually—and openly—called themselves "witches," who followed the old nature-gods, and (as he put it) "do magic, and make potions and cast spells and all that stuff—but for real." He said he could have been initiated and have become a "witch" himself if he had been willing to extend his visit, but he felt that he was "on a different path," and so continued his journey.

The reaction of his listeners (myself included) was a curious mix of aversion and fascination. In part we were taken aback that anyone would adopt such a negative label on purpose, but in equal part we were intrigued at the hint of deep secrets and dark, mysterious powers. In short, we were both repulsed and drawn—and drawn in part *because* of the repulsion. In retrospect, both of those reactions appear to be typical, and both have plainly played a part in the appeal and spread of the modern Witchcraft movement.

That dinner-party brush with modern Witchcraft left a deep impression on my mind, but it was the last time I had occasion to think about the subject for several years. By the fall of 1969 I had became a Christian—among the first to be touched by a wave of spiritual conversions that swept through the counterculture in the early 1970s (dubbed later by the media as the "Jesus movement").

Switching Viewpoints

From the beginning of my Christian commitment, I tried to look at my previous (occult) beliefs through the eyes of my new (biblical) worldview. As a participant in the spiritual explosion of the 1960s, I knew I had been part of something that was more than just a passing fad. I understood that the forces it had unlocked would profoundly affect our future. And I realized that my immersion in the counterculture gave me a unique opportunity to understand what was happening, and to communicate to my fellow Christians about it.

In 1973, with those concerns in mind, I founded the Spiritual Counterfeits Project (SCP)—an evangelical ministry and think tank based in Berkeley, California—to chronicle and critique the growing influence of Eastern and occult spirituality in our culture. Our intention was to keep watch on the expanding legacy of the counterculture as it worked its way like leaven through society.

And Berkeley was the perfect place to do the watching. Located on the eastern shore of San Francisco Bay, with its world-class university, ideal climate, and rich cultural mixture, Berkeley is a global crossroads—a place where people, religions, philosophies, ideologies, and movements from all over the world come together to compete for attention, adherents, and influence. At that time, northern California was also a center for the post-'60s spiritual ferment that was already generating the "Human Potential Movement," the "encounter group" craze, and other forms of secularized spirituality.

✣   ✣   ✣   ✣   ✣   ✣   ✣   ✣   ✣   ✣   ✣   ✣   ✣   ✣   ✣   ✣   ✣

Mind-manipulating "maximum leaders"...loomed much larger as threats to the social fabric—and to the souls of countless followers—than a few burnt-out hippies invoking ancient deities by the light of the silvery moon.

✣   ✣   ✣   ✣   ✣   ✣   ✣   ✣   ✣   ✣   ✣   ✣   ✣   ✣   ✣   ✣   ✣

The collapse of the '60s counterculture also stirred up the beginnings of the Neopagan movement on the West Coast, although it attracted less publicity. By the mid-1970s, signs of the emerging movement began to appear on the University of

California's Berkeley campus—which is where I first noticed it. Neopagan activists distributed leaflets attacking Christianity and praising paganism; they also held demonstrations on behalf of various pagan deities, idols, and fetishes*—such as parading a pâpier-maché "sacred phallus" effigy or "golden calf" statue through the university's main public plaza, accompanied by a retinue of followers in (presumably) "pagan" costume.

I made note of the phenomenon and began to collect information about it for SCP's files, but I paid no special attention to it otherwise. The pagans I had encountered seemed more like campus pranksters than serious religionists. And frankly, the idea of breathing new life into something as thoroughly dead as ancient pagan religion seemed far-fetched, to say the least. Mind-manipulating "maximum leaders" like Werner Erhard, Sun Myung Moon, and Jim Jones loomed much larger as threats to the social fabric— and to the souls of countless followers—than a few burnt-out hippies invoking ancient deities by the light of the silvery moon.

Ironically, Neopaganism turned out to be the slow but steady tortoise in the new religions race, while the big, attention-grabbing groups like TM, est, and the Moonies turned out to be flashy rabbits that faded before they got to the finish line. As the decade of the '70s drew to a close, Margot Adler wrote *Drawing Down the Moon* (first published on Halloween in 1979), her widely praised account of modern Witchcraft's origins and its development in the United States. The book quickly went to paperback and multiple reprintings. Its success was an announcement to the world

---

* According to Webster, a *fetish* is "an object...believed to have magical power to protect or aid its owner; *broadly:* a material object regarded with superstitious or extravagant trust or reverence."

that Neopaganism was here to stay, and that it intended to be a presence in the world of American religion.

Christian–Wiccan Dialogue

Neopaganism's staying power—and its steady growth—became increasingly evident during the 1980s. That reality was sharply underlined for me in 1986. In March of that year, SCP held a "Conference on Deception and Discernment" at an evangelical church in Berkeley, attended by several hundred pastors and laymen from across the country. I delivered one of the plenary lectures, on the subject of "Witchcraft and Neopaganism."

A local Neopagan elder came to the event, prepared to challenge what he assumed would be a typical, misinformed fundamentalist attack on his beliefs. In fact, he found nothing to challenge in my lecture, but he spoke up in response to a different speaker and publicly offered a contrary interpretation of Neopaganism. As a result, some of the Christians (myself included) stayed behind for an animated conversation that continued long after the main presentation was over.

Several things emerged from that encounter. One was the awareness that stereotypes and misunderstandings of Christianity are as common among Neopagans as stereotypes of Neopaganism are alleged to be among Christians. Another was the realization that both sides would benefit from a more structured conversation in which they could explain their beliefs and practices, and compare them with one another.

The result was a yearlong series of "Christian–Wiccan Dialogues" that ran from the summer of 1986 through the spring of 1987. The two sponsoring organizations were the Spiritual Counterfeits Project and the Covenant of the Goddess, one of the earliest and most influential Neopagan–Witchcraft organizations. We held a series of bilateral discussions, roughly one per month, with each side providing three or four people for each meeting. Each session dealt with a different topic and a different aspect of our contrasting worldviews.

The topics for discussion included

- the nature of Ultimate Reality
- the nature of Nature
- the nature of human nature
- the nature of Evil
- the nature of the spiritual–human interaction (prayer versus ritual magic)
- natural versus revealed religion
- the interaction of personality and spiritual practice ("salvation" versus "transformation")
- ethics and morality
- pluralism (one path or many?)
- authenticity (what is a Witch? what is a Christian?)
- issues of gender and sexuality

Those discussions were enlightening for all concerned. The Christians and Neopagans found little to agree upon, but they both learned a great deal about one another. Of equal significance, both sides learned how to communicate in the context of spiritual disagreement. One of the most important things we discovered is that, even in opposition, we could interact with mutual respect. We could be on opposite sides of a cultural conflict—and both sides acknowledged that, indeed, we are—without an equivalent level of personal hostility. For the Christians, it was a matter of taking seriously Paul's admonition that "our struggle is not against flesh and blood" (Ephesians 6:12), and applying it in a flesh-and-blood situation.

Personal Contacts

It took a lot of work—and a lot of honesty—on both sides to make that process work, but it not only proved to be possible, it proved to be worth the effort. Real communication was not only opened up, it has continued. I have maintained many of the contacts I formed during those dialogues —not just as an exercise in religious civility, but because I have found my Neopagan acquaintances to be intelligent, creative, thoughtful people who are interesting to know and enjoyable to talk to.

I have also found them invaluable as windows into their own religious world, which I will never be able to enter directly. Because of my background, there is much in Neopaganism I can empathize with. I have no trouble understanding why people are drawn to modern Witchcraft, or why they find it religiously fulfilling. I spent much of my formative adulthood in the counterculture—I am of that "tribe," so to speak. I might well be a Neopagan myself today, except for the fact that my "spiritual evolution" was interrupted by an encounter with Christ.

But interrupted it was, and as a result, I cannot partake of the spirit (or spirits) of their religion. There are clear limits to the rapport I can have with Neopagans. I can find common ground with them in some of the things we share as part of our common, created humanity—but I cannot take part in their religious observances, share in their religious sentiments, or enjoy their religious fellowship. I can never see their community from the inside as they do: as a member and a participant. To help me overcome that limitation, my Neopagan friends have been generous with their information and their commentary. The reason for their openness, as one of them recently explained to me, is that while they are "disappointed" that I don't "approve" of their religion, they do trust me not to distort the information they provide simply in order to cast them in a negative light. They know I will tell the unsensationalized truth about their beliefs and practices (thus clearing them of some of the standard slanders)—even though that also includes a highly critical assessment of their religion.

One of the reasons they have that level of trust is because of the work I did to follow up on our 1987 dialogues. In 1991, I wrote a lengthy article, "Witchcraft—From the Dark Ages to the New Age," for a special issue of the *SCP Journal*. The gist of that article was to demonstrate that the popular Neopagan version of their own history is a fantasy and a fabrication—that there is in fact *no* historical connection between the witchcraft of the Middle Ages and the modern religious movement that bears the same name. Despite my critical view of Neopaganism, the article got high marks from Neopagan readers for its fairness and accuracy. I sent a copy of the *Journal* to one of my contacts, a woman who is both a practicing Witch and an academically trained and published historian. She responded,

> Overall I think it's excellent. I felt that you under-stood Neo-Paganism well. The tone was good—opinionated (i.e., it's clear you're a Christian, and writing primarily for a Christian audience) yet not biased. I also thought that you hit on the major threads that created modern Paganism, and covered them succinctly. In general, I found it extremely accu-rate and well-written (Gibbons, 1999).*

---

* Throughout this book I have used the author–date system of notes. A brief description of the source appears in parentheses after the citation, and the full source information is given in the bibliography.

An Unexpected Development

After publishing that 1991 article, I turned my research attention to other topics (including UFOs, Deep Ecology, "angel" mania, and the "recovery" movement). I presumed that Neopaganism would continue to develop more or less along the lines I had indicated in the article—as a new but growing branch of the American "alternative religions" tradition.

And then, along came the rest of the 1990s.

The sudden appearance and wild popularity of witchcraft in the popular media during the latter half of the decade took everyone by surprise—including Neopagans. Starting in 1996, there was a series of sensational media productions featuring witchy characters and Neopagan themes. In the space of two short years, we were treated to no less than five Hollywood productions that all became major pop-culture events. They were the blockbuster teen movie *The Craft* in 1996; the debut of three new TV shows (*Sabrina the Teenage Witch* in 1996, *Buffy the Vampire Slayer* in 1997, and *Charmed* in 1998); and another mega-movie, *Practical Magic,* with Sandra Bullock and Nicole Kidman, also in 1998.

That late 1990s media explosion set off an enormous wave of interest in Neopaganism and a surge of experimentation that took many people well beyond mere curiosity. In short order, Witchcraft was transformed into a pop-culture phenomenon, and "Wicca" became a teenage fad that didn't fade, but turned into an enduring trend.

Those developments swelled the ranks of Neopaganism far beyond its own "structure" (such as it was), which was based on the various self-proclaimed Witchcraft groups and other organizations making up the active core of the movement. Suddenly, all of that was overshadowed by happenings in the popular media. Suddenly, there were tens of thousands of (mostly young) people running around calling themselves "witches," and taking their ideas about what that means, not from a tradition or a teacher of tradition, but from the Internet, or a movie, or a TV show. The movement had become a mass movement almost overnight, and it was quickly growing beyond anyone's ability to control, or direct, or even measure.

Today and Beyond—PantheaCon 2003

In 1998, I retired from active participation in the ministry of SCP. I did not, however, retire from my interest in Neopagans and Neopaganism. I have watched with fascination as the Neopagan movement has continued to change and develop. It has not only grown, it has also matured as the young radicals who shaped Neopaganism a generation ago have settled into adulthood.

The extent of those changes became evident to me when I had an opportunity to attend "PantheaCon 2003," a major pan-pagan conference held annually in the San Francisco Bay area. I had been invited by one of my Neopagan friends—a Wiccan elder and high priest. He knew I was writing a book on Neopaganism and suggested I could get a firsthand impression of the current state of the movement by going to the conference.

It was an offer I couldn't refuse. The conference was held in a large, convention-oriented hotel in Silicon Valley (roughly 2 hours commute from my home) over a long weekend. I attended one full 12-hour day on Saturday (from 11 A.M. to 11 P.M.). It was an exhausting but enlightening experience.

I had gone fully expecting to encounter sights that would make me avert my eyes, and people that would make me veer out of my way to avoid them. But there was very little of that. The "freaky fringe" was indeed present (including the "Sisters of Perpetual Indulgence"—the flamboyant, transvestite, anti-Christian "street-theater" group), but such participants were relatively few and far between.

My overwhelming impression of the conference-goers is that they were almost boringly *normal*. Many had families with children, ranging from toddlers to teens. You could have walked into any of the seminars I attended and thought you were in a graduate studies class at Berkeley or Stanford. That aspect of the experience was superficially reassuring, but it was also more deeply disturbing. It was disturbing because it signified to me, not just that Neopaganism is "mainstreaming" itself (the obvious observation)—but also that the "mainstream" is "paganizing" itself.

> The Neopagan movement and the larger society are approaching each other at warp speed (historically speaking) and, in fact, have already started to blend and blur at their boundaries.

The Neopagan movement on the West Coast was started some 35 years ago by people who were young, disaffected, and thoroughly countercultural. They were rejecting (and rebelling against) Christian morality, Christian values, Christian culture, and the Christian religion. As part of that package, they were also rejecting middle-class, bourgeois values and everything that went along with them.

Today, many of those same people have spouses, families, and children, and the middle-class values of stability, security, and prosperity are looking a lot more like virtues—and a lot less like vices—to them now. As a result, they are prepared to move back into the mainstream of society in search of a friendly haven for their family and community concerns.

And of course, they are carrying their paganism with them into the mainstream. But more than that—and more importantly—they are finding that the mainstream culture they are rejoining today is a lot more accommodating to them than the culture they left behind 35 years ago. Thirty-five years of cultural devolution have moved the mainstream far toward paganism at the same time that Neopagans have been moving toward the mainstream. The reality is that the Neopagan movement and the larger society are approaching each other at warp speed (historically speaking) and, in fact, have already started to blend and blur at their boundaries.

Twenty years ago, Christopher Nugent made an eerily prophetic observation. I marked it at the time, and it has stayed with me:

> As the idols descend, we have a convergence of the culture and the occult, a kind of "occulturation."...I would conclude that our culture may be becoming so demonic as to render particular cults redundant and superfluous (Nugent, 1983, pages 178, 180).

We are virtually at that point today. And the interesting thing is that what brings all these forces together—and binds them together—is their common refusal of Christ and Christianity. That same common choice is what gives unity and direction to all the various "lanes" of the broad highway "that leads to destruction" (Matthew 7:13). The non- (and anti-) Christian elements in our society are discovering a new solidarity in their shared rejection of Christ and the gospel. At PantheaCon, that point was brought home to me in a powerful way.

"I Hear That Jesus Loves Me..."

Several musical groups gave performances during the conference. On Saturday night, I dropped in to hear one of them, a singing duo called "Moonrise." The performers were two matronly Witches in their late 30s or early 40s, pleasant in appearance and demeanor, modestly dressed and modestly musically talented. In a different context, they could have been soccer moms at a picnic, with long hair, long dresses, and wire-rimmed glasses.

In clear and lilting voices, to their own guitar accompaniment, they sang a Pagan anthem entitled "Heretic Heart." In the words to the song, the singers say they have heard the rumor of Jesus' love, but openly proclaim they are turning down His offer because it is essentially useless and not worth responding to. They specifically declare that His love is going to go unrequited since He has no legitimate claim of any kind on them. Finally, in the song's refrain, the singers declare repeatedly that personal autonomy is the highest virtue and assert that the only real authority in life for anyone is their own self-assertive heart—the "Heretic Heart" of the song's title.

There were several more verses in a similar vein, but one verse was all it took to get the point across. You can't put it more plainly than they did: "Hey, God...I reject your love...go away and leave me alone...I am not one of yours."

Rejecting Christianity has been a basic part of Neopaganism from the beginning. It is one of several ways the movement has traditionally expressed its rejection of the main society. But today, in a fascinating historical irony, it is also one of the ways the movement finds itself increasingly in *harmony* with the main society, which is in hot pursuit of its own Christ-rejecting agendas.

Attending the conference was an intense experience— both demanding and enlightening. By the end of the day, I had learned what I came to find out. The state of the Neo- pagan movement is healthy, confident, and growing more so every day. The first generation of elders has begun passing its paganism on to the next generation of offspring This means that what was once a band of religious oddballs has become a functioning religious community. It has become an active, self-sustaining alternative culture, a fact that has enormous implications for the future of our society—and for the place of Christianity within it. The Neopagans are on a roll, and they know it. They sense that the Christian culture is in full retreat, and they are advancing energetically as it recedes.*

---

* More than one Neopagan of my acquaintance has objected to this charac- terization. Neopagans don't sense any obvious weakening of Christianity's presence or strength in our society. They are very aware that their move- ment has made important social gains over the last several decades, but they don't sense that their social opposition has significantly weakened. On the contrary, it seems to them that the strength of the so-called "Christian Right" is increasing rather than diminishing. If anything, from the Neopagan point of view, Christianity is more assertive of its social presence today than it has been for some time.

The key to these differing views, of course, lies in the differing perspec- tives. Neopagans see the imposing forms and institutions of Christian cul- ture, but cannot tell that their spiritual substance has fled; after all, if they don't know what the substance of Christianity is, they are not likely to notice when it's gone. Therefore they do not and cannot see that those imposing institutions are hollow facades, reamed out and ready to be brought down by their own empty weight in response to the right kind of social shock—or the right convergence of social forces.

I believe we are on the verge of social and spiritual changes that will make the last half-century look like the proverbial Sunday school picnic. The church is headed into a future that is unlike the past we have known, and Christians by and large seem unprepared to deal with the challenges that lie ahead of us.

On a superficial level, the mainstreaming of Neopaganism will mean learning to deal with Neopagans in routine social situations, including the workplace—for example, the Witch next door, or the Druid in the office down the hall. On a deeper level, it means that our culture as a whole is becoming more receptive to pagan values and more hostile to Christian ones—a process that will greatly change the way we relate to the society around us.

That, I believe, is the real significance of modern Witchcraft and the Neopagan movement. It is less important in its own right than it is as a herald and symptom of a larger transformation. We are well into a slow-motion cultural upheaval of historic proportions, and the rising fortunes of Neopaganism reveal much about the nature and extent of those changes.

This book, I hope, will help Christians understand some of the changes that have already occurred—and prepare for the rest of them before they actually arrive. To cope with the challenges before us, Christians not only need to understand Neopaganism, but also must be prepared to engage it. On a *personal* level, we must understand Neopaganism in order to guard our families from its influence; we must also be prepared to engage Neopaganism should it nevertheless appear within the family sanctum. On a *cultural* level, we need to actively counter the false picture of Christianity that Neopagans often present, as well as countering the false history it is based on. On a *spiritual* level, we must be able to actively present the gospel message to the Neopagan community in terms that they can hear and understand.

But before we can take the truth *to* Neopagans, we must first understand the truth *about* them. We need to know who we are talking to before the conversation starts. We owe them that respect in order to gain a hearing for the message that we bear.

A Note About Terminology

The terms "Wicca," "Witchcraft," and "Neopaganism" all refer to different aspects of the movement we are talking about in this book. Think of them as a series of concentric circles. At the center is "Wicca," the smallest circle. "Wicca" is the name that Gerald Gardner gave to the religion he and his associates created during the late 1940s and early 1950s. This is sometimes referred to as "Gardnerian" Witchcraft.

"Witchcraft" is the next and larger circle. The category "Witchcraft" encompasses both "Gardnerian" Witches (or "Wiccans") and people who call themselves "Witches" but who are *not* "Gardnerian"— including some who began as Gardner's followers and then broke away. There are a large number of subcategories within this second circle, but they are not especially relevant to the culture change we are discussing, and they are even losing their relevance within the Witchcraft movement itself. Modern Witches freely swap material between traditions and invent new materials with no tradition at all, so distinctions can get blurred very quickly, and language and the rules of usage are always changing. Margot Adler comments, "In the past, most writers broke down the Craft traditions into 'Hereditary,' 'Traditional,' 'Gardnerian,' 'Alexandrian,' 'Dianic,' and sometimes 'Continental.' All these terms now have vague boundaries, and mean less as the years go by" (Adler, 1986, pages 113–114).

"Neopaganism" is the third and largest circle. This term encompasses not only "Wiccans" and "Witches," but also includes the groups (and individuals) that try to "reconstruct" ancient, pre- and non-Christian religious systems—such as the Norse, Celtic, Greek, Roman, and Egyptian religions—as well as the followers of various obscure, forgotten, and neglected occult teachings from around the world. In that respect, Neopaganism could be described as "a congress of resurrected religious rejects."

But this simple concentric picture of Wicca/Witchcraft/Neopaganism has been complicated recently by the slang usage of "Wicca" in teenage culture and in the popular entertainment media. In teenage culture, "Wicca" now routinely refers to almost any form of modern Witchcraft, while blockbuster teen TV shows like *Charmed* and *Buffy the Vampire Slayer* often use "Wicca" as a synonym for a kind of superficial, "dabbler's" Witchcraft. In at least some pop-culture usage, therefore, "Wicca" seems to be turning almost into a term of derision.

In the meantime, I have tended to use the most inclusive term applicable for any given statement. When speaking of "Witches" (second circle), if my statement applies also to "Neopagans" (third circle), I incline to use the larger term.

I have capitalized "Neopagan," "Neopaganism," "Witch," and "Witchcraft" whenever they refer to the religion or religious movement, or to a follower thereof. Thus, as a thumbnail guide, I have capitalized "Witch" and "Witchcraft" in the same manner (and in the same places) that one would capitalize say, "Buddhist" and "Buddhism," or "Christian" and "Christianity." "Neopaganism" and "Neopagan" are almost always capitalized, since those words refer only to the modern religious movement and its followers.

This principle also means that, while the designations for modern Witches and their religion of Witchcraft are generally capitalized, those for biblical witchcraft, African tribal witchcraft, and European witchcraft—along with their practitioners—are not.

Witchcraft
Goes
Mainstream

✢ ✢ ✢

1

"Witchcraft"...
"Neopaganism"...
What Exactly Are We
Talking About?

✦ ✦ ✦

IF YOU WALK ONTO AN AVERAGE college campus and ask four different people what "witchcraft" is, you will probably get four different answers. I know, because I tried the experiment.

In the spring of 2002, I went to the University of California's Berkeley campus to sample the state of public opinion on the subject of modern-day witchcraft for a video documentary. The idea was to do a series of "man-in-the-street" interviews, selecting people at random and asking them what they thought the words "witch" and "witchcraft" refer to. I spoke with students, professors, tourists, and passersby. Here is some of what they told me:

- "A witch is somebody who was supposed to eat babies and get magical powers from the devil, but it wasn't real. It was all paranoid fantasy and social hysteria."

- "'Witch' was a word they used to condemn people who rebelled against the powers that be. Anybody who stood up to the Church and the establishment was likely to be called a 'witch'—especially women.

And that's still true. That's where the term 'witch hunt' comes from."

- "'Witches' are make-believe Halloween characters, like ghosts and skeletons and jack-o'-lanterns. They're ugly-looking and fly around on broomsticks scaring people."

- "A 'witch' is somebody who uses supernatural power in a bad way—using hexes and spells and stuff to hurt people—what they call 'black magic.'"

While none of those responses are "true," none are entirely "false," either. The real history of witchcraft is complex enough to provide at least some basis for all of those answers. Today however, confusion is multiplied because the word "witchcraft" can refer to several different things, depending on how it is used.

"Witchcraft" has at least four different meanings—four distinct ways the word is employed—and those different meanings get mixed up in the ways that people use and understand the term. We should therefore identify the four main categories of "witchcraft" before we go any further, so we can know what we are—and are not—talking about in this book. The four categories are

1. biblical witchcraft

2. anthropological witchcraft

3. historical witchcraft

4. modern religious Witchcraft

1. Biblical Witchcraft

In English versions of the Bible, several different Greek and Hebrew words are translated as "witch" or "witchcraft." All of those different words refer to different occult practices of the ancient Middle East. In some cases, all we have is a Hebrew word—the particular occult practice involved can't even be identified today. Therefore, it is difficult to give a single, specific meaning to the term "witchcraft" as it is used in Scripture. We can, however, give it a general meaning, since each of the Greek and Hebrew words in question have a similar reference, and all have a nearly identical connotation.

✛ ✛ ✛ ✛ ✛ ✛ ✛ ✛ ✛ ✛ ✛ ✛ ✛ ✛ ✛ ✛ ✛

While Scripture's pronouncements on witchcraft have an indirect, or "background," relevance to Neopaganism, the way the term was translated doesn't lend itself to scholarly precision or shed much light on the Witchcraft movement we see today.

✛ ✛ ✛ ✛ ✛ ✛ ✛ ✛ ✛ ✛ ✛ ✛ ✛ ✛ ✛ ✛ ✛

To begin with, biblical witchcraft (whatever it was) is essentially an Old Testament phenomenon. There are eight references to witchcraft in the Bible, and seven of them are in the Old Testament. In the Old Testament, the Hebrew term most often translated as "witch" is *mekashef* (which is also sometimes rendered as "sorcerer"). The exact root of the word is uncertain. It is believed to come from a word which means "to cut" or "to cut up," possibly referring to drugs or medicinal plants sliced and shredded into a magical brew.

> In the numerous instances in which *mekashef* occurs in the Old Testament, the idea seems to be of one who deals in medicines, charms or poisons...one who performs magical arts with drugs—in the modern sense, one who performs sorcery, witchcraft, or black magic (Nigosian, 1978, page 17).

But several other words are also translated as "witch." The so-called "witch of Endor" (1 Samuel 28:3-19) was clearly not a sorcerer in the usual sense, but a necromancer (one who conjures the spirits of the dead) or spirit medium. And in the famous statement from 1 Samuel, "rebellion is as the sin of witchcraft" (15:23 KJV), the word rendered as "witchcraft" is *qesem*, which refers to some (unknown) form of divination.

In the New Testament, the Greek word *pharmakeia* is translated once (in Galatians 5:20) as "witchcraft" and four times (in the Book of Revelation) as "sorcery"—or the related terms "sorceries" or "sorcerers." The same Greek word is also the root of our English word "pharmacy." Again, the central notion seems to be one of drugs, potions, and poisons—of either performing occult rituals while taking drugs, or possibly "spellbinding" others by giving them drugs.

In any case, the biblical references to "witchcraft" are hard to apply with precision today because the biblical translators were naming ancient occult practices with terms taken from the theological controversies of their own day—and they weren't always consistent in the way they did it. In the original languages, the biblical words translated as "witch" and "witchcraft" appear to refer to various forms of sorcery and black magic. Sorcery in that sense is a part of some, but not all, modern Witchcraft. Thus, while Scripture's pronouncements on witchcraft have an indirect, or "background," relevance to Neopaganism, the way the term was translated doesn't lend itself to scholarly precision or shed much light on the Witchcraft movement we see today.

2. Anthropological Witchcraft

Scholars of anthropology frequently refer to "witches" and "witchcraft," especially in studies of African tribal society. Some anthropologists use the word to mean any form of malevolent, "black" magic (that is, sorcery), particularly when it involves spirit-helpers or familiars. Another group of scholars, however, reserve the term "witchcraft" for a *special kind* of evil psychic power—a power to harm that is inherited, instead of being obtained through learning and initiation, as is the case with ordinary sorcery. Interestingly, this rather technical, scholarly distinction seems to have made its way into the popular lore of witchcraft via the entertainment media, as we shall see in chapter 4. But generally speaking, anthropological studies of tribal "witchcraft" are only indirectly relevant to modern Witchcraft. As Jeffrey Burton Russell points out, such studies serve mainly as a reminder that sorcery and black magic are indeed universal phenomena, which appear in all times, in all societies, and among all classes of people.

3. Historical Witchcraft

"Historical" witchcraft had a limited life span, with a beginning, a middle, and an end. It started in Europe at the beginning of the Middle Ages and ended in America at the end of the Renaissance. It is also called "European" witchcraft, "classical" witchcraft, "Gothic" witchcraft, and "diabolical," or "dualistic," witchcraft. In its fully developed form, it was alleged to involve worship of the devil, infant sacrifice, cannibalism of the sacrificed infant, and sexual relations with Satan, his seducing demons, or both.

Early versions of what later became witchcraft can be found as far back as 1022 in France, but witchcraft wasn't identified as a heresy by the Roman Catholic Inquisition until the 1200s. And the infamous "witch craze," with its sensational trials and widespread public executions, didn't begin until the time of the Renaissance (1400–1700). The notorious

Salem witch trials of 1692 were figuratively the last spasm of the Renaissance witch hysteria, which had largely died out in Europe half a century earlier. After 1700, witchcraft disappears from history altogether.

Modern-day Witches often claim that their religion is descended from the witchcraft of the Middle Ages, but that is not true. What *is* true concerning historical witchcraft is as follows: Witchcraft came into existence at a particular point in time when its components were woven together by circumstance to create something new. It passed out of existence at a later point in time when that process was reversed, and circumstance unraveled those same components. Historical witchcraft wasn't transmitted to later generations for the simple reason that, after its dis-integration, there was nothing left to transmit. (The origin, development, and eventual disappearance of historical witchcraft are discussed in chapters 5 and 6.)

It is important for us to understand what historical witchcraft was, and how it relates (and doesn't relate) to modern Witchcraft and the Neopagan movement. In recent years, a lot of Neopagans have backed away from the claim that modern Witchcraft is directly connected with the witchcraft of European history. But even the Neopagans who no longer claim to be descended from historical witchcraft still claim to be inspired by it. A lot of their self-understanding as modern Witches is based on their understanding of what historical witchcraft was. A lot of their (mis)understanding of Christians and Christianity is likewise based on their perception of who historical witches were in relation to their accusers. As they see the witches of history, so they tend to see themselves in relation to the world of today.

The real nature of historical witchcraft (and its relationship with Christianity) is a subject of ongoing controversy, not only among scholars, but also within the Neopagan community. In fact, it is one of the subjects on which it is most important for Christians to engage Neopagans in dialogue and debate—both directly and indirectly, both individually and collectively, both face to face and in the media. This is one of the places where the battle is currently being fought over how we will understand Christianity's place in our history—and its place in our future. Christians need to be part of that discussion at a grassroots level.

4. Modern Religious Witchcraft

Almost 250 years after historical witchcraft ceased to exist, modern Witchcraft appeared. It was essentially the creation of one man, in England, in the 1940s. But as it grew, and especially when it came to the United States in the 1950s and 1960s, modern Witchcraft mushroomed into a populist magical mystery cult that has become one of the most dynamic and rapidly growing movements in America.

Religious Witchcraft was originally conceived as a goddess-centered nature religion (and given the name of "Wicca"), but in the decades since it came to America, the movement has not only increased in numbers and influence, it has also diversified far beyond its original concept. What began as an effort to re-invent a simple vision of witchcraft (and claim it as a "survival") has expanded into a collection of "revivals" and "re-creations" that includes the ancient Celtic, Greek, Roman, and Egyptian religions. Increasingly, it also draws in enthusiasts of various superseded, forgotten, and discarded traditions from around the world (for example "Shamanic Healing Circles" and "Toltec Wisdom").

But the movement is more than just a revival of bygone ways. It also includes purely modern elements. This larger movement incorporates a number of political causes and enthusiasms (chiefly of the left-wing variety), such as feminism, environmentalism, "gay" activism, and antiwar activism. Clearly, this is more than the dabbling of those with a taste for the quaint and ancient.

This expanded version of the movement is what is meant by the term "Neopaganism." In that context, it should be pointed out that while all modern Witches are Neopagans, not all Neopagans are Witches. It is an imperfect parallel to say that if Neopaganism is a "religion," then Witchcraft is one of its "denominations," but it does make the point that Witchcraft is only one "flavor" of Neopaganism. It also serves to illustrate how different the movement has become from what it started out to be.

And the movement is poised to become more different yet, as Neopagans are discovering that they have interests in common with a wide variety of other religions and spiritual movements. In fact, in the minds of some people, "Neopaganism" itself has become a divisive term and a limiting concept. They believe that the movement has evolved beyond its roots, that it should drop the "Neo" part of its name and become simply the "Pagan movement"—a motley alliance of minority beliefs and alternative religions, the main unifying thread of which is that all of them are not Christian. And they have taken this belief with them into interfaith activism. In interfaith circles, the term "Pagan" is used to refer to a wide variety of religious groups, including indigenous, tribal, Shinto, Hindu (and Neo-Hindu), Taoist, and Neopagan groups—among others.

Nevertheless, even as Neopaganism defines itself in increasingly inclusive terms, the fact remains that it began as a witchcraft "revival" and is still heavily weighted toward its Witchcraft component. Modern Witchcraft continues to be Neopaganism's most active public presence and its most compelling public image.

Describing Modern Witchcraft

Although Witchcraft has attained a higher public profile, it still has not come sharply into focus in the public mind. Even though more people have a generally positive impression of Witchcraft today, not many have a clear idea of what it really consists of. In fact, as a religion, modern Witchcraft is remarkably difficult to pin down.

Witchcraft is individualistic to the point of being anarchic, with no centralized authority or even any agreed-upon definition of what a "Witch" is. In effect, a Witch is whoever says they are a Witch, and Witch beliefs and practices amount to whatever individual Witches actually believe and do. The problem with this approach is that the people who say they are Witches actually believe and do so many different things that no single description fits them all. In fact, the Witches themselves have been stymied in several attempts to come up with a definition.

One early (and failed) attempt was promoted by the occult publisher Llewellyn in 1973. Under Llewellyn's sponsorship, a "Council of American Witches" was organized, but it soon fell apart—precisely because of conflicts over questions of definition. Problems were immediately evident in the responses submitted to the basic question "What is a Witch?" Below are some of the answers Llewellyn received:

- "'A Witch above all worships the Triple Goddess and her Consort, the Horned God, in one form or another. A Witch works Magick within a definite code of ethics. A Witch acknowledges and uses the male-female polarity in his/her rites. A Witch takes total responsibility for her actions, herself and her future.'"

- " 'Witchcraft is an initiatory mystery religion whose adherents seek, through self-discipline, to live a life dedicated to the pursuit and practice of knowledge, wisdom and compassion under the guidance of the Gods.' "

- " 'A Witch is a member of a religion which by its own internal definition is monotheistic.' "

- " 'Wicca can be defined as a pagan mystery religion with a polarized deity and no personification of evil.' "

(All of the above quoted in Adler, 1986, page 100.)

On the West Coast, Witches did manage in 1975 to create the "Covenant of the Goddess" (CoG)—an alliance of Witchcraft groups that has not only survived but gone on to become one of the prominent voices of Neopaganism in the United States. But CoG survived only because it *avoided* definitions. After struggling with the issue, CoG decided that defining a Witch is an impossibility and declared that Witchcraft's unstructured individualism is in fact a virtue. In their statement, CoG's organizers said,

> We could not define what a Witch is in words. Because there are too many differences. Our reality is intuitive. We know when we encounter someone who we feel is worshipping in the same way, who follows the same religion we do, and that's our reality, and that has to be understood, somehow, in anything we do (quoted in Adler, 1986, page 104).

Neopagans pride themselves on their religious creativity and believe that their ability to "make it up as they go along" is one of the strengths of their community. Margot Adler says in effect that the creation of new traditions is itself becoming a tradition in Neopaganism:

New traditions are springing up in the Craft almost every day. In my travels across the country, I found that easily half the people I interviewed in the Craft were either forming their own traditions or changing the ones they were involved with (Adler, 1986, page 129).

Under those circumstances, it is obviously difficult to speak in general terms and say that "Witches" believe this or that, or that "they" behave in such and such a way. Any declaration along those lines should come with a disclaimer attached, warning that the statement is riddled with exceptions.

Nevertheless, if we keep that disclaimer in mind, it *is* possible to discern a kind of religious attitude—if not a fully developed religious ideology—behind the differences of detail in modern Witchcraft.

Witchcraft's Religious Attitude

Witchcraft's religious attitude begins with rejection, distinction, and opposition. Witchcraft asserts its existence, as the sociologists say, "against the rejected background" of the main culture. Its identity is proclaimed in terms of its *difference* from, and its *opposition* to, the Christian-based culture and religion(s) of the West. Witchcraft is not only anti-authoritarian within its own ranks, it also actively opposes the authority of the prevailing culture in general.

The contagious excitement of cultural insurrection is modern Witchcraft's functional substitute for missionary zeal.

Margot Adler makes that stance of active opposition clear, saying of her own book, *Drawing Down the Moon*, that it "stands against all of the totalistic religious and political views that dominate our society" (Adler, 1986, page viii). Much of the motive force behind the growth of Neopaganism lies in this vital sense of "standing against" the powers that be in contemporary culture. The contagious excitement of cultural insurrection is modern Witchcraft's functional substitute for missionary zeal.

Adler goes on to describe the Neopagan religious attitude in four additional points (one of which, again, explicitly repudiates a cardinal Christian teaching). The four points can be summarized as

1. animism/polytheism/pantheism

2. feminism

3. there's no such thing as sin

4. spiritual reciprocity

1. Animism/Polytheism/Pantheism

Adler says that animism, polytheism, and pantheism are overlapping terms to describe the basic pagan attitude toward the divine (Adler, 1986, page 25).

"Animism" sees a spiritual vitality in all things, thus blurring the distinction between animate and inanimate in our universe. "Polytheism" means to Neopagans that "deity" is plural rather than singular, many rather than one. First and foremost, this puts the Neopagan approach in opposition to the biblical concept of monotheism—and all of its implications. However, even though "the gods" are numerous, there is still a basic "divinity" that underlies them all—indeed, that underlies *all* things. This is where "polytheism" overlaps "pantheism" in the Neopagan scheme of things.

"Pantheism" is a loaded term in any religious discussion, and many Witches would deny that their beliefs are "pantheistic." But it is hard to use any other term when Adler asserts that Witchcraft is "a...religion of immanence"* and says that it leads to "the understanding of one's own divine nature. Thou art Goddess. Thou art God. *Divinity is immanent in all of Nature.* It is as much within you as without" (Adler, 1986, page ix, emphasis added). Certainly "pantheism" is the right word to describe belief in a divinity that pervades all of nature and that shows up in the individual as "the divine within."

To Neopagans, the universe is alive with the energy of consciousness, and that conscious energy *is* the divine—the invisible ground and substance of everything that exists. Pantheism in that sense also includes several related ideas. If the divine pervades all of nature, then all of nature is sacred. From that connection follows the ecological emphasis of modern Witchcraft; Witchcraft itself is frequently referred to as an "earth-based" religion. The spiritual practice of Witches is often organized around the yearly cycle of Nature's four seasons, as seen in the so-called "wheel of the year"—the repetitive round of seasonal high points such as solstices and equinoxes and the ancient agricultural festivals of sowing, growing, and mowing.

Also related to Witchcraft's pantheism are the ideas of "enlightenment" and occult "empowerment." If the divine is hidden within Nature, the objective of the religion becomes

---

* "Immanence" is the quality of being "immanent"—that is, according to Webster, "being within the limits of [humanly] possible experience or knowledge." This is as opposed to Christianity's "transcendent" character—"transcendent" meaning "going beyond the universe or material existence."

to "uncover" that divinity, "realize" one's divinity, or "tap into" the divine in order to manipulate its energies by means of magic. In that connection, the use of magic or some other form of occult working (such as divination or spirit invocation) is virtually universal among Neopagans—though again, there are exceptions, and the details of the actual occult practices vary widely.

2. Feminism

From its very earliest days, modern Witchcraft has been female-centered and goddess-oriented. Gerald Gardner's original "Wicca" was an attempt to recreate an imagined goddess-cult of pre-Christian Europe. His ideas were later enlisted as support for the political goals and social critique of activist feminism. Today, Adler describes the feminine focus of Witchcraft this way:

> In our culture which for so long has denied and denigrated the feminine as negative, evil or, at best, small and unimportant, women (and men too) will never understand their own creative strength and divine nature until they embrace the creative feminine, the source of inspiration, the Goddess within (Adler, 1986, page ix).

3. There Is No Such Thing as Sin

That is exactly the way that Adler states her third point. If it seems odd that two of the five main elements in Neopaganism's "religious attitude" are devoted to invalidating Christianity, it is worth remembering that the single most defining thing about Neopaganism is its *detachment* from the main (that is, Christian-based) culture. Neopaganism begins— both in its history and, for the individual, psychologically— by *breaking* with the prevailing religious environment.

Neopaganism must assert itself *against* the dominating influence of Christianity simply to create a breathing space for itself to exist in this society.

The specific Christian beliefs most often targeted for denial and repudiation by Neopagans are the concept of "sin" and the uniqueness of Christ. This almost visceral rejection seems to be one of the few genuine universals of the modern Witchcraft movement, and it appears to hold true across the Neopagan spectrum. In our 1986 "Christian–Wiccan Dialogue," for example, opposition to the concept of sin was one attitude that united all of the Wiccan participants, regardless of their (sometimes acrimonious) differences of opinion on other subjects.

4. Spiritual Reciprocity

Adler expresses the notion of spiritual reciprocity concisely: "The energy you put into the world comes back" (Adler, 1986, page ix). In colloquial terms, we would say, "What goes around comes around." Many Witches (but not all) would subscribe to some version of what is called "the threefold law," or "law of three"—the idea that whatever you do will eventually come back to you with triple force. Many Witches (but again, not all) believe in some form of reincarnation, which gives the concept of spiritual reciprocity greater scope to do its work (in other words, what you do in this lifetime may not come back to deliver its effect—and your due reward—until several lifetimes later). In any case, the idea of spiritual reciprocity, often in the form of "the threefold law" is frequently put forward as a basis for "Wiccan ethics." The assumption is that people who believe that their actions will come back to haunt them, both for good and for ill, will take care to act more responsibly and considerately—that is, to pursue empathy and eschew self-ishness.

With this moral confidence in hand, modern Witchcraft sets forth its basic ethical guideline, sometimes known as the "Wiccan Rede." "Rede" is Old English for "advice" or "counsel," but this piece of advice is not as ancient as its name. Like much else in Neopaganism, it is given an appearance of antiquity by couching it in obsolete forms of expression. The precise origin of the Wiccan Rede is subject to speculation, but it is unquestionably modern. Its usual formulation is, "An it harm none, do as ye will." In contemporary idiom, that translates to "As long as it doesn't hurt anybody, do anything you want to."

The Rede resembles a passive version of the "Golden Rule," but undercut by its bow to the primacy of self-will. The admonition not to hurt others is a classic piece of moral advice as far as it goes, but as stated, it is the equivalent of saying "let your conscience be your guide." Christians will understand the inherent weakness of that approach. In Romans chapter 2, Paul shows how the conscience strives toward God's righteousness, yet is distorted by original sin. This makes it variable in its judgments and subject to rationalizations—"sometimes accusing, sometimes excusing" (see verse 15). When the desire of the will (or the will of desire) is pitted against the call for empathy in appraising the needs of others, only the naive expect empathy to prevail.

But you don't have to be a Christian to wonder if the Wiccan Rede is a stong enough basis for moral guidance. There is controversy on the subject even among Neopagans. In *Witchcraft Today: An Encyclopedia of Wiccan and Neopagan Traditions,* author James R. Lewis notes,

> Some feel that this is too slender a "rede" on which
> to base an ethic adequate for a religious movement

as large as Neopaganism. There are others who feel that the kind of libertarian ethic implied by the Wiccan Rede is precisely what is needed not only by the craft, but by modern society in general (Lewis, James R., 1999, page 303).

Once again, the diversity of Neopagan opinion renders generalizations difficult. For almost anything you can say about modern Witchcraft, there will be Witches somewhere to stand up and say, "Not true of us!"

Nevertheless, there are some unmistakable commonalities that unite the Neopagan movement and bond together those who make it up. Keep in mind the statement issued by the Covenant of the Goddess in 1975: "Our reality is intuitive. We know when we encounter someone who we feel is worshipping in the same way, who follows the same religion we do."

In that context, the common threads of Neopaganism are less in the details of beliefs and practices than they are in a sense of agreement on outlook, attitude, mood, and perspective. In summary,

- The Neopagan religious attitude begins by breaking with the prevailing (Christian) religious attitude, and in particular with its monotheism and its transcendence. Neopaganism's outlook sees the divine not only as many, but also as pantheistic, and therefore as available—both for enlightenment and for occult empowerment.

- Neopaganism's viewpoint is female-centered and goddess-oriented, earth-based and environmentally focused.

- Neopaganism strongly repudiates the concept of sin—and, needless to say, the concept of salvation based upon it.

- The Neopagan attitude fundamentally rejects the idea that we are accountable for our behavior to a higher moral authority and a revealed moral standard. Instead, consistent with its pantheism, Neopaganism believes that ethical behavior arises naturally out of the workings of "spiritual reciprocity." In effect, Neopaganism asserts an ethic of self-will, tempered by mysticism (for example, belief in the "law of three").

At every point, and in every respect, Neopaganism stands in contrast, and outright antagonism, to the Christian understanding of reality. Neopaganism's aversion to Christianity is more than just a sociological device for carving out its religious identity. It also reflects a deep spiritual antipathy toward the moral basis of Christianity: Christianity's (to them) suffocating sense of sin and judgment—the "bad news" that makes the "good news" good. Ultimately, Neopagans reject the good news that God has given us a Savior because they reject the bad news that we need one to begin with. And ironically, it is this part of its religious mood and attitude that puts Neopaganism increasingly in harmony with the mood and attitude of the secular society around us.

2

The Halloween Witch Is Dead: The Changing Face of Modern Witchcraft

✣ ✣ ✣

THE HALLOWEEN WITCH IS DEAD. The old crone on a broomstick with a black cat, a peaked hat, and a wart on her nose is history. She has been replaced by a young, beautiful, sexually magnetic maiden who reveres Nature, honors a goddess, practices magic, and wields mysterious psychic powers. Such indeed is the image of the modern, Neopagan Witch today.

That is quite a transformation—from repulsion to allure—and it has happened very rapidly: essentially within the span of a single generation (about 30 years). Moreover, the process itself seems to be accelerating—examples of the changes in Witchcraft's public image have become more frequent and more dramatic near the end of that 30-year phase.

It isn't easy to assess the meaning of historical change from within the history that's being changed. We can't get enough distance from current events to tell the difference between a transient fad and an enduring trend. Nevertheless, the changes in Witchcraft's public image have been happening fast enough, and are far-reaching enough, that they are plainly an important development.

And of course, those changes in the public's attitude toward Witchcraft have not happened in a vacuum. Context is critical. What's happening to Witchcraft is part and parcel of a much larger transformation happening to society as a whole. Unraveling the factors behind Witchcraft's rising popularity can give us insight into the larger process of cultural change. And the reverse is also true—if we see the larger patterns, we can better understand how those cultural changes speed up the mainstreaming of marginal movements and worldviews, such as Neopaganism.

Most people have probably already noticed at least some signs of Witchcraft's increasing presence and status in society. If they watch daytime television, they have seen Witches promoting their viewpoint to a sympathetic hearing on the *Oprah Winfrey Show* and other afternoon "chat" programs. If they watch cable news, they have seen Witches interviewed on Fox, CNN, and MSNBC. If they read newspapers, they have seen the articles that predictably appear every Halloween, explaining that Witches really don't deserve their infamous reputation. And if they pay attention to the entertainment world, they have certainly noticed the recent spate of movies and TV shows dealing with Witchcraft as a theme. But unless they are closely attuned to the world of teenagers—its spin-offs and its subcultures—they are seeing just the tip of the iceberg. It is among the Internet-savvy younger generation that modern Witchcraft is seeing its most explosive growth—and its most thoroughgoing image makeover.

Numbers and Influence

It is hard to be specific about the numbers involved. There is considerable emphasis on secrecy in modern Witchcraft, and Neopagan organizations don't make their membership rolls available for counting. Wild guesses have ranged as high as 5 million adherents of Wicca alone (Edwards, 1999, page

23), but better-informed estimates put the numbers at considerably less than that. One sociologist who spent ten years as a "participant–observer" of the Neopagan community concluded that the total number of Neopagans in the United States was between 150,000 and 200,000 in 1999 (Berger, 1999, page 9). Five years later, those numbers may have as much as doubled. If her estimate is correct, that would put the projected number of Neopagans in the U.S. at nearly half a million by 2004.

In another attempt to assess the numbers, the Covenant of the Goddess conducted a yearlong poll of the Neopagan community beginning in 1999; they calculated the total number of both Witches and Pagans to be 768,400. If *that* estimate is correct, then by 2004, the figure could be near a million and a half.*

But of course the real numbers, whatever they are, are changing all the time, and in some ways are inherently unknowable. People can enter the Neopagan movement—or depart from it—without leaving any traces at all. People can and do become interested in Wicca without joining any group or identifying themselves as "Witches" in any public way. They can also put that interest aside and move on to other fascinations without any outward signs of the transition. If we want to get a picture of how the modern Witchcraft movement is developing, we will have to rely on other kinds of information.

If you wanted to gauge the presence and influence of Christianity in this country, you would look to our churches, which are easy enough to see—in most cases, just by driving

---

* The difference between these figures illustrates the difficulty of trying to measure Neopaganism's "membership." For a sensible discussion of the numbers question, see the essay "How Many Wiccans Are There in the U.S.?" at www.religioustolerance.org/wic_nbr.htm.

down the street. Generally speaking, Christian churches are publicly accessible and tend to be publicly active. In a word, Christianity is socially "visible." Not so with Neopaganism. Although there are several organizations that represent Witchcraft to the general public, most of what modern Witches do together, as Witches, happens outside of public view.

To gauge the presence and influence of Witchcraft in our midst, we need (among other things) to know the movement's history—its origins and development (see chapter 7). But to understand where, how, and why the movement is growing *today*, we need to look at three areas of activity: first, at what's happening among teenagers; second, at what's happening on college campuses; and third, at what's happening on the Internet.

Those three connected subcultures form a matrix within which Neopaganism flourishes. They are connected because the denizens of the teen culture soon move on to the college scene, and cyber-literacy is increasingly taken for granted in both of those overlapping worlds. And, as we shall see, all three are also *dis*connected from the rest of us in important ways—fashioned into a world apart by a combination of unruly hormones, proliferating technology, and turbulent social change.

The Changing Demographics of Neopaganism

The Web site witchvox.com claims that it is "the busiest religious site in the world," having registered more than a million and a quarter "hits" by the end of its first full year of operation in 1998 (Nightmare, 2001, page 118). In a Web survey conducted on the site in September 1999, it was determined that 60 percent of respondents were under 30 and 62 percent were female (Edwards, 1999, page 23). The observation that Wiccan enthusiasts are predominantly young and female may seem like a stereotype, but it appears to be borne out by the data.

That surge of enthusiasm for Witchcraft among the young, especially among young women, is a distinctly new development—one that began suddenly, in the late 1990s. It also stands in sharp contrast to the conditions that prevailed before the trend got started. In the early 1990s, one of the most dynamic segments of Neopaganism was the "women's spirituality" branch of the feminist movement. But, while "women's spirituality" was attracting plenty of women who were already politically active, very few of them were youthful. In 1993, journalist Cynthia Eller wrote a book praising and promoting feminist spirituality *(Living in the Lap of the Goddess: The Feminist Spirituality Movement in America)* in which she openly lamented the lack of younger women in the movement. Eller noted "how few women [in feminist spirituality] there are below thirty....There are women in their teens and twenties, but not many" (Eller, 1993, p. 18).

Five years later, that situation had been turned completely on its head. In 1998, "*Spin Magazine* in its 'Grrrl [sic] Power' issue ranked witchcraft as the top interest among teenage girls" (Nisbet, 1998). Not surprisingly, merchandisers were among the first to respond to the growing fascination. Teen-themed promotions for products such as Finesse Shampoo and Cover Girl Cosmetics (along with many others) featured witches in their ad campaigns. And the appeal to young women extended beyond the teenage culture per se. "*Young and Modern* magazine featured two pages on witchcraft with the banner headline 'Witchy Ways!'....*Jane* magazine featured Phyllis Curott (a high-profile witch) as one of their 'Gutsiest women of the year.'" (Edwards, 1999, page 25). According to one commentator, "Sorcery and witchcraft have become the hottest themes in youth culture...for the first time in modern Western civilization" (Harvey, 2002).

Why Such a Change?

What accounts for such momentous change within such a moment of historical time? The easy, if oversimplified, answer is that the change is accounted for by the sudden "explosion" of Witchcraft characters, stories, and themes in the media during the mid-1990s (see chapter 4). Indeed, there can be no doubt about the connection between the two. When *The Craft* was released in 1996, it triggered a dramatic rise in the number of people contacting Neopagan groups and Web sites, such as the Covenant of the Goddess (www.cog.org) and the Witches' Voice (www.witchvox.com). Neopagans have told me that the response was so strong, so sudden, and so unexpected that they were literally overwhelmed by the surge of inquiries.

That same high level of interest in Witchcraft was sustained over the next few years by a whole series of movies and TV programs featuring young, stylish, hip, and glamorous women—who happened to be Witches. Almost overnight, Witchcraft became the "in" thing for any teenage girl who also aspired to be young, stylish, hip, and glamorous (in other words, almost every one of them). Interestingly, even as Witches were being portrayed in positive roles, Witchcraft itself retained its aura as a form of "anti-establishment rebellion"—which naturally made it even more attractive to teenagers in general.

Yet it must also be said that the media explanation *is* oversimplified. There was more to Neopaganism's late-1990s success story than a few Hollywood screenwriters and popular actresses making Witchcraft look good to impressionable kids. Our culture in general (and the youth culture in particular) *responded* to Witchcraft because they were *ready* for Witchcraft.

✣ ✣ ✣ ✣ ✣ ✣ ✣ ✣ ✣ ✣ ✣ ✣ ✣ ✣ ✣ ✣ ✣ ✣

A 1986 Federal Court of Appeals decision **(Dettmer v. Landon)** had effectively declared "The Church of Wicca" to be a constitutionally recognizable "religion," with the same legal rights and standing as other religions.

✣ ✣ ✣ ✣ ✣ ✣ ✣ ✣ ✣ ✣ ✣ ✣ ✣ ✣ ✣ ✣ ✣ ✣

Witches had been working for decades to change the popular image and legal status of their movement, and by the 1990s, their work was starting to pay off. Several Witchcraft organizations had been created during the 1970s, and they quickly began to give modern Witchcraft a higher public profile and a better public image. A 1986 Federal Court of Appeals decision *(Dettmer v. Landon)* had effectively declared "The Church of Wicca" to be a constitutionally recognizable "religion," with the same legal rights and standing as other religions.

Teenagers were untouched by any of those developments directly, of course, although they were affected indirectly by Neopaganism's newfound public-relations self-confidence. But teens *were* affected directly by other trends that prepared them to embrace Witchcraft with enthusiasm when it broke out of the occult ghetto and into mainstream entertainment. By the early 1990s, there was a broad awareness of something called "dark spirituality" among teenagers in America. Appealing to disaffected and alienated youth, dark spirituality incorporated fantasy and science-fiction themes (especially as portrayed in comic books and on television), and it permeated the fantasy role-playing scene, as in the controversial game "Dungeons and Dragons." More of a mood than a movement, dark spirituality emphasized the pursuit and use of power by occult means, including witchcraft, sorcery, and spirit invocation. The occult theme was largely drawn from fantasy fiction and often acted out in fantasy role-playing games.

By the mid-1990s, dark spirituality was associated primarily with the "goth" movement. The goth movement (named for the medieval Gothic period) had come from Britain during the 1980s and had firmly taken root among American youth. Following the lead of such "pop-goth" bands as Depeche Mode and The Cure, goth teens were fascinated by gargoyles and vampires, and specialized in gloom, depression, and nihilism (the music of The Cure has been called "British Mope-Rock"). Goths were self-described as "pale-faced, black-swathed, hair-sprayed nightdwellers, who worshiped imagery religious and sacrilegious, consumptive poets, and all things spooky" ("Goth," 1998).

In the 1990s, the "spiritual underbelly" of high school was dominated by goth style and imagery, but it also included all manner of social exiles and outcasts (such as dopers, gays, and satanists) who existed on the fringes of teenage society. In 1997, an informal study of local teenagers by the *Lexington* (Kentucky) *Herald-Leader* showed how thoroughly this counterculture had spread throughout area schools. "Most said there's a subculture at nearly every school that includes Anne Rice-influenced gothic kids, faux vampires and outcast kids who dabble in the occult. After all, in the Bible Belt, what could be more shocking than experimenting with witchcraft, vampirism or Satanism?" (Isaacs, 1997).

The author reassuringly concluded that most signs of teenage involvement in the occult merely indicate a temporary rebellion against parental and social boundaries—though she did note that "a small percentage" of those who flirt with occultic interests move on to a heavier involvement with more serious practices. She did not assess the effect of "normalizing" occultism in the minds of the rest of the kids—those who were dabblers or even just observers. In fact, this process—making deviant spirituality into a normal part of the social environment—was a major preparation for the late-1990s eruption of Witchcraft (and more broadly Neopaganism) in the youth culture.

Teen Witch and Teen Witches

The evidence we have available, mostly from advertising and journalism, indicates there is a high level of awareness of Witchcraft among teenagers, especially girls, coupled with a generally positive attitude toward it. How often do this awareness and this attitude come together to create an active interest—or go on to create an actual involvement? It is difficult to know directly. In the absence of direct information, book sales may be our best indication.

If there is one book that is tied to the teen culture's enthusiastic embrace of Witchcraft, it is 1998's surprise hit *Teen Witch: Wicca for a New Generation,* by Silver Ravenwolf (a Wiccan pseudonym). Written for girls 11 and up (Radio U, 1999), *Teen Witch* has sold 150,000 copies, according to information on the author's Web site (www.silverraven wolf.com). The book is a 250-page "how-to" manual of modern Witchcraft that promises to teach teens how to become "a pentacle-wearing, spell-casting, completely authentic witch!" Among the spells available for casting are "such uniquely teen rituals as the Bad Bus Driver spell, the

Un-Ground Me spell, and the Just-Say-No spell" (Mulrine, 1999).

According to the book's frontispiece,

> Now, for the first time, [teens] can explore what it's like to be a real Witch with a book written especially for you.
>
> - Find out how the Wiccan mysteries can enhance your life
> - Begin your journey with the Teen Seeker Ceremony
> - Combine common herbs from the supermarket to make your magickal formulas
> - Create your own sacred space
> - Read true stories of Wiccan teens
> - Work magick with real spells
> - Learn the Craft techniques for gaining love, money, health, protection, and wisdom
> - Discover how to talk to friends, parents, and other people about your involvement with WitchCraft

The concept—and the success—of *Teen Witch* was directly related to the youth-market Witchcraft explosion in the media during the late 1990s. 1996's hit movie *The Craft* had created a ready-made audience among teens for learning more about Witchcraft, and it almost certainly inspired Ravenwolf's decision to make teenagers the focus of her book. Partly because of those pop-culture connections, *Teen Witch* was not well received among "traditionalist" Wiccans in the Neopagan movement. Those who saw Witchcraft as an esoteric religion, transmitted by teaching and initiation, thought that Ravenwolf had sensationalized their beliefs. The book was widely disdained in the Witchcraft community for being crass, superficial, and exploitive.

But that didn't seem to slow it down. Within its first year, *Teen Witch* was flying off the shelves at Borders, Barnes & Noble, and other mainstream bookstores. It quickly went to multiple reprintings and became the all-time bestselling title for its publisher, the occult-oriented Llewellyn Publications. That kind of success attracts attention—and imitators. Other publishers tried to jump aboard the already rolling bandwagon with books like *The Teen Spell Book: Magick for Young Witches* (2001), followed by *Where to Park Your Broomstick: A Teen's Guide to Witchcraft* (2002), and *Witchin: A Handbook for Teen Witches* (2003)—among many others.

The surprising success of *Teen Witch* prompted Ravenwolf to start writing Wiccan popular fiction aimed at the same audience. One day, in a reverie, she imagined that the teens in the cover art for *Teen Witch* were real people. She gave them names and identities and came up with the idea for the Witches' Chillers series of supernatural/ horror/mystery novels for Llewellyn Publishers. The central character in the series is Bethany Salem, a 16-year-old high school sophomore and Witch-in-training. Along with several of her teenage Wiccan friends from a local coven, Bethany uses witchy spells and psychic skills to solve crimes and fend off dangers—in stories with titles like *Witches' Night of Fear, Witches' Key to Terror,* and *Witches' Voodoo Moon.* An advertisement for the series spells out its unsubtle appeal: "Do Teens Have Power? You Bet! Experience the Thrill of a Witches' Chiller."

Ravenwolf is very clear that the purpose of her books is to encourage teens to investigate the world of Witchcraft for themselves. On her Web site, she says, "Although the story is entirely fictional, I set about to devise a world where the teens use real magick, not the fairy tale stuff." And she not only makes the "magick" appealing, she also makes it accessible: "Woven into the Witches' Chillers series is a positive spell in each book that teenagers can do for themselves."

Even the Disney entertainment machine is exploiting the teen–Witchcraft connection, with a book series for adolescent girls called W.I.T.C.H., about five teenage girls who practice Witchcraft. According to a statement by Disney Publishing Worldwide, the series was introduced in the U.S. in April 2004—after several years of what a Disney executive called "an unprecedented global response to the characters and the concept" in other countries.

Collegiate Pagans

For many teens, high school merges into college as seamlessly as summer merges into fall. By 1999, what had begun among high schoolers had also moved with them onto the college campuses. There, the "teen wave" of Wiccan enthusiasm merged with the "goddess" contingent of feminism that had found a home in academia during the 1980s. The result is that Neopaganism has become securely ensconced as part of the social and academic scene at many colleges and universities. Today, according to college officials, increasing numbers of incoming students "identify Wicca and other pagan practices as their official religion" (Wereszynski, 2002).

What has startled observers is not just the extent of that change, but the speed with which it is taking place. "On college campuses in the past several years, many pagan groups that were once underground have become official student organizations"—in 1998, "the Pagan Educational Network received its first request from a college student wanting to start a pagan group on her campus" (Reisberg, 2000). Five years later, in 2003, contact information was available on the Internet for Neopagan student groups at 99 colleges and universities in 35 states (Pagans on Campus Web site). The schools on the list span the spectrum of educational institutions, from large state universities (the University of Texas, Penn State University) to advanced technical and research schools (MIT, Rensselaer Polytechnic Institute) to small, private liberal arts colleges (Reed College, St. Olaf's College) to elite Ivy League schools (Yale), and traditional women's colleges (Smith College, Wellesley College).

One result of the increasing pagan presence on campus has been an increasing recognition of Neopagan religion by university administrators. At Syracuse University, members of the student Pagan Society use the campus chapel to hold candlelight Pagan ceremonies. The Reverend Thomas Wolfe, dean of the chapel, was "worried some would object to having Wiccan rituals performed in the same spiritual center used by Christian, Jewish and Muslim students, [but] said he's faced no objections" (Wereszynski, 2002).

In addition, some schools now include Neopagan holidays on the approved list for student observation, along with those of Christianity, Judaism, and other traditional faiths. At the University of Arizona and Lehigh University, for example, believers can be excused from class on Wiccan holidays. "'We acknowledge an individual's right to engage in their religious practices as they see fit,' said Lehigh spokesman Andrew Stanten. 'It is our firm belief that we embrace all kinds of thoughts'" (Wereszynski, 2002).

In *National Review Online,* the Provost of Boston University calls campus Wicca "part of the florid undergrowth of the contemporary liberal university" and says that "the widespread recognition of neo-pagans and similar groups shows how far the spiritual immune system of higher education has been compromised. Little inanities that once would have been brushed aside now settle in as opportunistic infections" (Wood, Peter, 2001). Others see the movement as connected to particular social developments. In October 2000, the *Chronicle of Higher Education* took note of the "growing pagan movement on campuses in the United States." In an article titled "Campus Witches May Wear Black, but Don't Look for Hats or Broomsticks," the author suggests that the rapid rise of campus Wicca is a result of converging cultural trends:

> It's no coincidence, scholars and followers say, that paganism is growing in an era when environmentalism and feminism are among the movements that have dominated campus discourse.
>
> "Paganism reverberates with [those] two very powerful and culture-changing movements we've had now for several generations," says John K. Simmons, a professor of religious studies at Western Illinois University (Reisberg, 2000).

In this we can see some of Witchcraft's appeal for college students and other young adults. It manages to appear both "ancient" and "modern" simultaneously. On the one hand, it claims to be part of a venerable tradition stretching all the way back to the dawn of human religion. On the other hand, it addresses modern concerns so explicitly that it often looks like political pandering. This odd combination of opposite qualities (achieved mainly by fabricating the "tradition") enables collegians to satisfy their desire for continuity and connectedness at the same time they satisfy their desire to disconnect from society and take a countercultural stance against it. It enables them to hang on to something like cultural rootedness at the same time they stand at the cutting edge of cultural change. In that respect, Neopaganism seems almost tailor-made to capture the fancy of the college generation.

Like teen Witches, collegiate Witches also have their own age-appropriate literature. The college-level equivalent of *Teen Witch* is *Rocking the Goddess: Campus Wicca for the Student Practitioner* by Anthony Paige. Paige is a graduate of SUNY Purchase College, where he started a Wiccan student group. In a recent interview, he candidly expressed the attraction that modern Witchcraft has for contemporary students: "Wicca appeals to some college students because 'there is no sense of sin...There is a karmic law, but there's no scorn or condemnation,' said Paige, who was raised a Roman Catholic" (Wereszynski, 2002).

The content and purpose of the book are well-described by the publisher's promotional copy:

> Wicca is the fastest-growing religion in America, and it thrives on college campuses—in underground covens, classrooms, on the Web, and through campus associations. Now, in this comprehensive, thoroughly modern handbook, journalist and practicing Pagan Anthony Paige gives you the lowdown on everything you need to know to Rock the Goddess and celebrate Pagan rituals on campus and off. Whether you're a practicing Pagan or new to the tenets of Wicca, this practical handbook—written by a student for students—explores today's college Wicca scene.
>
> Filled with invaluable resources, history, role models, spells, Web sites, and personal stories from college witches nationwide, *Rocking the Goddess* is an indispensable guide to an old religion for a new generation, one that will help you feel the mystery, experience the magick, and find the witch within (Branwen's Cauldron).

Today the link between teenagers, college kids, and Witchcraft seems to be firmly established. It is not a fad or a passing fancy, and it will almost certainly be a feature of our social landscape for some time to come. But another element turns that teen–collegiate linkage into an even more potent instrument for propagating Neopaganism—and that other element is the Internet.

Urban Primitives and Computer Mystics

One of the real surprises of the 1980s was the emergence of a strong connection between Neopaganism, high technology, and the computer culture. The relationship came to light in 1986, in the revised edition of Margot Adler's *Drawing Down the Moon*. In surveying Neopagans to bring her research up to date, Adler discovered that "their job profiles are pretty unusual, with an amazingly high percentage in computer, scientific and technical fields" (Adler, 1986, page 446).

Why should there be an overlap between such seemingly disparate realms as the primal world of nature religion and the high-tech world of computers and the Internet? At first impression, the connection seems unlikely and surprising. But in fact, it is one of several superficial ironies in Neopaganism that actually do make sense on a deeper level.

Another example appears in the fact that while Neopagans exalt Nature to the point of divinity and revere Nature to the point of worship, the movement itself is distinctly an urban phenomenon, concentrated in the cities rather than the countryside. That is not a new relationship. Rousseau's philosophy of naturalistic innocence arose from the over-refined culture of European aristocracy and probably couldn't have arisen anywhere else. Those who are most concerned with their connection to nature tend to be those who are most aware of their *dis*connection from nature. Such people are reacting to their real experience, even though they misinterpret their predicament—which is predictable enough, from a biblical point of view.

The relationship between Neopagans and computers is more complicated. Margot Adler herself was taken aback by the results of her 1985 questionnaire:

> The most unusual finding in this job survey is that so many people involved with Paganism were in technical fields. Out of 195 answers, 28 people or roughly 16 per cent were either programmers, technical writers or scientists—and I'm not even counting the lab technicians or the students who said they were studying computer programming (Adler, 1986, page 447).

When asked the reason for that connection, the Neopagans themselves offered a variety of answers, but came to no consensus. One said that computers are "elementals in disguise." Another said that both activities attract the same kind of people—namely oddball, solitary, creative types. Others offered that it's simply "where the jobs are" (Adler, 1986, page 449). But one Witch, a "techno-pagan" who uses actual, physical computers as components of his metaphysical rituals, suggested a more basic connection—within the human mind.

> Magic is the science of the imagination, the art of engineering consciousness.... "Both cyberspace and magical space are purely manifest in the imagination," [he] says.... "Both spaces are entirely constructed by your thoughts and beliefs" (Davis, 1995).

He is suggesting, in an appropriate blending of occult and technical jargon, that the magical worldview is fundamentally compatible with the outlook that prevails in the computer culture. And that suggestion is borne out by the history of the computer culture itself. A great deal of the so-called computer revolution arose within a California subculture that was heavily influenced by "New Age" thinking and was therefore wide open to gnostic and occult spirituality. The hippie counterculture, especially in its '70s and '80s "New Age" version, has always affected the outlook of computer pioneers. From the beginning, a quasi-occult worldview was thoroughly woven into the way that many of the people in "Silicon Valley" thought about computers—and for that matter about life in general.

A great deal of the so-called computer revolution arose within a California subculture that was heavily influenced by "New Age" thinking and was therefore wide open to gnostic and occult spirituality.

New Age elements are rife throughout the post-1960s Bay Area culture that laid the groundwork for much of what we call cyberculture. A psychedelic, do-it-yourself spirituality directly feeds the more utopian elements of this Northern California subculture of Virtual Reality designers, computer artists and computer programmers....For many of these folks, computers are the latest and among the greatest tools available for the achievement of the

Aquarian goal: the expansion of consciousness by whatever means necessary....For the more futuristic New Agers, the self is an information-processing entity that changes its nature, depending on the information-flows it receives and the various media to which it connects (Davis, 1993, pages 610–611).

In the magical worldview, Reality is not a "thing," but a "process"—constantly changing, constantly in flux, and subject to manipulation by the directed force of will. Indeed, to the magician, the very "self" that is our identity has no fixed form or boundaries, but is expandable to the limits of divinity. Computers seem to offer a down-to-earth version of that same dream, and a tangible fulfillment of its yearnings. Through computers, the prospect of practical omniscience beckons; so too, the promise of virtual omnipresence, as the mind extends its grasp at will across the reaches of the global network. Magic and technology are two versions of the same impulse—the impulse to self-will—and it is inevitable that they reconverge. It is no accident that our feats of computer technology are rising to the level of virtual magic at the same time that Witches are embracing computers as instruments of actual magic.

Witchcraft and the Internet

The early blending of the computer culture and the magical worldview had several important results. One result of that connection can be seen in the fact that the content of much computer entertainment is heavily oriented to occult and pagan themes. The "gaming" subculture itself is also suffused with Neopagan sympathies and enthusiasms—thus providing one more overlap between Neopaganism and the world of teens and collegians.

But another result has been even more important. The relationship between Neopaganism and the computer culture means that Neopagan enthusiasts were in attendance at the birth of the Internet, and Neopagans were therefore among the first to stumble upon the power of the Net to link scattered individuals together into an entity that is greater than the sum of its parts.

The Internet has been central to the development of the Neopagan movement for two reasons. First, it strengthens the hand of culturally marginal types in general by allowing people to connect together who would otherwise remain isolated from one another. Second, it does so while maintaining the individual's privacy and anonymity.

M. Macha Nightmare, author of *Witchcraft and the Web,* discusses those functions of the Internet and describes the difference the Net has made to Neopagans:

> Prior to the advent of the Internet and the World Wide Web, Witches and Pagans were isolated from one another....Several covens and traditions could exist in the same city, or even in the same neighborhood and never even know about one another.... Most Witches lived their lives in the figurative broom closet. Discretion was the safe and prudent approach when it came to our religion. We kept ourselves, and our groups, to ourselves.
>
> The Net changed all that. On the Web, isolated individuals and groups found one another....The Web allowed community to be created where none had been. The anonymity of online communications liberated witchen folks to express their thoughts, feelings and experiences in relative safety. So, in a sense, the Web became our church (Nightmare, 2001, pages 23–24).

Other Neopagan writers have also emphasized the Net's features of "networking" and "anonymity" as critical to the emergence of Neopaganism as a movement. Starhawk says, "The Internet has allowed the Pagan movement to grow tremendously, because it has provided a very safe way for people to connect with it" (Vale and Sulak, 2001, page 15). Rowan Fairgrove says, "Millions of people are meeting in chat rooms, communicating, finding validation for what they do, making new friends—especially those with non-mainstream interests. It's a very powerful experience when you discover you're not really alone—that's the biggest difference the Internet has made" (Vale and Sulak, 2001, page 41).

Enabling Alternative Culture

While isolated individuals remain powerless to challenge the main culture—or to build a "countercultural" alternative to it—connected individuals can do both. And the privacy of the Internet means that cultural dissenters can make their connections without having to "come out" in a public way that would subject them to reproach or reprisal. The combination of those two factors means that cultural dissent in general becomes more feasible, less costly, and easier to find and connect with. As an illustration, those same two characteristics of the Internet have also helped to create the homosexual movement—a different "cultural minority," but one that overlaps Neopaganism significantly in membership. In "Queer Witches and the World Wide Web: Breaking the Spell of Invisibility," self-described "Faggot Witch Sparky Rabbit" writes,

> One of the biggest obstacles faced by Queer men and women is the cloak of invisibility put on us by the dominant culture's hetero-sexism....One of the worst

experiences many Queer people share is the feeling, from childhood on, that "I am the only one of my kind in the world."…So when the Web became available—*bam!!*—Queers were all over it from the git-go. When I was first learning about computers and the Internet, in the mid-nineties, a friend of mine said, "The Internet is made up of Pagans and Queers." I don't believe that statement was statistically correct, but it definitely was an accurate expression of what many Queer Pagans I know were experiencing on the web; there were a Hell of a lot more of us out there than any one of us had ever guessed (Quoted in Nightmare, 2001, pages 174–175).

"Breaking the spell of invisibility," also known as "minority empowerment," also known as "linking otherwise isolated individuals," was the single most important contribution of the Internet to cultural dissent of every kind—Neopaganism included. It was a development that made everything else possible, as numerous "alternative cultures" arose and many of them turned into outright cultural resistance movements. That has certainly been true of the so-called "erotic minorities" (read "deviant sexual proclivities"), including not only homosexuality, but also pedophilia and Bondage/Dominance/Sado-Masochism (BDSM), all of which have established "communities" of like-minded enthusiasts on the Net. The same is also true of extremist zealotry of both left and right, for example eco-terrorism and militant racism. In fact, there is scarcely any form of deviance—whether cultural, social, spiritual, or otherwise—that has *not* been empowered by the Internet. For that reason, the Net has been called "the clearinghouse of contemporary heresy," where "magicians are just one more thread in the Net's rainbow fringe of anarchists, Extropians, conspiracy theorists, X-Files fans, and right-wing kooks" (Davis, 1995).

Moreover, the very existence of that "rainbow fringe" serves its own culture-changing function. Because the Internet gives marginal causes a power and presence in society they wouldn't otherwise have, it desensitizes people to cultural deviance in general, and eventually makes it seem routine. Sheer repeated exposure to cultural insubordination breeds at first awareness, then acceptance, and finally, acceptability.

The Web as "Church"

In the case of modern Witchcraft and Neopaganism, the Internet has clearly been a critical factor in the mushrooming growth of the movement since the 1980s. When M. Macha Nightmare says, "the Web became our church," it is more than just a figure of speech. The Internet functions for Neopagans in several ways that are parallel to the way the church functions for Christians.

Just as Christianity is most visible and most accessible through its churches, Neopaganism is undoubtedly most visible and accessible on the Internet. A serious involvement with Witchcraft in particular is more available to outsiders via the Internet than it is in any other way. In fact, without having access to the Internet, it is almost impossible to get a real impression of how vigorous and expansive the Neopagan movement has become.

The rapid rise and surprising success of the Web site Witchvox.com perhaps best illustrates the growing presence of Witchcraft and Neopaganism on the Web. Wren Walker and Fritz Jung founded "The Witches' Voice" in 1996. They acquired the domain name "Witchvox.com" and inaugurated their Web site in 1997 with 56 pages of content and a section of Neopagan links and contacts. Its declared purpose was to create and disseminate educational materials for Pagans and non-Pagans alike, fight discrimination against Pagans, and act as a tool for networking Pagans by providing an index of "Pagans, Pagan groups and Pagan shops," together with "their e-mail addresses, events and work-shops" (Nightmare, 2002, page 117).

The Web site was an instant hit with Witches and Neo-pagans of every persuasion. The resources offered by "The Witches' Voice" evidently addressed needs that were strongly and widely felt within the Neopagan community.

> By the end of its first year, Witchvox was offering 385 pages which were viewed on personal computers the world over. Within that time, the site had received 1,235,237 hits. It listed several thousand Witches, Wiccans and Pagans on its state/country pages, 385 circles and events, 250 witchen and metaphysical shops (most submitted by customers), 976 Pagan Web sites (with complete contact info), and a site map.... Truly, The Witches' Voice is something for us Witches to crow about (Nightmare, 2001, page 118).

But even that auspicious beginning was just a trickle in advance of the torrent to come. In the five years since its inauguration, Witchvox.com has grown as explosively as the community it serves. By October 2003, the Web site had received almost 96 million hits (95,748,682, to be exact) since its inception, and over 2 million hits (2,005,473) for the month of October in that year alone. Its contact list (now entitled "Witches of the World") contained 2520 pages of text, with over 46,000 named contacts—including individuals, groups, publishers, shops, bookstores, and so on, all around the globe. There were extensive listings for all 50 states of the USA, all provinces of Canada, all regions of the United Kingdom, and all states of Australia, as well as 40 other countries worldwide. There was also a separate catalog of electronic contacts ("Witchvox Links") that listed 6917 Internet links, including some 5000 Neopagan Web sites (out of an estimated 9000 Pagan Web sites total).

If, as Neopagans say, they are making up their religion as they go along, then the Internet is one place where that work of creation is being done.

By any measure, those statistics are impressive. But they indicate more than mere numerical inflation. Beneath the surface of those numbers runs a constant, invisible stream of activity that constitutes Neopagan "networking"—Neopagans communicating, setting up meetings, arranging to do rituals, actually doing rituals online, disseminating news about festivals, celebrations, lectures, and workshops, sharing spells and rituals, swapping information and opinions, arguing, agreeing, organizing events, co-ordinating political activism, and so on, and so on. This is where Neopaganism lives on a day-to-day basis, and to find it you have to pass beyond the portals of the Neopagan Web sites—to scan the online Neopagan bulletin boards, frequent the Neopagan chat rooms, and subscribe to the Neopagan listserves. To say that Witchvox.com lists 46,000 Neopagan contacts only hints at the teeming activity that goes on all the time at the grassroots of the Internet, but which never gets counted or catalogued.

Incidentally, that is another way that the Internet functions for Neopagans much as the church does for Christians. It is where they find contact, interaction, edification, encouragement, and teaching; indeed, for many Witches and Neopagans, the Internet becomes the primary means, or even the sole means, of "fellowship" with their co-religionists. It is also where the next stages of Neopaganism are being created. If, as Neopagans say, they are making up their religion as they go along, then the Internet is one place where that work of creation is being done. It has been said that the Witchcraft of tomorrow is taking shape today in the chat rooms of the World Wide Web.

The modern Witchcraft movement has always put a high priority on changing the public's perception of Witches and their craft. During the 1970s and '80s, that public relations work went forward cautiously, as a few out-of-the-broom-closet Witches spoke out publicly on behalf of their beliefs. Federal court decisions during the 1980s validated the constitutional status of religious Witchcraft, giving the movement a claim to legitimacy that opened new doors of growth and positive publicity. But the real point of transition, both for the movement and for the image of Witchcraft, came during the 1990s. The mushrooming interest in the subject that followed hard on the heels of the mid-1990s media blitz fundamentally altered the composition of the movement. It also put a newer, hipper, more youthful face on Witchcraft for the general public to see.

Those converging changes created a new center of gravity for the Neopagan movement. The early close connection between Neopaganism and the Internet had helped to create the movement by bringing its participants together. Then the late-1990s "youth revolution" transformed the emerging teenage/college/Internet connection into a powerful tool for bringing the message of modern Witchcraft to outsiders. In the space of half a decade, Witches took the Internet from an inward-looking tool of movement-building to an active tool of cultural outreach.

Apart from the Internet, the most important catalyst in the process of modern Witchcraft's image makeover has been the influence of the entertainment media. We will take a look at that part of the equation in chapters 3 and 4.

3
Teens and the Media: Witchcraft in Popular Entertainment

T HE WORLD OF ADOLESCENTS has always been separate from the world of adults. The so-called "generation gap" has always existed, and reflects the need of children to form an independent identity which can then make its peace (or not) with grown-up society. Today, as always, teenagers express their solidarity and separateness in a number of ways (jargon and clothing come to mind as obvious examples) that deliberately exclude adults from participating—or even from comprehending.

The Generational Tug-of-War

Part of that process of adolescent separation has traditionally involved experimenting with behavior that deliberately flouts the standards of adult society. Predictably, that includes dabbling with disapproved ideas as well as disapproved acts. The teen world has always been a hotbed of exotic "spiritual" exploration. Ouija boards and fortune-telling games are a staple of teen girl slumber parties precisely because they are known to lie outside the boundaries of accepted grown-up behavior. Adolescent boys act out the same impulses with so-called "legend tripping"—nighttime visits to cemeteries, "haunted" houses, and other places connected with death and the dark side of the unseen (that is, "spiritual") world.

The passage through adolescence has always been a source of anxiety for parents in general, and for Christian parents in particular. The teen years are a volatile phase in the process of forming a lifelong identity. Religious conversions occur more frequently during the teen years than at any other time of life (Clark, 2003, page 9). Parents who take seriously their calling to cultivate the seeds of Christian faith in their offspring are justifiably concerned about this vulnerable time in their children's development.

Again, none of these concerns are new. The "generation gap" is a timeworn cliché for the very good reason that it is a universal experience. It is part of everyone's life at least once, often twice (that is, first as a child, then again—in reverse—as a parent). The formula of teenage vulnerability is likewise widely understood: as adolescents start to engage with the wider world, inexperience plus experimentation produces casualties—physical, mental, and spiritual. As always, parents do what they can to minimize the threats and maximize their children's ability to deal with them.

But recently, the balance of power in that generational tug-of-war has shifted in ways that are new and disturbing. Traditionally, society itself has been a powerful source of support that parents could draw on to provide protection, rescue, or recovery from the dangers that teens routinely encounter and sometimes run afoul of. The mainstream society has always been a dominating, collective force for validating family stability, family values, and family-friendly institutions. In the Christian-based culture of the West, that has meant society's endorsement of the whole range of personal and social obligations that we have come to call

"Christian morality"—including monogamy, fidelity, and parental responsibility.

Today, those traditional social supports are eroding with alarming rapidity. At the same time, teenagers face new stresses that greatly intensify the sense of continual crisis that haunts their experience to begin with. And teens are further isolated by new conditions that create even more distance between them and the larger society. That is not a helpful combination.

Consider the novel anxieties that today's teenagers have to contend with: school shootings, school muggings, terrorism, hate crimes, racial tensions, "date rape," sexually transmitted diseases, gangs, and drugs—all in addition to the "normal" teen worries about delinquency, pregnancy, popularity, bullying, alcohol, and automotive mayhem. It is enough to test the mental stability of a saint, much less that of a teenager already giddy from riding the hormonal roller coaster.

The Disconnected World of Teenagers

At the same time that teens are being overloaded with fears and worries, they are also being pushed more and more into their own self-contained world to deal with them—a world where they are much less responsive to outside influences, and much less reachable by outside sources of help and support. Again, teenagers have always lived in their own unique world to some degree. It is an essential stage in their development to do so. But all of the things that tend to make that world self-contained and exclusionary have recently been intensified—and some new ones have been added. The result has been to create a kind of psychological hothouse for developing adolescents, in which increasingly artificial conditions are maintained by teens being increasingly disconnected from the wider social world.

Some of that disconnected environment for teens comes from economic and social changes that have nothing to do with the teenage culture per se. For instance, the great increase in single-parent families we have seen since the 1960s means that more children are being left on their own, more of the time. In her illuminating study of teen culture *(From Angels to Aliens: Teenagers, the Media, and the Supernatural)*, author Lynn Schofield Clark points to "changes in the postindustrial economy" that have further isolated teenagers and driven them into their own self-referential world.

> More parents now work in service positions that offer lower pay and less security (and hence encourage multiple simultaneous jobs), and the few who are fortunate enough to have higher-paying positions regularly work long hours. This, combined with the fact that more mothers work outside the home, means that a great number of parents are away from their homes and their teenage children—more than was the case with the previous generation of teens—making them "a tribe apart" as author Patricia Hersch has described them (Clark, 2003, page 7).

The Internet is another factor that works to make the teenage universe even more disconnected and self-contained than it otherwise would be. We have already seen that the Internet was crucial in creating the Neopagan movement. The same qualities of privacy and anonymity that make the Internet such a powerful networking tool also make it an easy way to "bypass the parent-filter"—to disengage from the "real" world and enter into a "virtual" world that is shielded from adult attention.

> Not only has the Internet provided a way for pagans to network and share ideas, beliefs and spells, it's a neat and clean way for curious youth to avoid the scrutiny of parents while exploring once-forbidden subjects. Any Web-savvy child can be indoctrinated into a pagan worldview and start casting spells before a parent catches on to this new interest. A 15-year-old on the Website Witches' Voice writes:
>
> "A friend told me about a religion that worships both a male and a female deity. I was interested and she gave me Silver Ravenwolf's book, *Teen Witch*. I started reading and never put it down. I got on the Internet and learned more and more. I finally did a devotion ceremony and I considered myself to be Wiccan" (Harvey, 2002).

The world of teenagers today is not only more self-contained and self-sufficient than it used to be, it is also self-validating —in the literal sense that for many young people, the Self has become the final arbiter of what is real, what is true, and what is valuable. And that is the effect of yet another social trend—one that began in the 1950s, flowered during the 1960s, and remains a potent social force today. It is what sociologists have called "the rise of personal autonomy." As the traditional sources of authority in society (including religion) have steadily lost credibility since World War II, they have also lost their power to define Reality and set the standards of Truth. As the old authorities were being rejected, the individual's own will and intellect gradually rose to replace them as the ultimate judge and measure of all things.

Individuals see themselves as final arbiters of what they will believe and how they will embrace practices related to those beliefs...Teens, like their parents and other adults today do not seem to be very interested in learning about ultimate truths from authoritative sources like the Bible or religious traditions. They consider *themselves* to be the ultimate authority on what it might mean for them to be religious or spiritual (Clark, 2003, page 9).

But religion isn't the only source of authority to suffer a loss of prestige and credibility. For many people, science itself—usually seen as the opposite of religion—is also losing its power to dictate what we believe in. "Soulless science" and out-of-control technology are often thought to be implicated in many of today's crises, especially the abuse of our environment, thereby disqualifying them as reliable guides to belief or behavior. "Baby Boomers" (today's parents) were raised in an atmosphere of virtual science-worship in the years after World War II. Their children, noticing science's failed promises and destructive side-effects, are much less trusting of it. In the end, "the rise of personal autonomy" has meant that the Self replaces *all* other forms of authority, not just the religious ones. For many young people today, that includes "a rejection of the authoritative claims of science, *particularly those that exclude the possibility of any realities beyond that which was knowable in the material world*" (Clark, 2003, page 52, emphasis added).

For teens today, the net effect of those converging trends is to open the door to the spiritual realm while simultaneously closing the door on sources for understanding what they will find there. It is one more way that young people find themselves pushed into their own separate world—and left to their own devices for dealing with it. Teenagers are presented with a huge new array of choices to make about the world and their place in it. As their alienation from the larger society has intensified, they have increasingly looked to one another—and to the media—for help in building a worldview out of the raw material of their own experience.

Teens and the Media

If teens are ready to take their role models, their values, and their worldview from the media, the media are more than ready, willing, and able to provide. Among other things, teenagers represent an economic resource to be exploited by means of advertising—which is the media's natural function and purpose.

> Courting and cultivating the lucrative youth market has been an important part of the work of the media industries for decades. In recent years, however, the desire to appeal to teens has become even more intense. This is because today's teens represent the largest demographic group of young people ever— even surpassing their parents' generation, the "baby boomers" (Clark, 2003, page 14).

Teenagers are not only more numerous today than ever before, they are also richer than they have ever been, with more disposable cash at their command than any previous generation. The rise of MTV during the 1980s pioneered a new wave of entertainment (and companion advertising) designed to appeal specifically to teenagers. Today, a lot of the money that flows through teen pockets goes for various forms of media-delivered entertainment—a category that includes VCRs, DVD players, "home theaters," video games, and personal computers with Internet access, as well as "going out" to the movies in the old-fashioned way. When you add to that list the all-pervasive impact of television programming, it is evident that teenagers are drenched in visual media to an extent unprecedented in history. Converging with that trend, we have also seen a sharp rise in the amount of media programming "dedicated to issues of the supernatural and paranormal—long popular topics for the plots and subplots of teen culture stories" (Clark, 2003, page 15).

For teens today, even the Internet connection is a gateway to the visual entertainment industry. Among the more than 17 million teens who are online today, the three most popular uses for the Internet are "sending e-mail, surfing the Web for fun and visiting entertainment sites...in fact, the top Web site at the turn of the millennium, according to the youth- and young adult-oriented magazine *Yahoo! Internet Live,* was dedicated to Sarah Michelle Gellar, star of *Buffy the Vampire Slayer*" (Clark, 2003, page 15).

Development of Identity

It goes without saying that this media-drenched environment affects the way teens develop their concepts of self and personal identity—how they understand who they are and what their place is in the world around them.

> A great deal of evidence suggests that the media play an important role in how young people form and articulate their identities. Young people learn from and identify with characters they watch and with celebrities they admire...They share their interests in media with their friends as a means of expresssing both their own individuality and their shared tastes. This sharing then informs teens' individual tastes, as well, for the two processes of using the media in individual and collective identity construction reinforce one another (Clark, 2003, pages 15–16).

The power of the media to shape the emerging identities of young adults lies in two things. It lies first in the stories that the media tells. Specifically, it lies in the dramatic power of their narratives—their power to convey ideas and values by means of storytelling, and especially their power to engage teenagers' attention because of the stories' *relevance* to their lives. Secondly, the media's power to mold teen identities lies in the commercial manipulation of teenage wants, needs, and fantasies, both with overt commercial advertising and by means of its entertainment content.

✛ ✛ ✛ ✛ ✛ ✛ ✛ ✛ ✛ ✛ ✛ ✛ ✛ ✛ ✛ ✛ ✛

Young people today live in a world of their own that is very different from the teen culture of earlier generations.

✛ ✛ ✛ ✛ ✛ ✛ ✛ ✛ ✛ ✛ ✛ ✛ ✛ ✛ ✛ ✛ ✛

Teen-oriented entertainment is highly engaging to young people, not only for the obvious reason that it features appealing teenage characters they can identify with, but also because its dramas provide teens with powerful psychological tools that can help them cope with the stresses and anxieties of adolescence. In that respect, the media's stories serve an important function in the process of forming an adult identity.

> Horror stories, particularly those with strong super-natural elements, allow young people to experience and relieve fears about death, the afterlife, and in general, the forces in life that they believe are beyond their control—which includes quite a bit, from the teen perspective (Clark, 2003, pages 63–64).

For most teenagers, the number one "force beyond their control" (aside from their parents) is their own sexuality. Thus the supernatural elements in the media's stories are magnetic to them because they also serve as a metaphor for sex in the teen experience. In many of these programs and films, "the young people at their center have either inherited or stumbled on their powers in their teen years, and they find that they have no choice but to use them. Having these powers is their 'destiny,' regardless of how much they may long for a normal teen life" (Clark, 2003, page 69).

Because of this ability to engage the deep, intense concerns of teenage life, media entertainment (along with peer-group influence) is displacing more traditional sources of guidance and support in the process of teenage character- and identity-formation. For example, "as anthropologist Victor Turner argued, the experience of watching films together can, in some ways, serve the same function as the older rituals that marked rites of passage" (Clark, 2003, page 6).

Young people today live in a world of their own that is very different from the teen culture of earlier generations. As the media increasingly cater to the tastes and cravings of teenage consumers, what teens see in and through the media is increasingly a reflected image of themselves. Increasingly, their world of values and beliefs is self-created, without reference to external realities or expectations. Teen-oriented media becomes a kind of youth-culture echo chamber—an ideal environment for commercial manipulation. Without any standards other than profits and ratings, the media is "both responding to interest in Witchcraft and creating it, in a rapid feedback loop" (Harvey, 2002). In fact, the mid-1990s explosion of Witchcraft in the media can be seen as part of that process, and as a sign of the new (teen) center of gravity in media marketing and entertainment.

Changing Images of Witchcraft in Popular Entertainment

Of course, witches didn't have to wait until the 1990s to make their appearance in popular entertainment. Witchcraft's sinister and sensational reputation has made it an ideal device for authors who want to add drama to their plot lines or spice up their character development. From the three "weird sisters" of Shakespeare's *Macbeth* to the devil-worshiping conspirators of the movie *Rosemary's Baby,* most witch depictions in literature and entertainment have been drawn from the classic stereotypes associated with medieval witchcraft—resulting in characters who range from menacing to actively evil. One of the first works to (partially) break out of that mold, both in print and visual media, was *The Wizard of Oz* (print version, 1900; movie version, 1939), which offered a "good witch" character in the person of Glinda to counterbalance the classic "bad witch" stereotype embodied in the ugly, black-clad hag who was Dorothy's antagonist.

As the 1960s began, the classic stereotype was significantly broken again, this time in an important but easy-to-overlook medium—comic books. In 1962, "Sabrina the teenage witch" made her debut appearance in the popular *Archie* comic-book series. Sabrina soon became a regular character in the *Archie* series, then went on to star in her own Saturday morning animated TV program, and in 1996 finally graduated to become the feature character in a live-action TV movie on Showtime—which was followed by a spin-off live-action TV series (both the Showtime movie and the TV series were part of the late-1990s Witchcraft surge in the entertainment media). Sabrina was a pioneer of Witchcraft's image change in several ways: she was one of the earliest characters to break out of the "bad witch" mold; she is easily the longest-lived; and from the beginning, she has been designed to appeal directly to a teen and pre-teen audience.

Almost as if following Sabrina's comic-book lead, within a few years two popular television comedies also broke decisively with the "bad witch" stereotype—and one of them didn't even have a witch in it. *I Dream of Jeannie* ran between September 1965 and September 1970. It starred Barbara Eden as a genie who becomes the magical servant of an American serviceman when he discovers and then opens the bottle in which she has been imprisoned. The comedy in this sitcom revolves around Jeannie's tendency to use her magical powers in ways that disrupt her master's "normal" military life. Jeannie was a genie, not a witch, but she helped to break the negative stereotype with her role as a female who uses occult power in funny, nonthreatening ways.

The other trailblazing sitcom of the '60s did have a witch in it. *Bewitched,* starring Elizabeth Montgomery as witch Samantha Stevens, ran from September 1964 through July 1972 (overlapping *Jeannie*, but three years longer-running). The series was extremely popular with viewers; in fact, it was the biggest-hit series produced by ABC up to that point and was rated second among all programs aired during its first season.

The story line in *Bewitched* involves an entire family of witches who are immortal. One member of the family, the beautiful Samantha, marries a mortal husband ("Darrin," played by Dick York) and pledges to renounce her supernatural powers, much to the disapproval of her witchy relatives, who constantly try to interfere in the marriage and generally use their magic in mischievous ways. Samantha herself is also tempted to rely on her magical powers in order to get things done around the house. As in the case of *Jeannie*, the humor in the series is drawn from the friction between the magical world of witches and the mundane world of ordinary people (the "mortals," in *Bewitched*'s scheme of things), who unfailingly fail to understand the freakish events that intrude on their otherwise ordinary lives. According to one reviewer, "The fun never ends when you mix witchcraft with mortal intellects who painfully attempt to explain to themselves the strange things that go on" ("Bewitched").

Sabrina, *I Dream of Jeannie,* and *Bewitched* were frivolous, but not trivial. None of them could be considered active propaganda for the Witchcraft movement per se. "Sabrina" and "Samantha Stevens" resemble real Witches about as closely as "Barney" resembles a real dinosaur. There is very little in either portrayal that modern Witches would recognize as part of their beliefs. But that doesn't mean they are irrelevant to the rise of modern Witchcraft. Sabrina, Jeannie, and Samantha were all an expression of the 1960s' penchant for turning the values of the main culture inside out. The counterculture had already given respectability to previously rejected ideas, including both Eastern religions and astrology. In that context, a comic-book or a television series based on reversing the values normally attached to witches and magic seemed like a perfectly natural development—especially as it was done in a lighthearted manner. In their function as statements of dissent from prevailing cultural values, all three characters helped set the stage for the more complete reversal of attitudes toward witchcraft and occultism that was to come some two decades later.

The Pendulum Swings

In the meantime, however, that process of cultural change was temporarily interrupted by a cultural pendulum-swing. As the '60s ended, the counterculture's quick descent from idealism into decadence gave rise to a cultural and spiritual backlash, symptoms of which included the "Jesus movement" and the rise of evangelicalism to prominence and political influence during the 1970s. Popular entertainment in the 1970s and early 1980s also reflected the new, more serious, and more religious mood that was asserting itself in society at large.

As evangelicals became a presence in public discussion, they brought biblical ideas and images to the forefront of public attention. In particular, they popularized the biblical imagery associated with the end times, the second coming, and the ongoing spiritual battle between God and His angels versus Satan and his demons. The result, in the words of Lynn Schofield Clark, is that "evangelicalism has inadvertently provided a framework for thinking about and representing evil in popular culture" (Clark, 2003, page 26). That development was particularly evident in the treatment that the entertainment industry gave to stories dealing with occultism and the supernatural during the 1970s and 1980s. "Horror" films, long a staple of the B-movie circuit, began to incorporate religious themes into their stories, even as they moved into the "A" category of major Hollywood productions.

Hollywood had invoked the real existence of the devil in *Rosemary's Baby* (1968) to great dramatic effect and impressive box-office success. *The Exorcist* (1973) went even further, portraying the conflict between good and evil as a war between God and the devil, who worked "through the vulnerable and the corrupt and [was] to be fought only with the traditional power of Christianity" (Hutton, 1999, page 332). The Omen trilogy (1975, 1978, and 1981) made the Christianity of its movies even more explicit—and more evangelical—by taking its story from premillennial eschatology, with its scenario of the end-times rise of Antichrist.

In all of those blockbuster films, occultism and supernatural power were virtually identified with demons, the devil, and evil (though only *Rosemary's Baby* featured witches per se in its story). *The Exorcist* in particular was a watershed film because it strongly established the new, biblically based imagery of good and evil. At a time when the mainstream religions were losing adherents and influence (especially among the young), the movie's conflict was defined as a showdown between a religious authority figure (a Catholic priest) and a disembodied demon over the soul of a teenage girl. The demon, moreover, had gained entry to the teenager's soul through her dabblings with the Ouija board—a plot device that dramatized the concerns evangelicals were raising about the occult and the danger it poses to young people.

The Omen trilogy reinforced that biblical imagery of good and evil, and strengthened it even further by tying it to biblical prophecy. In all three of the Omen movies, occult power serves the devil and his Antichrist in their opposition to God as that conflict is played out in the book of Revelation. The Omen movies also reinforced the disturbing idea that lay at the center of *The Exorcist*'s plot—that someone's identity could be taken over and completely changed from within by some (occult) force outside of themselves, and outside of their control.

The rise of evangelicalism was part of a social pendulum-swing. The influence of evangelicalism brought biblical images of good and evil to the forefront of the public's imagination. But the pendulum-swing of the 1970s was both brief and shallow. The biblical images of good and evil carried their own undeniable power, and they were quickly picked up by popular entertainment. But evangelicalism didn't make enough of an impact on the general culture to sustain the biblical *meaning* of those images beyond the decade in which they appeared—which is not much of a pendulum-swing, as such things go.

As those biblical images were handled by the entertainment media, they were also changed. Hollywood is very much a channel for the Spirit of the Age (the "Zeitgeist"), and the Zeitgeist's resistance to the biblical point of view eventually affects everything that Hollywood does. By the late 1980s, Hollywood was using the biblical imagery of evil to convey a nonbiblical message. And by the mid-1990s, Hollywood was using that biblical imagery to convey an overtly paganized message. The transformation was both rapid and complete.

The Witches of Eastwick is an example of biblical imagery in the process of transformation. The film, released in 1987, was loosely based on the 1984 novel by John Updike—a professing Christian. Three single, suburbanite women (played by Michelle Pfeiffer, Cher, and Susan Sarandon) dabble in magic, feminism, and witchcraft; they succeed in invoking a real, if somewhat trivialized, devil (played with obvious relish by Jack Nicholson), who appears in response to their magically amplified sexual yearnings. Nicholson's devil then uses their witchcraft to ensnare them into his net of ego, lust, and greed. The movie also invokes some of the classic witch stereotypes derived from the Middle Ages (see chapter 6), depicting witchcraft as connected not just with the devil, but also with magical powers such as levitation, and with unbridled sexual license as well.

But there is no hint here of Christianity as a counterpoint and nemesis to the forces of darkness, as there was in films of the previous decade. *The Witches of Eastwick* depicts the churchgoing Christianity of New England as pervasive, but impotent and irrelevant. The only Christian character of any significance in the movie is a comic figure—a woman who sees the devil and his evil for what they are, but is so unhinged by her knowledge that she becomes incoherent. By the end of the film, the devil is brought low, not by "the traditional power of Christianity," but by the women he had abused, who use the power of witchcraft to wreak their revenge and then to banish him from this world altogether.

The movie dramatizes (and satirizes) the blending of feminism, "goddess spirituality," witchcraft, and female sexual assertiveness that was a cultural fad of the 1980s. It is basically a feminist revenge-fantasy that uses the Christian imagery of evil to set up its intended target, but mocks and marginalizes Christianity while it vindicates witchcraft in principle as a form of personal power. It is hard to imagine an application of biblical imagery any more antithetical to actual biblical values.

Hard to imagine, that is, until it happens.

What happened next was a sudden eruption of Witchcraft themes in popular entertainment during the mid-1990s—a development that took everyone by surprise. It significantly changed the public's perception of Witchcraft, and even the shape and direction of the Witchcraft movement itself. Moreover—and more importantly—it changed the role that Christianity plays in popular entertainment's imagery of good and evil. In that rapid, radical change, two media productions stand out as part of the process: the surprise teen movie hit *The Craft,* and the surprise teen TV hit *Buffy the Vampire Slayer.*

4
Witchcraft in Popular Entertainment: *The Craft, Buffy,* and Beyond

✛ ✛ ✛

Aｆｔｅｒ *Tｈｅ Wｉｔｃｈｅｓ ｏｆ Eａｓｔｗｉｃｋ* ｉｎ 1987, the biblical imagery of good and evil that evangelicals brought to public attention seemed to disappear from popular entertainment —in fact, so did the whole subject of witchcraft. Movies that dealt with horror and the supernatural continued treating good and evil in religious terms, but those terms were no longer identifiably biblical; now they were drawn from a vague, generic, humanistic "spirituality"—which in turn was drawn mostly from Eastern and occult sources.

For example, *Jacob's Ladder* (1990) featured hallucinatory demons and hell scenes presented as dreams of its dying protagonist—a concept based on the elaborate death-mysticism of the Tibetan Book of the Dead (Brooke, 1990, page 30). *Flatliners* (1990) explored the same subject in more "scientific" terms, as its characters sought visions of "the other side" by deliberately subjecting themselves to a near-death experience. In *Ghost* (also 1990), the depiction of the afterlife and the evildoers' descent into hell is drawn from the accounts of spirit mediums and the teachings of

91

the kabbalah (a form of Jewish mysticism with deeply occult roots). Yet, despite their occult-related themes, none of those movies touched on witchcraft or dealt with the issue of occult power per se.

The Pendulum Swings Back

And then along came *The Craft*—which did both of the above, in spades. Released in 1996, the sensational movie about teenage Witches was a huge box-office success, and exposed the public to information about real Neopagan Witchcraft for the first time. The movie was a compass-setting event, both in popular entertainment and in popular culture generally. *The Craft* revolutionized the media's approach to teenagers, reshaped the media's imagery of good and evil, and redefined the public's idea of modern Witchcraft—all in a single stroke. It was also the first in a series of movie and video productions about Witches and Witchcraft that came out of Hollywood in quick succession for the next two years, and still continues intermittently today.

The movie tells the story of four teenage girls from a Catholic high school in Los Angeles, each of whom is an "outsider" in some way—different from and not accepted by the rest of the students. "Rochelle" is "multiracial" in an all-white school, "Bonnie" is disfigured by burn scars, "Nancy" is a poor kid in a rich kid's school, and "Sarah" is a new girl from out of town. The first three dabble in magic to get some power and control in their lives, then recruit the new girl to make four for a "coven" to explore Witchcraft more deeply. They discover real power in their spell-casting, but quickly lose control of it—and themselves—as their magic becomes progressively nastier and more destructive. Sarah casts a love spell and creates an obsessive, unwanted admirer, whom she then humiliates. Rochelle gets revenge on one of the snotty white girls by making her hair fall out. Nancy causes the death of her drunken, abusive stepfather in order to collect the insurance money (or, as Rochelle puts it, "not to be white trash or something"), and she later murders Sarah's obsessive admirer out of jealousy.

The Craft presents a picture of modern, Neopagan Witchcraft that actually resembles the real thing, instead of being based on the standard medieval stereotypes.

The four teen Witches not only visit general mayhem on those around them (including several deaths), they finally turn their powers against one another. In a dramatically staged ceremony, Nancy "invokes the spirit," a ritual of (something like) voluntary possession, which imbues her with tremendous magical power. Sarah tries to leave the coven, provoking a showdown with Nancy, who is backed up by the other two. It is a duel of good Witch versus bad Witch. In the end, the good Witch wins, the bad one is banished (strapped to a bed in an insane asylum), and her craven allies lose their witchy powers—while the good Witch (Sarah) gets to keep hers.

On one level the movie is a simple "cautionary tale"— easy to understand, and even familiar in its moral lessons. On that level, *The Craft* is a story about the temptations of power and the consequences of abusing it; the lesson is that the lust for control leads to the loss of control. But there are other levels, and other lessons—and it is because of them that the movie has had its effect on popular culture and popular entertainment.

To begin with, *The Craft* presents a picture of modern, Neopagan Witchcraft that actually resembles the real thing, instead of being based on the standard medieval stereotypes. That is not an accident, of course, nor is it the result of merely casual research. The movie's producers sought out a prominent Witch from the occult community in Los Angeles to act as a consultant on the script; she worked with them for two years to bring the film version of modern Witchcraft substantially into line with the real-life version.

The consultant—Pat Devin—was interviewed in 1998 about her work on the film. Devin said that a Sony Pictures publicist had originally contacted the owner of a well-known occult bookstore (The House of Hermetic) in Los Angeles, seeking someone with an insider's knowledge of modern Witchcraft. The bookstore owner in turn directed Sony to Devin, who was then serving as Co-National Public Information Officer for The Covenant of the Goddess, one of the oldest and most influential Neopagan groups.

In one of the fascinating highlights of the interview, Devin tells how she ran up against—and dealt with—the compromises in her beliefs that Hollywood required. At their initial meeting over lunch, the director of the movie (Andrew Fleming) leaned across the table and said, "Pat, you'll have to remember that this is a movie. It's Hollywood. It's not intended to be a documentary about the Wiccan religion. It's intended to make money. It will, hopefully, be entertaining. Do you think you can work with that?" (Devin, 1998).

Devin decided that she could.

> I decided to try to get as much truth into what was, after all, a teenage date spooky movie, as I could. I knew the results would not be perfect, but I felt

obligated to try, as the movie was going to come out in any event. I knew that I would be criticized for my attempt to be as authentic, if generic, as possible. But, of course, had I chosen to just make it up, I'd have been criticized for that (Devin, 1998).

Devin was right about the criticism—many Neopagans felt the movie cheapened and sensationalized their religion. Margot Adler went so far as to call it "the worst movie ever made!" (Vale and Sulak, 2001, page 28). But Devin succeeeded in her effort to get as much accurate information as possible about modern Witchcraft into the script. In the interview, she details some of her contributions.

My goal for the rituals and chants was that they be authentic, if generic, and that they contain nothing that could not be easily found in at least two books, or plausibly created by teenage girls....I wrote the Initiation scene, using widespread and common wording for the challenge. I suggested several possible ritual acts for that scene. Andy chose a drop of blood in the wine, which is based on a rite of my 1734 group. I asked my High Priestess' permission before suggesting it. I wrote the opening chant....I belong to two covens—one Dianic Feminist Separatist and one in the 1734 Tradition. The words in the scene are similar to what you'd hear in my Women's circle (Devin, 1998).

The Craft and Teen Culture

Neopaganism may have been sensationalized for the sake of the movie, but it was still identifiably Neopaganism. The fact that the movie's portrayal of modern Witchcraft was recognizably true to life is what made its impact so substantial.

Despite Margot Adler's horrified reaction, *The Craft* gave a big publicity and recruitment boost to modern Witchcraft for two reasons. The first reason is a matter of simple psychology: The lessons of the movie's "cautionary tale" are largely lost on teenagers, but its dangled lure of occult power definitely is not. A sense of attraction to the dream of control (especially the dream of controlling others) is what the movie lastingly conveys. The second reason is a practical one: because the Witchcraft in the movie resembles the real thing, the lure of occult power is linked to a collection of ideas, rituals, and objects in the real world that teens will actually encounter when they investigate further. Thus, curious teens have a framework of information and involvement waiting for them to plug their curiosity into.

And there were a *lot* of curious teens coming out of the movie theaters in 1996. Devin does the arithmetic:

> *The Craft* was seen by approximately one million people in its first weekend. If one in ten of those people are intrigued enough to look into the subject further, maybe read a book (and now there are shelves full of books!), that's 100,000 people who will at least be more educated about our reality. If one in ten of *those* people chose to pursue the subject further, that's 10,000 people out of the first weekend.
>
> I began calling myself a Witch at 16 because Donovan wrote a song called "Season of the Witch." I do not underestimate the impact of the media on teenagers, and this movie was brewed up for the teenage audience (Devin, 1998).

The effect was explosive and virtually instantaneous. Within days of the movie's opening, inquiries began to pour into the various Witchcraft groups and Neopagan organizations. They were all caught off-guard; even those that had

had some advance knowledge of the movie were stunned by the size and suddenness of the response. And it is realistic to assume that the number of direct inquiries was more than matched by the number of those who went looking for further information on their own, without contacting anyone.

That unexpected surge of teenage interest in Witchcraft posed a problem for the movement in more ways than one. In the first place, it was a wave of fascination they were largely unprepared to deal with. Neopaganism was not a young person's movement; few Witches had any experience in dealing with teenage inquirers, and no group had any kind of organized teenage outreach. In the second place, the prospect of having teenagers "convert" to Witchcraft while still under their parents' roof was a hot potato, to put it mildly—not just emotionally, but legally as well. Any Witchcraft organization that deliberately drew a child away from its parents' religion stood a very good chance of being sued out of existence. As a result, the Neopagan groups generally took a hands-off approach in dealing with minors. The combined result of their unreadiness and their wariness is that the organized Witchcraft movement lost control of the Witchcraft phenomenon in popular culture. Teenagers drawn to Witchcraft were forced to rely chiefly on one another, as Margot Adler points out:

> The fact is that most Pagan groups won't take teenagers—they're afraid of repercussions from unsympathetic parents. So in fact most teenagers just find like-minded friends, because there are very few groups that teens can enter until they're 18 (Vale and Sulak, 2001, page 28).

Thus, as teens embraced Witchcraft, Witchcraft itself became part of the self-contained, self-referential world of teen culture, disconnected even from its roots in adult Neo-paganism.

However, the organized Neopagan movement also grew in membership as a result of *The Craft*. Many of those who reacted to the movie were young adults rather than minor children, and the Witchcraft groups responded to their inquiries with enthusiasm. In addition, many of the teenagers who were drawn to Witchcraft through peer influence would later drift into the established movement once they were no longer minors. There was certainly not a complete separation between the Witchcraft of teen culture and that of organized Neopaganism.

Still, *The Craft* created a whole new "branch" of modern Witchcraft among young people that quickly took on a life of its own. Pop-culture Witchcraft was both different and separate from the pre-existing Witchcraft movement, since much of its content came from sources that traditional Witches disdain, such as popular entertainment. Pop-culture Witches in their turn are often inclined to see traditional Witches as stodgy and hidebound, unhip, and out of touch. It is one of the ironies of the movement that, even as modern Witches are striving to establish their "tradition" of some 60 years *as* a tradition (see chapter 7), they are already faced with a cadre of younger, self-proclaimed "Witches" who are out of touch with that tradition and largely indifferent to it. The differences between the two "cultures" have not been bridged in the years since *The Craft* was released, and in important ways the two are working at cross-purposes today (see the conclusion).

The Craft and the Symbolism of Good and Evil

The Craft firmly established modern Witchcraft's new image in the public mind: dangerous, but exciting—and above all, *real*. The film also swelled the ranks of the Witchcraft movement, in that it directly caused large numbers of people to identify themselves as "Witches," and led many of them to join various Witchcraft groups and organizations. But the movie also had an even deeper cultural impact.

The Craft not only transmitted some real detail about modern Witchcraft's spells and rituals, it also conveyed key elements of Witchcraft's ideology and worldview. Most importantly of all, it redefined the place that both Witchcraft and Christianity occupy in the symbolism of good and evil. It especially redefined the images of good and evil that prevail in teen-oriented entertainment, and in popular culture generally.

One of the movie's subtle yet powerful messages is conveyed through its "stage setting"—the place(s) in which the story occurs, and the people among whom the characters move and act. By using a Catholic high school as the setting for its drama, and in identifying its main characters by their alienation from that setting, *The Craft* almost exactly reproduces modern Witchcraft's understanding of its own emergence from the "rejected background" of the main, Christian-based society. And by tying that viewpoint to youthful characters teens can identify with, the film brings modern Witchcraft's self-understanding down to the personal level, and conveys it in a forceful way.

The Craft also conveys another key element of Neopagan ideology, and it does so even more directly. One of the secondary characters in the movie is a woman who runs an occult bookshop that the four teenagers frequent in their quest for information and supplies. As an attractive, middle-aged female (and evidently a Witch), she hardly qualifies as a "crone," but she definitely plays the role of an elder "wise woman" in relation to the quartet of youngsters who come into her store. If there is a Neopagan "authority figure" in the movie, she is it. Early in the movie, she singles Sarah out as the sincerest "seeker" among the four, and confides to her the true nature of magical power: "True magic is never black nor white. It is both, because nature is both—loving and cruel, all at the same time. The only good or bad is in the heart of the Witch."

Not only does that commentary convey a Neopagan understanding of good and evil (see chapter 1), it also lays down the moral framework for the rest of the film. In effect, the central conflict in the movie (between the good Witch and the bad one) is an extended example of how that advice works out in life, confirming that "the only good or bad is in the heart of the Witch." Thus *The Craft* systematically communicates a Neopagan way of looking at the world, both by direct instruction and by narrative illustration.

But the movie's real impact lies in the fact that it reshuffles the imagery of good and evil in popular entertainment. Witchcraft has traditionally been used as symbolic of evil, but *The Craft* does more than simply turn that symbolism upside down and portray it as something good. In *The Craft*, Witchcraft has been *taken out of the good-versus-evil conflict altogether, and put into a morally neutral category.* Consistent with the comment by the shopowner quoted above, Witchcraft is seen as neither good *nor* evil. It is simply a source of power. It is a tool in the conflict, but it is above the conflict, not favoring either side but accessible to both, to be either used or misused—depending on the user.

Christianity, likewise, has been removed from its role as opposite number and nemesis to witchcraft, occultism, and black magic. In *The Craft*, Christianity plays a role as part of the background to the action, but plays no role at all in the action itself. It remains a looming, vaguely menacing presence as the religious face of "mundane" society, but it is otherwise irrelevant to the characters and their actions. That is Neopaganism's working attitude toward Christianity writ large.

✣ ✣ ✣ ✣ ✣ ✣ ✣ ✣ ✣ ✣ ✣ ✣ ✣ ✣ ✣ ✣ ✣ ✣

The Craft...dispensed with the familiar, biblically based symbolism used to signify good and evil in popular entertainment—and replaced it with an entirely new and different symbol system.

✣ ✣ ✣ ✣ ✣ ✣ ✣ ✣ ✣ ✣ ✣ ✣ ✣ ✣ ✣ ✣ ✣ ✣

What *The Craft* accomplished is simple but profound, straightforward but not necessarily obvious. It dispensed with the familiar, biblically based symbolism used to signify good and evil in popular entertainment—and replaced it with an entirely new and different symbol system, from which many of the familiar images have been removed (and in which the ones that remain have been given different meanings). In both its timing and its content, *The Craft* well illustrates the larger culture's shift away from biblical values and toward pagan ones. And as with so much else in popular culture, it is both cause and effect of the changes that are taking place.

Beyond *The Craft: Sabrina, Charmed,* and *Buffy*

Although *The Craft* was the central event in Witchcraft's mid-1990s image makeover, it was just one of several media productions that were part of that process. 1996 also saw the inauguration of *Sabrina the Teenage Witch,* a TV series that turned the teen–Witchcraft connection into a half-hour sitcom. The following year brought *Buffy the Vampire*

Slayer, an hour-long teenage/horror/sci-fi/comedy/adventure series that was wildly popular with its target audience and even drew a surprising amount of serious scholarly attention. The media's three-year Witchcraft spree climaxed in 1998, which saw another new TV series *(Charmed)* and another new movie *(Practical Magic)*, both of which featured young actresses at the peak of their careers and at the height of their popularity with younger audiences.

As we have already noted, the *Sabrina* of 1996 was just the latest episode in the long and successful media career of a character first introduced by the *Archie* teenage comic books back in 1962. Since she was launched that year as a minor character in *Archie's Madhouse #22,* "Sabrina" has graduated to progressively larger roles and wider audiences. She went from a minor comic-book character to a major one in 1969; in 1971 she became the main character in an animated kiddie TV series; the same year, she gained her own comic-book series with the debut of *Sabrina the Teenage Witch #1.* In 1977 she was made the star of yet another animated Saturday morning TV cartoon series—*Sabrina, Superwitch,* on NBC. In September 1993, Sabrina got her own series of 48-page annual special comic books (originally called *Sabrina's Halloween Spooktacular,* but changed the following year to *Sabrina's Holiday Spectacular*). In the spring of 1996, *Sabrina the Teenage Witch,* the live-action TV movie, was shown on the Showtime cable network to positive reviews and enthusiastic audience response. The movie starred Melissa Joan Hart, otherwise known to millions as "Clarissa" in Nickelodeon's hit show *Clarissa Explains It All.* By September of that year, the hit Showtime movie had been spun off into the prime-time sitcom for ABC's "TGIF" Friday-night line-up of family-oriented fare, with Melissa Joan Hart once again in the title role.

Both the movie and the sitcom spin-off tell the story of a teenage girl (Sabrina Spellman) who lives with her two eccentric aunts, Hilda and Zelda; on her sixteenth birthday, she learns that her aunts are actually a pair of 2000-year-old witches, while their cat Salem is a warlock who is being punished (by reverse reincarnation) for his attempt at world domination. She also receives the gift of magical power that runs in her family and begins the process of training for her "witch's license."

Sabrina gets its humor from the same comic formula used by *I Dream of Jeannie* and *Bewitched* (see chapter 3)—namely, from the friction between the "insider's" understanding and the outsider's incomprehension. Since Sabrina is a novice witch, her spells often misfire, requiring her to smooth over or explain away the results. She also has to keep her witchy powers secret from her boyfriend, Harvey; her two girlfriends Jenny and Valerie; her stuck-up nemesis, Libby; and the nosy, suspicious vice-principal, Mr. Kraft. And that is the gist of the story line, such as it is—one scrape after another, one comic misadventure after another, extracting laughs along the way from the cluelessness of the mundane world. That simple formula, incidentally, is part of the program's appeal to teenagers—by identifying with Sabrina's "insider" knowledge, they are able to turn the tables on the adult world, which is otherwise constantly telling teens that *they* are the clueless ones, and that "grown-ups" have the superior knowledge and understanding.

Charmed's Odd Mixture of Witchcraft and Scripture

Charmed was a different kind of program. It was not a sitcom, but a supernatural teenage drama. Witchcraft was a central element of the plot, but it was also mixed with soap-opera themes, and even with biblical themes of apocalyptic conflict. The series tells the story of three young sisters who live together in an inherited mansion in San Francisco. In the first episode, the three (played by Shannen Doherty, Alyssa Milano, and Holly Marie Combs) accidentally "discover" that they are hereditary Witches, destined to become the most powerful Witches ever (foretold by an ancient prophecy as "the Charmed Ones"), whose mission is to fight evil and protect the innocent. They also receive supernatural "powers" as part of their inheritance, each sister acquiring a different ability: One sister can move objects with her mind, one can freeze time, and one can see visions of the future. The novice Witches are assisted in their role as fighters of evil (and in learning to use their powers) by "White-Lighters," immortal beings who seem to combine the functions of guru and guardian angel. "The Charmed Ones" are opposed (and regularly attacked) by demons and evil warlocks, who are constantly scheming to steal the Witches' power.

Even in this brief description of the program's story line, we can see that the scriptwriters are creating a hodgepodge fantasy world with components drawn from many different sources. Neopagan Witchcraft is one of those sources—but not the only one—and some of the other components are incompatible with it. That mixture makes for an odd picture of Witchcraft on the program—accurate in its smaller details, but distorted in its larger dimensions. The reviewer for Witchvox.com took note of both aspects of the series, observing first of all that the scriptwriters appear to be "taking pains not to offend Pagans too much":

> On the up side of the rainbow bridge—the pronunciations were good, the tools were explained well and some ethical considerations were mentioned. The altars looked messy enough to be real —I guess not even Hollywood magick can do anything about

wax drippings—and the sisters wore—gasp!—regular clothing even when casting spells! (Walker, 1998).

But the same reviewer also complained about the alien elements in the script, which are numerous and discordant. Both the "mission" the sisters are given and the "powers" they receive seem more derived from comic-book superheroes than from anything modern Witches do. In addition, *Charmed* creates an imaginary distinction between "Witches" (who inherit their magical abilities) and "Wiccans" (who take up the religion and learn their magic secondhand).

The idea that Witchcraft and its "powers" are inherited has proved stubbornly persistent in popular entertainment—as has the parallel idea that Witches are immortal (or at least extremely long-lived). Both the 1960s' *Bewitched* and the 1990s' *Sabrina* helped to popularize that linked misconception, and *Charmed* just continues the tradition. The source of those two ideas is unclear, as is the question of how they became joined together. The idea that a Witch's powers are inherited could be derived from a similar concept in anthropological witchcraft (see chapter 1), and the immortality factor is presumably borrowed from vampire legends—but how and why they happened to come together around the witch-figure in popular entertainment is anyone's guess.

However, the Witchvox reviewer was most put off by the alien elements in the script that seemed to have biblical overtones. In the show's opening episode, some of the chanting before an altar apparently invokes "The Maker," without specifying who or what such a being might be. The reviewer responded to that sour note with her first and most emphatic complaint:

O.K., let's get the flawed stuff out of the way right now.

1. There is no "maker" that Witches regularly chant about in front of an altar. There is Goddess and God and a lot of other deities, or the One.

No maker, no maker, no maker (Walker, 1998).

Her second emphatic complaint had to do with the war of the Witches versus the demons and warlocks the program depicts. It doesn't ring true to a Neopagan worldview. Indeed, the whole idea of an apocalyptic struggle between the forces of good and the minions of evil echoes biblical themes far more than Wiccan ones, and *Charmed*'s imaginary warfare seems closer to *The Exorcist* or the Omen movies than to anything in Neopaganism.

But *Charmed*'s deliberate mixing of incompatible traditions had a specific inspiration. By using biblical themes to spice up a pagan tale, *Charmed* was following the lead of another pop-culture blockbuster that had made its debut the previous year (1997)—*Buffy the Vampire Slayer.*

Buffy the Vampire Slayer—Taking It to the Next Level

In effect, *Buffy* was an aftershock of *The Craft*'s pop-culture earthquake. Following hard on the heels of *The Craft, Buffy the Vampire Slayer* took the same symbolism of good and evil that *The Craft* had introduced (that is, depicting Witchcraft and its power as morally neutral, beyond good and evil), then brought *back* in some of the older, biblical imagery—but with a new and different meaning.

Buffy took the biblical symbols of good and evil that had been introduced into popular entertainment during the 1970s (such as the idea of apocalyptic conflict), emptied them of their biblical meaning, then re-used them as building blocks of an essentially pagan narrative. It was a mixture that proved to have a magnetic appeal for teenage audiences—and it was the demonstrated formula that the *Charmed* scriptwriters were trying to follow.

Buffy was first written and produced as a Hollywood movie in 1992, starring Kristy Swanson and Donald Sutherland, but it drew mediocre reviews and even more mediocre box-office receipts. The project was plagued by problems from the outset, and its creator and chief writer (Joss Whedon) walked off the set at one point because he felt his idea for the film was being ruined by the director and the actors. It wasn't until 1996 that he was able to sell the story concept again, this time as a TV series over which he retained artistic control—and this time it was an instant and continuing success, supported by rave reviews and an ardent audience response.

Buffy is second only to *The Craft* as a milestone in the ongoing spiritual devolution of American culture, especially as that process is reflected in popular entertainment. *Buffy* brings together in a single narrative many of the attitudes that are driving our cultural transformation, and conveys them in a powerful way to a large and receptive audience of teens—that is, to the people who will basically be deciding where our culture is headed over the next several decades.

Buffy's story line begins with an imaginary "ancient prophecy" (another gimmick that the *Charmed* scriptwriters would copy the following year), which foretells that "in every generation there is a Chosen One. She alone will stand against the vampires, the demons and the forces of darkness." In this generation, the "Chosen One" turns out to be Buffy Summers, a 16-year-old high school student from "Sunnydale, California." Sunnydale, despite its smiley-face name and its outward appearance of utter normality, is located over a "Hellmouth," a gateway between the worlds through which demons try to escape their perdition by entering into our universe; once among us, they take over the bodies of vulnerable human beings and turn them into vampires.

When Buffy discovers that she is the Vampire Slayer, she gains allies as well as enemies in her mission. There is "Giles," Buffy's "Watcher," who represents "The Council," a shadowy group that oversees the Vampire Slayers. Giles, the school librarian, is a tweedy, bookish type who also happens to be a walking encyclopedia of the occult. Then there are Buffy's close friends, "the Scooby Gang" (a reference to *Scooby Doo, Where Are You?* Hanna-Barbera's cartoon mystery series of the early '70s, whose characters chased monsters every week), as well as "a shifting gang of human and undead friends and enemies who alternately help and hinder her mission" (R., 2002).

Buffy was an instant hit with its target audience of teenage viewers. The show's overall numbers, while not spectacular, were solid. *Buffy*'s Nielsen ratings reached as high as 5.2 in its second season (which translates to over 5 million households—not just viewers—tuned into the program) but they consistently ran in the 3's and 4's—strong enough to make it the hottest show in the lineup of the fledgling WB Network. But the real measure of the devotion that *Buffy* inspired can be seen in the endless array of *Buffy*-themed paraphernalia that was eagerly snapped up by the program's legions of teenage fans. There were posters, trading cards, cosmetics, costume jewelry, keychains, video games, board games, card games, fantasy role-playing games, wallpaper, notepaper, stationery, pencils, calendars, greeting cards, notebooks, folders, binders, backpacks, lunchboxes, action figures, soundtrack albums, picture books, story books, puzzle books, and so on...and on, and on.

And then there are the Web sites. An Internet search conducted for "Buffy the Vampire Slayer" yields "about 1,130,000" entries according to the Google search engine, which offers some 800 of them for immediate access via the Internet. A random sampling indicates that most of them fall into one of three catgories: teen-oriented fan Web sites, media commentary and reviews, and scholarly articles and publications. By far the greatest amount of Internet "traffic" flows to the fan Websites—and through them, via Internet "links," to other sites, often including Witchcraft sites. We have already noted that the Web site most visited by teen Web surfers is devoted to the actress who plays Buffy, Sarah Michelle Gellar.

Not only was *Buffy* a huge hit with teenagers, it has also been the subject of a surprising amount of serious academic attention. There have been international conferences to discuss the series, and there is an online scholarly publication (*Slayage: The Online Journal of Buffy Studies,* http://www.slayage.tv) dedicated to analyzing all aspects of the subject. The extent and seriousness of scholarly interest can be seen in the fact that in 2002, an online bibliography of academic articles dealing with the series ran to 19 pages (Badman, 2002).

Joss Whedon—Social Engineer

One of the reasons the program attracts that kind of attention is that it builds a complex fantasy world for its characters—with plot twists that raise contemporary issues, and dialogue that probes philosophical questions while at the same time remaining hip, cool, and closely attuned to the conversational rhythms of teenage life. The show explores the issues that dominate teenagers' lives—such as friendship, jealousy, sex, rules, good and evil, and so on—and presents them in a format that is already familiar to them (the teenage horror/comedy/adventure movie). *Buffy's* star, Sarah Michelle Gellar, succinctly stated both the design and the appeal of the program: "We basically just take high school and use horror as the metaphor for it" (Clark, 2003, page 49).

The success achieved by *Buffy's* unique mixture of "melodrama, horror, film noir and hip teen comedy" (Clark, 2003, page 46) can be traced directly to the creative talent and professional skill of the man who conceived it, brought it into being, and wrote much of its content—Joss Whedon.

Whedon, frequently referred to as a "genius" in the media, is a young (born 1964), third-generation screenwriter who is the very definition of the term "industry insider." TV was not entertainment for Whedon, it was his environment; it was the atmosphere that enveloped him as he was growing up. Both Whedon's father and his grandfather wrote for television; his grandfather wrote for various sitcoms in the '50s and '60s *(Leave it to Beaver, The Dick Van Dyke Show, The Donna Reed Show)*, while his father wrote for such shows as *Benson* and *The Golden Girls*, in addition to helping produce a number of other programs. Whedon himself has done screenwriting for several blockbuster movies, including *Toy Story, Twister,* and *Speed.*

"I designed Buffy to be an icon, to be an emotional experience, to be loved in a way that other shows can't be loved....I wanted her to be a cultural phenomenon."

Whedon is very much a child of his times. Not only is he a master of the visual media (the most dominant and pervading influence in teen culture), he also embodies many of the attitudes that have placed his generation at the cutting edge of cultural change. Whedon makes no bones about the fact that he is a dedicated pro-feminist, environmentally sensitive, gay-friendly, antireligious, atheistic unbeliever. He also makes no bones about the fact that his work expresses those convictions and is designed to convey them to as many people as possible, believing (sincerely, no doubt) that society would be better off if more people thought as he does. And finally, he makes no bones about the fact that he is consciously using his skill at media manipulation to implant those convictions in the hearts and minds of his audience. In effect, Whedon acknowledges that his work is (among other things) a form of social engineering. And he believes, with good reason, that his efforts are being successful.

In a revealing interview with *Salon* magazine, Whedon discusses some of the concerns that motivate his work.

> I believe that religion has contained within it an enormous amount of misogyny, and that cannot be denied. That's something that I will always bridle against....I have nothing against religion as a concept, or as people practice it. Religious institutions, on the other hand, I believe cause people to fly planes into buildings. It's very dangerous....It's not any huge secret that I'm an atheist (Miller, 2003).

As a professional in the visual media, Whedon's natural impulse is to convey those concerns by using his professional abilities. *Buffy* is the vehicle he created to do that. In an interview with *Onion* magazine, Whedon showed that he understands how to push people's buttons in a deep and personal way—and how to use that skill to implant his viewpoint in as many people as possible.

> I designed Buffy to be an icon, to be an emotional experience, to be loved in a way that other shows can't be loved....I wanted her to be a cultural phenomenon. I wanted there to be dolls—Barbie with kung-fu grip. I wanted people to embrace it in a way that exists beyond, "Oh, that was a wonderful show about lawyers, let's have dinner." I wanted people to internalize it, and make up fantasies where they were in the story, to take it home with them, for it to exist beyond the TV show. And we've done exactly that (Robinson, 2001).

Three years later, as the series was ending, Whedon was even more direct about his purposes, and about his sense of accomplishment. The interviewer for about.com asked him, "Can you believe the impact Buffy has had on popular culture?" Whedon responded,

> I always intended it to have the kind of impact on popular culture that it did. I wanted Buffy to be a pop icon. I wanted her to be remembered. I wanted her to be in people's interior lives. I wanted her to be a hero to kids and she was designed very specifically for that so it wasn't a big surprise when it worked. It should have been (Topel, 2004).

Buffy, Witchcraft, and Cultural change

Buffy the Vampire Slayer is complex enough that it can be analyzed from many different angles, as the volume of scholarly literature shows. But two aspects of the program concern us here. They are, first, *Buffy*'s contribution to the process of cultural change; and second, *Buffy*'s specific effect on the biblically-based imagery of good and evil used in popular culture and entertainment.

Buffy's contribution to the process of cultural change begins with giving its viewers a complete new universe to enter into and be a part of. The universe Joss Whedon wants his audience to "take home with them," to "be in their interior lives," is the same mental universe he already lives in—a universe that is very much in harmony with the Neopagan "attitudes" outlined by Margot Adler in chapter 1. As a self-described "atheist," Whedon is not personally Neopagan but, like Neopagans, he tends to see traditional, biblically based beliefs as a barrier to social progress. Thus he tends to be supportive of cultural dissent and cultural deviance in general, including such trends as modern Witchcraft, "lesbian chic," and various other departures from conventional standards and behavior. He also personally supports many of the social and political causes that Neopaganism favors (such as feminism and environmentalism). The overall view of reality that *Buffy* implants in its audience reflects that order of values.

The series treats Witchcraft per se in two opposite ways at the same time. On the one hand, Witches have condemned *Buffy* for its distorted and overtheatrical version of Witchcraft, which is made to seem more like sorcery (with "powers" like levitation and shape-shifting) than a religion. *Buffy*'s dialogue also refers to "Wiccans" in unflattering terms, implying that they are dabblers who are only scratching the surface of "real" Witchcraft.

On the other hand, even that dismissive attitude assumes that there *is* such a thing as "real" Witchcraft. And to show what "real" Witchcraft might be, the series has featured several positive and likeable characters in Witch roles. In one notable case, Willow Rosenberg, one of Buffy's "Scooby" sidekicks (and one of the show's most popular and best-loved characters), "grew" over several seasons from a shy, socially clumsy, geeky girl into a powerful, self-confident, initiated

Witch who had an out-of-the-closet lesbian affair with one of the other characters on the program, who was also a fellow Witch in Willow's coven.

Because of such portrayals, Neopagans have generally responded positively to the show, despite having some misgivings about it. The reviewer for *New Witch* magazine (motto: "not your mother's broomstick") summed up her reaction this way: "Overall, *Buffy* has provided one of television's most diverse and well-rounded views of witchcraft.... It's not 'real' paganism, but it's been a mostly positive view of what it means to be a witch—or just deal with one....It's hard not to be enchanted by the image of two young women clasped in each other's arms, floating a foot off the dance floor" (McGuire, 2002, page 20). Looking beyond *Buffy* to the bigger picture, one scholar notes that "the series' use of witchcraft is a part of a larger discursive field in popular media in which Wicca is presented as trendy and empowering for teenagers" (Winslade, 2001).

However, while *Buffy*'s endorsement of Witchcraft (and feminism and lesbianism) to teenagers is the program's most obvious contribution to our culture change, it is not the only one—or even the most important one. *Buffy*'s deeper significance lies in the fact that *it has taken the biblical concepts and images in popular entertainment, emptied them of their biblical meaning, and turned them into mere components of a pagan narrative universe.* Christianity's contribution to our culture's symbolic language has been appropriated, de-Christianized, and re-used for other purposes. That transition effectively represents a terminal degradation of Christianity's cultural presence and potency—at least in the part of our culture that affects the generation now rising to adulthood, power, and influence (in other words, teenagers).

Like so much else about *Buffy*, its function as a cultural chrysalis—in which Christian imagery is turned into pagan symbolism—is the unique, personal contribution of its creator, Joss Whedon. Whedon is surrounded by Christian imagery but is personally a stranger to the Christianity that gives it meaning. As a trader in visual images, it was therefore inevitable that he would use the Christian symbols available to him without regard for their Christian content. In his interview with *Salon* magazine, he said as much, with no apparent consciousness of cultural vandalism.

> So I am an atheist, but...I do use Christian mythology. Buffy—resurrected much? She pretty much died for all of us by spreading her arms wide and...well, I won't go into it. That's what I was raised with....I grew up around Christianity and Judaism and those are the prevalent myths and mythic structures of my brain (Miller, 2003).

De-Christianizing Christian Symbols

Whedon's de-Christianized use of Christian imagery shows up in several ways. It can be seen in his treatment of 1) apocalyptic conflict, 2) demons, and 3) vampires. All three are components of *Buffy*'s narrative world, and all are drawn from sources with deep Christian roots and shared Christian values.

The program's concept of an end-times showdown between the forces of good and evil is based on the Bible's story of that conflict through the ages, and especially on the story of its climax as told in the Bible's final chapter, the book of Revelation. In all of that grand, sweeping account—from the fall of Adam in the Garden of Eden to the fall of Babylon the Great at the end of the age—the central theme is one of temptation, fall, judgment, and redemption, and the central actors in the drama are those who advance the agenda of redemption versus those who hinder and oppose it.

The program's concept of demons and demon possession is likewise based on biblical ideas of spiritual warfare, in which the cosmic conflict between good and evil comes down to a war within (and for) the possessed person's soul, with exorcism being the weapon wielded in the name of God, and redemption being the goal. In the same way, the vampires in *Buffy* are also derived from vampire legends that originally had a strong Christian content. "In *Dracula*, crosses are used as a weapon against vampires, and the staking of a vampire is accompanied by a prayer. Moreover, the killing of a vampire was associated with saving its soul, returning it from the Devil to God" (Clark, 2003, page 47). Christianity was the context that gave a greater meaning to the gruesome imagery of blood and death, and the meaning it conveyed was the familiar Christian one of temptation, fall, judgment, and redemption.

None of that content makes it through the filter of Whedon's secular–atheistic worldview. His self-confessed alienation from the Christian meaning of those symbols ensures that the symbols themselves will acquire new meaning at his hands. In Whedon's version of apocalyptic conflict, for example, demons and vampires are "evil" simply because they want to hurt people, and the Slayer's mission to fight evil mainly amounts to dispatching them before they can do more damage. That conflict routinely threatens to break out into a "final" battle as a result of some malicious scheme hatched by the demons, but without the larger picture to provide motive and context, the struggle with the demons boils down to a simple contest of wills and skills. "The Apocalypse" becomes little more than a ramped-up version of "us versus them."

This process of emptying Christian symbols of their Christian meaning has even been noticed by secular observers. According to Lynn Schofield Clark, *Buffy* and similar programs were "groundbreaking in the way they re-introduced otherworldly enemies into popular fictional television after a several-decade hiatus. In this way, they also did something else: they told stories of a spiritual battle between good and evil with an almost complete disinterest in organized religion" (Clark, 2003, page 47). And it is a battle, Clark says, that "despite its Christian overtones, makes no reference to Christian categories that are central to evangelicals, such as Jesus Christ and personal salvation" (Clark, 2003, pages 40-41).

The twin themes of vampires and demons underwent a similar loss of Christian content in Whedon's version. When a person is turned into a vampire on *Buffy,* "the soul leaves the body and is replaced by a demon. Staking kills a demon; the soul of the person is already long gone. Thus in *Buffy,* tales of vampires and those of demon possession blur, with little hope for the redemption of the lost ones, as there was in earlier vampire lore such as *Dracula* and as there is in demon possession practices" (Clark, 2003, page 52).

Secularism, Syncretism, and the Decline of Evangelical Influence

What's happening here is simple enough to understand: because Whedon doesn't grasp the Christian concept of redemption, the way he uses Christian symbolism won't convey redemption as part of its meaning. The meaning of a symbol is not built in—it depends on a shared understanding between author and audience. The meaning of symbols is sustained in the way they are used, just as the meaning of words is sustained in their usage. The Christian symbols that Whedon uses have been drained of their Christianity because he is unable to use them in a Christian way and because his audience is unprepared to grasp their Christian meaning. There is no longer any shared understanding between author and audience that would support the Christian meaning of things like apocalyptic conflict, vampires, demon possession, and so on. And so—just like that—the meaning of so-called "Christian" symbolism has been completely lost.

That loss is one more result of the extreme cultural borrowing and blending ("syncretism") that typifies our age. Today, we have access to ideas from all over the world and from any time in history. It has become routine for us to cut cultural products (such as religions) loose from their cultural context and turn them into spiritual consumer goods for people with different cultural values, or none at all.

In another sense, Whedon's borrowing and blending typifies the secularism that came to dominate our culture well before he appeared on the scene. The secular appetite consumes all values and cultures equally, "digesting" them by breaking them down into their disconnected components and using the pieces in new and different ways. In that respect, Whedon is the perfect product of a secularized society, and *Buffy* is a perfect example of secularism's impact on traditional beliefs.

Thus *Buffy*'s de-Christianizing of Christian symbols is both a symptom of and a milestone for our changing culture. The 1970s' renewal of Christian vitality (and the reinvigoration of evangelical influence on society that went along with it) was a startling breath of fresh air at the time, but its lasting effects have been minimal. The short arc of evangelical influence on the larger culture can be charted with some clarity in the popular entertainment media.

At the beginning of the 1970s, evangelicalism introduced into public attention a new "concern about evil and...largely defined the terms of the conversation about evil and the realm beyond this world" (Clark, 2003, page 45). This could be seen in the strong Christian imagery of good and evil established by such movies as *The Exorcist* and the Omen trilogy, which extended the "evangelical effect" into the 1980s. But by the end of the 1980s, the evangelical imagery of good and evil had been turned into an object of mockery and satire in *The Witches of Eastwick*. Then in the mid-1990s came the pop-culture revolution, in which *The Craft* took Christianity simply (and literally) out of the picture—painting it not so much as bad or wrong, but as trivial and irrelevant. At the same time, *The Craft* painted modern Witchcraft as being beyond good and evil, but of great value and importance nontheless.

The real story is the dismemberment of Western culture's Christian legacy—its "digestion" by secularism in a process that empties Christianity's culture contribution of its Christian content.

The next stage of culture change happened quickly. The very next year, *Buffy the Vampire Slayer* brought back all of the biblically based symbolism that *The Craft* had dispensed with—but in a form that was biblically neutered and emptied of its biblical meaning. Lynn Schofield Clark assessed the matter succinctly:

> While evangelicals and other conservative Christians may feel that stories and images of supernatural battles between good and evil in some sense belong to them, they cannot control how these stories will be used, and reconfigured, once they enter the realm of the media—and particularly the entertainment media....Evangelicalism has been successful in introducing its definition of and concerns about evil into the public consciousness, [but] loses control of

what happens once that definition gets woven in to the culture (Clark, 2003, pages 39, 227).

As the evangelical definition "gets woven in to the culture," it interacts with the changing image of Witchcraft in the media to produce hybrids like *Buffy the Vampire Slayer* and *Charmed*. Of course, the changing image of Witchcraft in the entertainment media can be seen in a number of other instances as well, including the hugely successful series of Harry Potter books and films. We will take a look at some of those other instances in the conclusion, as we consider the place of narrative and storytelling in the process of cultural change.

But the real story here is not modern Witchcraft's image change, as important as that development may be. The real story is the dismemberment of Western culture's Christian legacy—its "digestion" by secularism in a process that empties Christianity's cultural contribution of its Christian content and then renders its disconnected components to be used for other purposes. That story is perhaps best illustrated by Witchcraft's changing status vis-à-vis Christianity in popular entertainment, a story that we have followed as far as *The Craft* and *Buffy the Vampire Slayer*.

We will try to assess the overall meaning and direction of those changes in the conclusion. In the meantime, as Witchcraft goes mainstream, we need to understand what we are seeing. We can't understand *what* is "going mainstream" (or what that means), unless we understand where it came from and how it came to be among us today. Having looked at the way Witchcraft is perceived in the media, it is time to take a look at what Witchcraft actually is—both in history and today.

5
Three Myths About Modern Witchcraft

Despite the public's exposure to Neopagan themes and concepts through the media—or perhaps because of it—there remains widespread confusion about what modern Witchcraft is and where it comes from. In particular there is confusion about how the Witchcraft of today relates to the witchcraft of the Middle Ages.

Among the general public, there are three basic ways of thinking about contemporary Witchcraft. Most people probably believe some version of one of the following statements:

1. "modern Witchcraft is a flaky New Age delusion"

2. "modern Witchcraft is the revival of an ancient, pagan religion"

3. "modern Witchcraft is a dangerous satanic cult"

Unfortunately, all three of those statements are false.

The belief that Witchcraft is a New Age delusion is based on a simple ignorance of history. The other two beliefs about Witchcraft, however, are based on an actively false version of history. As a matter of fact, the contending "Pagan" and

"Christian" views of Witchcraft (statements numbers 2 and 3, above) are really just conflicting interpretations of the *same* false version of history! They are opposite spins on the same erroneous assumption—namely, that modern Witchcraft is a descendant or development of classical European witchcraft, and that there is some historical connection or continuity between the two.

That assumption is not only false in itself, but once accepted, it distorts all further discussion. To "undistort" the discussion, we need to correct the false history, dispense with the misleading myths about modern Witchcraft based upon it, and examine in their stead some of the serious but largely undiscussed issues that Witchcraft really does raise. In a word, we need to "winnow" our ideas about Witchcraft—in order to separate the factual substance of the matter from the chaff of myth and fabrication.

Myth Number One: The New Age Delusion

The belief that Neopagan Witchcraft is simply another delusion coming out of the "New Age movement" is superficially plausible but historically wrong. The sources of modern Witchcraft predate the so-called "New Age" by almost a century; the actual beginnings of modern Witchcraft predate the New Age by almost half a century.

What came to be called the New Age movement is really a delayed outgrowth of the 1960s counterculture. The counterculture promoted the hope–hype that we are "evolving" into a new phase of history and human development (remember the "Age of Aquarius"?). That hope became the "New Age" mentality, as we know it, some 20 years later, emerging as an updated version of the counterculture's mass-market, pseudo-mystical, pop-therapeutic wing (pioneered by the likes of TM's Maharishi Mahesh Yogi, and the apostate priest turned psychotherapist, Alan Watts). But the "New Age movement" didn't acquire its identity as such until the late 1980s, when journalists and commentators began using that terminology on a regular basis.

In contrast, modern Witchcraft has been under construction since the beginning of the twentieth century. It acquired a coherent identity in the 1940s and actually began to take organized form during the 1950s. All of the foundation and some of the superstructure for modern Witchcraft were already in place, therefore, before the "New Age" even began.

Modern Witchcraft has a unique and traceable history all its own. Modern Witches did not need the New Age to jump-start their movement, and they have not needed New Age notoriety to stimulate its growth. In fact, many Witches resent being associated with the New Age at all, and some go out of their way to distinguish themselves from anything bearing that label.

People tend to think that modern Witchcraft and the New Age movement are connected for one basic reason—namely, that both emerged into widespread public attention at about the same time (during the mid-1980s). But that timing is coincidental. The rise of modern Witchcraft and the later rise of the New Age movement are both related to the spiritual disintegration of society as a whole, and both benefited from the widespread mood of spiritual discontent that infused our society from the 1960s onward. Both movements flourished in and partly because of that social environment. Other than that, however, they are not particularly related to one another.

Myth Number Two: The "Enduring Pagan Tradition"

For many years, with the help of an uninformed but sympathetic media, apologists for modern Witchcraft promoted a view of its past that claims a lineage stretching back to the witches of European history—and beyond them, to prehistoric times.

There are several versions of the basic story line connecting modern Witchcraft with the witchcraft of the Middle Ages. Not all Neopagans accept the story as historical fact, but many do, and even more of them support the underlying theory that there is a traceable thread of continuity between medieval witchcraft and its modern namesake.

For that matter, many Neopagans think the thread of continuity extends all the way back to Stone Age religions of fertility and Nature-worship. Longtime Witch Isaac Bonewits sardonically refers to this expanded version of the story as "the myth of the Unitarian, Universalist, White Witch-cult of Western Theosophical Brittany."

An Outline of the "Charter Myth"

The basic scenario of the myth goes something like this: What came to be called "witchcraft" is really the Ancient Wisdom of Nature that is common to humanity worldwide, and it goes back literally to the Stone Age. Paleolithic people worshiped the god of the hunt and the goddess of crops and fertility; those two primal figures eventually generated all the complex pantheons that we know today. Divine names changed with time and location, and divine qualities fragmented into various subdeities. But beneath the change, the basic deities endured, and the forces and functions that they symbolized remained the same.

The religions of Nature are inherently at odds with the religions of The Book—and vice versa. When Christianity first appeared amidst the Nature-worshiping paganism of Europe, the antagonism was mutual and spontaneous. From the outset of the conflict, Christendom's cultural strategy was one of cultural co-optation. The Roman Church undercut paganism by taking over important pagan forms and symbols and putting them in Christian dress—for example, renaming pagan festivals as part of the Church's liturgical year, erecting Christian churches over pagan shrines and sacred sites, and recasting popular pagan myths as the lore of Christian sainthood.

That strategy of co-optation was substantially "successful," in that the Roman Church did in fact attain cultural and religious dominance within a few centuries. But in the nature of things, the strategy could never be entirely successful, just as the dominance could never be complete. Some pagan diehards insisted on continuing their homage to Dionysus or Demeter (or whoever) out of sheer spiritual inertia, simply because that's what they had always done. Others refused the new "Christianized Paganism" not because they cherished paganism, but because they rejected Christianity.

In the end, whatever Christendom could not absorb, it condemned. The pagan gods who *could* not be converted (typically those connected with sex and fertility) were demonized instead. Their pagan followers who *would* not convert were hounded and sometimes killed. With their gods turned into devils and the flames of persecution at their heels, the followers of the Old Religion went underground in order to survive.

But even hiding couldn't save them from the gathering fury of Christian bigotry. Beginning about 1300, the Inquisition directed a 400-year reign of terror against anyone who resisted the patriarchal repression of the Catholic Church, especially pagans, heretics, healers, midwives, and women in general. As many as nine million may have died at the stake in this slow-motion "holocaust," and the period is therefore known as "the burning times."

By the end of the 1600s, the witch-mania began to wear itself out. But the terror and repression had succeeded in driving the followers of the old ways deep beneath the surface of society. In the face of ostracism at best and persecution at worst, the Old Religion was kept alive by families and by small, secretive, local groupings. When England finally repealed its Witchcraft Laws in 1951, those secret followers of the craft came quite literally "out of the woods" to make themselves known as "witches." They also began a campaign to rehabilitate the image of their misunderstood religion. The modern Witchcraft movement has grown from that resurfacing of a long-submerged tradition.

✦ ✦ ✦ ✦ ✦ ✦ ✦ ✦ ✦ ✦ ✦ ✦ ✦ ✦ ✦ ✦ ✦

There is no identifiable continuity between the witchcraft of the Middle Ages and the modern-day religious movement that bears the same name.

✦ ✦ ✦ ✦ ✦ ✦ ✦ ✦ ✦ ✦ ✦ ✦ ✦ ✦ ✦ ✦ ✦

Such is the "Charter Myth" of modern Witchcraft. As noted, there are several variations on the basic theme. One of them (a radical feminist version) claims that an original, goddess-worshiping, matriarchal paradise was overthrown by a conspiracy of patriarchal males, who replaced the gentle, all-accepting Goddess with the jealous, judgmental, moralistic, male deity that prevails in religion to this day.

Challenging the "Charter Myth"

In recent years, every claim of the Charter Myth—from the idea of a dawn-age matriarchy down to the very existence of medieval "witchcraft" itself—has been subjected to a withering historical critique. Every link in the chain of presumed continuity has been broken. The blunt fact is that current scholarship has actively falsified the Charter Myth on almost all of its important assumptions (see appendix B).

This is what current scholarship does indicate: There never was an original matriarchy. There was no worship of a universal Mother Goddess and no primal tradition, transformed over time, to be finally defined (by a hostile Church) as "witchcraft." Last and most importantly, there has been no passing down of any tradition from medieval witches to anyone in our own time. There is no identifiable continuity between the witchcraft of the Middle Ages and the modern-day religious movement that bears the same name. The most that can be said is that bits and pieces of mythic and magical lore from long ago are still to be found today. But fragmentary religious and occult survivals do not constitute a tradition, and they offer no support for any claims of continuity.

To their credit, many Neopagans have acknowledged those realities of historical research and no longer accept a literal version of the Charter Myth. Margot Adler writes about changing attitudes within the Neopagan community in her recent essay, "A Time for Truth."

> During the past 10 years, there has been what Ronald Hutton...calls a "tidal wave of accumulating research" that has essentially swept away many of the assumptions upon which the "Old Religion," Wicca, was based. Two of the most basic that have been revised are the notion of an unbroken tradition and the belief that our religion had a history of persecution that rivaled or even exceeded the Jewish Holocaust....Scholars have never accepted the myth of an unbroken Wiccan tradition, and now most

Wiccans are being asked to look honestly at their history (Adler, 2000).

Some Wiccans are apparently finding that kind of honesty difficult to come by. As Adler notes in her essay, the "new breeze that is blowing through Wicca is not being celebrated by the more literal among us. In some groups, there is open hostility to this revisionist history."

The reason is not hard to find.

Functions of the Charter Myth

For many, the Charter Myth's presumption of continuity is central to modern Witchcraft's sense of identity. Therefore, modern Witches have promoted the myth in one form or another for four understandable (and largely undisguised) reasons:

1. *As a way to gain a personal feeling of spiritual connectedness and religious continuity.* Every religion needs a tradition, and all believers need to feel a part of something tried and true, something with a history that is longer than their own. Few people can sustain themselves solely on a faith in their own spiritual resources for very long. Psychologically, a contrived tradition—or even an imaginary one—is better than no tradition at all.

2. *As a strategy to gain social acceptance and legal status.* Partly on the basis of its claimed historical lineage, modern Witchcraft asserts parity in the religious marketplace. The Federal Court of Appeals decision that declared "The Church of Wicca" to be a constitutionally recognizable religion (*Dettmer v. Landon*, 1986) relied on the bogus claim of modern

Witchcraft's continuity with medieval witchcraft and, through it, with ancient pagan religion. Partly on the basis of that claim, the religion of Witchcraft was given official recognition and First-Amendment protection—in the armed forces and in government policy generally.

In *Dettmer v. Landon,* the 4th Circuit Court of Appeals used the supposed long history and tradition of "witchcraft" as a basis for its ruling that modern Witchcraft is indeed a legitimate, officially recognizable "religion." In its opinion the Court said,

> Another...parallel to recognized religions is witchcraft's long history....Evidence [for this] includes a handbook for chaplains published by the United States which states that witchcraft enjoyed a following in Northern Europe during the Middle Ages as an ancient pagan faith, losing public expression when systematic persecution began in the 15th century. It regained some popularity after the repeal of English Witchcraft laws, and the handbook estimates that there are between 10,000 and 100,000 adherents in America.

3. *As a tactic to gain a rhetorical advantage over their perceived competitor and adversary (Christianity) by claiming "victim" status.* In that connection, Neopagans have promoted the idea that the witch hunts of European history were an outburst of Christian bigotry against women, healers, midwives, and gentle, Nature-worshiping pagans. They have also promoted the idea that modern Witches are heirs not only of that history, but of those resentments as well. Among

other things, the concept provides a platform for taking the moral high ground against Christianity and supplies a rationale for righteous anger directed against it.

4. *As a way to define their boundaries as a community and their identities as individuals.* Neopaganism began as a rejection of the main religious culture, grew as a protest against it, and has established itself as a systematic alternative to it—a genuine "counter-culture." Inevitably, Christianity (at least as perceived by Neopagans) becomes the "rejected background," *against which* the identity of Neopaganism is defined.

Thus, for many in the movement, an abiding antagonism to Christianity is basic to being Neopagan. Now that the historical basis for that resentment is being dismantled by scholars, the Neopagan community faces a crisis of identity that is just beginning to assert itself—as Margot Adler has already noted.

From its inception, the modern Witchcraft movement was built on the explicit claim that the "old ways" had been suppressed by Christianity, but had survived and were being rediscovered. For many Neopagans, those beliefs are part of their religious self-image, something that can't be changed without destabilizing the sense of personal identity that goes along with it—a prospect that is simply too daunting for most people to deal with. Those Witches and Neopagans who do answer Adler's call for honesty and are able to acknowledge that the myth is factually false, generally respond by insisting that the myth is "metaphorically" true—that is, that it asserts a continuity of spirit, sympathy, and attitude, rather than a continuity of teaching or practice, or of any actual tradition.

Many Witches claim, as Adler does, that their lack of tradition is actually a positive virtue, in that it unshackles modern Witchcraft from the dead hand of the past and liberates its potential for creative development. Adler quotes other Neopagan commentators to the effect that "nothing prevents us from embracing our syncretistic origins while still preserving the unique worldview of modern Wicca, except for our own self-consciousness" (Adler, 2000). In other words, since modern Witches don't *have* a tradition, they aren't *bound* by one, and are thereby freed to create their religion by blending together whatever elements appeal to them.

In any case, the myth of the enduring pagan tradition is disbelieved by all serious historians and, these days, by increasing numbers of honest Neopagans.

Myth Number Three—The Satanic Cult

Witchcraft's Charter Myth is not the only way to see the supposed connection between medieval and modern witchcraft. There is another, very different, way to read that same dubious claim. In the interest of honest history, it is important to correct the parallel misconception that modern Witchcraft is a satanic religion of devil-worship.

That belief is common among conservative Christians—ironically, because they have bought the same false version of history that some Neopagan apologists have sold to the general public. Modern Witches claim their beliefs are directly descended from medieval witchcraft. According to accounts of the time, historical witchcraft involved worshiping the devil and was strongly at odds with Christianity. So, when Christians believed the Neopagan claim that a continuous line of descent unites modern Witchcraft with its medieval predecessor, they naturally gave the claim a negative value rather than a positive one as the Neopagans had done. Because modern Witches identify themselves *with* medieval witches, Christians identify them *as* witches in the medieval mold. By their very claim to be the spiritual heirs and descendants of historical witchcraft, modern Witches automatically gave themselves an evil image in Christian eyes. The creators of modern Witchcraft seized upon medieval witchcraft for their inspiration in part *because* of its anti-Christian reputation—which of course is inseparable from its devil-worshiping reputation. Therefore, when modern Witches stress their identification with medieval witches, in a real sense they are helping to sustain the historical confusion.

That confusion is compounded by the fact that today, some avowed Satanists also refer to *themselves* as "witches"—apparently because they too identify with the anti-Christian reputation of classical witchcraft. And *that* confusion is compounded yet again by the fact that the Neopagans themselves don't all agree that the Satanists should be excluded from their number (Pike, 2001, page 113).

For that matter, some modern Witches enjoy the sense of dread and menace the classic "witch" image inspires in ordinary people, and they haven't always struggled to separate themselves from it. There is no doubt that Gerald Gardner (one of the founders of modern Witchcraft) liked to "put on the horns," so to speak, and adopt a style and appearance that played to popular stereotypes of the demonic. Outraging conventional sensibilities was one of Gardner's hobbies, and he sometimes exploited the public's (mis)perception of Witchcraft for his own amusement.

For all of those reasons and then some, the confusion persists—especially among Christians—that modern Witchcraft and devil-worship (or Satanism) are one and the same. But that negative image is as false as the positive one in Witchcraft's Charter Myth. Today, there is no reason to believe either of them. Both images are bogus because both are based on the same spurious version of history, invented to serve the purposes of the Witchcraft movement. As usual, ideology impoverishes history. Historical witchcraft and modern Witchcraft each have their own unique pedigrees. Their real histories are more complex, more credible, and ironically, more interesting than any of our fantasies about them.

Historians Study Witchcraft

Witchcraft appeared during the Middle Ages, rose to crisis proportions during the Renaissance, then abruptly disappeared—raising several obvious historical questions: Where was witchcraft before the Middle Ages? Where did it go after 1700? And what did it consist of while it was here?

Nineteenth-century scholars, under the influence of the "Romantic movement" in philosophy and politics, offered speculative answers to those questions (one example: Witchcraft was a quasi-political movement of peasant resistance to the Catholic aristocracy). But by the time the study of history had become an academic profession (in the late 1800s), a different mood enveloped the academy. An aggressive skepticism characterized scholarly thinking, and "debunking" was a favored mode of academic discourse. The scholarship of the day was dominated by rationalism, secularism, and anticlericalism—attitudes that dismissed witchcraft as the deluded creation of ignorant medieval priests.

Prior to 1920, therefore, historical scholarship largely discounted witchcraft as a fantasy of the Inquisition.

> Witchcraft, according to the liberal view, was a gross product of the superstitions of the Catholic Dark Ages, beyond which we have infinitely progressed

and with which we have little in common....Emotionally committed to liberalism and viewing the Church as an obstacle in the road of progress, they reject the possibility of there being any real currents of witch belief and practice and insist that not the witches, but the Inquisitors, invented witchcraft.... Some witches may have believed in their own powers, but only because the ideas propagated by the Inquisition had rendered them hysterical (Russell, 1972, pages 30-31).

That stance of militant skepticism inevitably generated a counterstance of militant credulity. As Christopher Nugent observes, "A scientism that sees no evil inclines to generate its opposite, a moral hysteria that sees nothing but evil" (Nugent, 1983, page 104). A group of writers, led by traditional Catholic apologist Montague Summers, "believed in the reality of Satan and accepted all trial reports as accurate and literal" (Adler, 1986, page 45). The rationalists assumed that the lurid charges lodged against the witches were all false; Summers, contrariwise, assumed that they were all true. Although Summers never attained academic credibility, he exercised wide popular influence, along with Dennis Wheatly, another author of the "antirationalist" school. And their influence lingers—even today, the works of those two are the source for many of the details in our popular image of the devil-worshiping witch.

In 1921, the increasingly sterile debate between the rationalists and the antirationalists was swept aside by a sensational new theory of witchcraft from an unexpected source—Margaret Murray's book *The Witch Cult in Western Europe*. Although Murray was a professional scholar, her expertise was in Egyptology, not European history. She had a hobbyist's interest in British folklore, however, and it led her to construct an interpretation of witchcraft that not only seized the imagination of the public, but held it for more than 40 years. Her work was eventually discredited during the 1960s, but not before her theories had helped to energize the growth of the modern Witchcraft movement during its critical early years in the 1950s. Murray's influence will be discussed at greater length in chapter 7, but in essence, she wrongly gave credibility to the "theory that victims of the early modern witch trials had been practitioners of a surviving pagan religion" (Hutton, 1999, pages 194–195) That is just what the creators of Neopagan Witchcraft wanted to hear, and they eagerly used her speculations to bolster their own eccentric theories of history.

Murray's work was subjected to criticism during the latter stages of her career, and it was subjected to outright rejection after her death in 1963. By the 1970s, the demolition of her scholarship, her theories, and her reputation was complete. The decline and fall of the "Murrayite thesis" threw the study of European witchcraft into confusion. For four decades, it had been commonly assumed that witchcraft was a pagan survival. Once that "common knowledge" was gone, some other theory was needed to replace it.

New Theories: Cultural Pathology or Political Mythology?

The old style of rationalism had been rendered obsolete by half a century of scientific and intellectual changes, but the basic motives behind the viewpoint hadn't changed. After Murray, skeptics changed their approach, but not their attitude. Secular scholars were reluctant to attribute any reality to witchcraft's weirder dimensions, but the weirdness still had to be accounted for somehow. As a result, the theories of witchcraft that are popular today deal with the topic in psychological, sociological, and political terms, focusing on why people *believed* that witchcraft existed, and why the witch *hysteria* existed—even though witchcraft itself *didn't* exist—indeed, by definition, *couldn't* exist.

The school of thought on the subject that is currently most influential among historians could be called the "delusional" school. The leading exponent of the delusional school is historian Norman Cohn, whose views are put forth in his book *Europe's Inner Demons: An Enquiry Inspired by the Great Witch-Hunt*. Cohn takes the old-style rationalist argument that witchcraft was a hysterical fantasy, and brings it up to date by adding elements from psychoanalysis and sociology. Instead of claiming that witchcraft was a delusion created by the demented mentality of the Inquisition, Cohn says that it was a deep, psychological disturbance that overtook the whole population of Europe. The disturbance was centered around a twisted fantasy of infanticide, cannibalism, and deviant sexuality that existed in Europe long before witchcraft appeared on the scene. One commentator summarized Cohn's argument as follows:

> There was a standard definition of a sinister, conspiratorial organization working to undermine society at large; this definition was operating at least as early as the Roman persecution of Christians, and has simply changed hands and altered appropriate details as it has pursued its course over the centuries. The early Christians, the heretical Cathars and Albigensians, the Knights Templar and the so-called witches were all tarred in turn with the same brush, as can be seen in the fact that the accusations against them were all so similar. In Christian times, the central elements in the stereotype included repudiating Christ, worshipping the devil, murdering and eating

babies, and holding orgiastic celebrations full of promiscuity and incest (Davis, 1993, page 309).

According to Cohn, that basic nightmare stereotype surfaced again during the early Middle Ages, at which point it also blended with a network of surviving folk beliefs about spirits, goblins, goddesses, and night-flying hags. As the stereotype became more elaborate and more detailed, it attached itself to certain socially marginal types and—voilà!—the myth of witchcraft was born, eventually to bloom into the terrible witch hysteria.

✢ ✢ ✢ ✢ ✢ ✢ ✢ ✢ ✢ ✢ ✢ ✢ ✢ ✢ ✢ ✢ ✢

According to Cohn, Europe's nightmare fantasy turned into the witch mania because of an "unconscious resentment against Christianity as too strict a religion, against Christ as too stern a taskmaster."

✢ ✢ ✢ ✢ ✢ ✢ ✢ ✢ ✢ ✢ ✢ ✢ ✢ ✢ ✢ ✢ ✢

Whence the Delusion?

Cohn's theory is easily the leading view among academic historians, but it is not without its critics and competitors. One of its weak points lies in his explanation of where the "nightmare fantasy" came from, and how it embedded itself in the collective mentality of Europe. For answers, Cohn relies on the dubious insights of psychoanalysis and the increasingly discredited views of its founder, Sigmund Freud. In his concluding postscript (appropriately titled "Psycho-Historical Speculations"), Cohn says that "for many Europeans, [the fantasy] came to embody part of their innermost selves—their obsessive fears, and also their unacknowledged, terrifying desires" (Cohn, 1977, page 259). And where do these fears and desires come from? Cohn's answer is pure Freud—incorporating not only Freud's ideas, but also his personal attitudes toward religion.

Freud regarded religion in general (and Christianity in particular) as a repressive and constraining force in human affairs, irksome to the untamed appetites of our animal nature. In Freud's view, this repression generates resentment, which *unconsciously* brings back what has been repressed, but projects it outward and perceives it to be "out there" rather than within. That is also Cohn's view—and when all is said and done, his analysis of the Great Witch Hunt boils down to restating Freud's critique of religion (including Freud's special, hostile focus on Christianity). According to Cohn, Europe's nightmare fantasy turned into the witch mania because of an

> unconscious resentment against Christianity as too strict a religion, against Christ as too stern a taskmaster. Psychologically, it is *altogether plausible* that such an unconscious hatred would find an outlet in the obsession with the overwhelming power of Christ's great antagonist, Satan, and especially in fantasies of erotic debauches with him....The tens of thousands of victims who perished [are] victims of an unconscious revolt against a religion which, consciously, was still accepted without question (Cohn, 1975, page 262, emphasis added).

" 'Altogether plausible' to whom?" is the operative question. If one finds Freud's assumptions questionable, then Cohn's "plausibility" diminishes accordingly.

Many Neopagans, understandably enough, reject Cohn's claim that medieval witchcraft was nothing more than a delusion. Whatever their motives, their criticisms will sound eerily familiar to Christians who are in the habit of complaining about the limitations of the secular mindset. Cohn routinely dismisses as "fantasy" all reports about witches that don't fit in with his idea of what is and isn't real. Margot Adler puts the point concisely:

> One of the problems with Cohn's argument is his limited conception of what is possible in reality. For example, he considers all reports of orgies to be fantasy....Here he is surprisingly ignorant of the history of sex and ritual. Orgiastic practices were a part of religious rites in many cultures of the ancient world. And while most modern group sexual encounters lack a religious dimension, one only has to read reports about modern sex clubs to know that orgiastic experiences are not merely a product of fantasy (Adler, 1986, page 82).

Another Skeptic's Explanation

Cohn's theory is the leading explanation of medieval witchcraft among academic historians, but not the only one. An alternative theory that also expresses the skeptical outlook is put forth in the work of British historian H.R. Trevor-Roper. Trevor-Roper (in contrast to Cohn) essentially says that witchcraft was indeed a creation of the Inquisition—not as a sick delusion, however, but as a more or less deliberately crafted tool in pursuit of religious domination. Unfortunately, the Inquisition's tool got out of hand and took on a malignant life of its own in the form of the Renaissance witch hysteria.

Trevor-Roper says that, in its struggle with heretical groups, the Inquisition created the stereotype of witchcraft to use as a weapon of religious politics against its opposition. For centuries, the Church had pretty much ignored the fragments of paganism and folk magic that lay scattered about Europe after the fall of Rome. To the extent that the Church paid them any attention, it was to deny that they had any significance. St. Boniface went so far as to declare that it was unchristian to even believe in witches.

But as the Church's struggle with heresy intensified at the beginning of the Middle Ages, that attitude changed. Gradually, says Trevor-Roper, fragments of the old, non-Christian ways were assembled into an elaborate system of demonology that turned into the concept of "witchcraft." The Inquisition used the concept of witchcraft as a model for attacking groups that resisted the dominance of the Catholic Church. For several hundred years, that model was applied sporadically and locally. Its use probably would have died out at that stage, but the model was revived in response to the social crises of the Black Death and the Hundred Years' War. Then, very suddenly, it became universal, spread throughout Europe by the new technology of the printing press. Finally—and fatally—it was given fearful urgency by the religious passions of the Reformation and Counter-Reformation. At that point, there was no stopping it; the witch hysteria had become a social reality in its own right and had to simply run its course, like some virulent disease.

Beyond Skepticism

The theories of both Cohn and Trevor-Roper can contribute something to our understanding of historical witchcraft, but neither approach can stand on its own as an adequate account of its subject. Cohn suggests that the pattern of witch accusations reveals the deep psychological roots of witchcraft fear. He is partly right, but he rejects the possibility that those deep psychological roots also generated any actual witch behavior. Trevor-Roper suggests that the myth of witchcraft was "the creation of social and political struggles. And only when the social structure of the society changed could the myth be destroyed" (Adler, 1986, page 54). Again, he is partly right: There is no question that the ideological battles of the Catholic Church helped to determine how the idea of witchcraft developed. At the same time, Trevor-Roper's skeptical worldview limits his understanding; his picture of reality can't accommodate the possibility that any real witches existed.

The existence of actual witch behavior would, to say the least, change our assessment of the forces at work behind the witchcraft craze. Unfortunately, historical study alone won't solve that riddle. There is no historical evidence to tell us whether anyone did any of the things that witches were accused of. All we have are records of accusations, trials, and confessions—all of which are suspect in some way and historically inconclusive. The historian is left to weigh the possibilities and draw his own conclusions according to the assumptions of his worldview.

But there is other evidence suggesting that Europe's flap over witchcraft may have had some basis in fact. Studies in comparative religion, folklore, and anthropology have turned up practices among the Africans, Asians, and South Americans that are strikingly similar to the practices of witchcraft alleged by the Inquisition. Mircea Eliade, for instance, points out that the practices of tantric yoga are a virtual duplicate of the European witchcraft allegations. Eliade's conclusions are a challenge to those who would dismiss the lurid aspects of witchcraft as mere fantasy.

> Even a rapid perusal of the Indian and Tibetan documents will convince an unprejudiced reader that European witchcraft cannot be the creation of religious or political persecution....As a matter of fact, all the

features associated with European witches are—with the exception of Satan and the Sabbath—claimed also by Indo-Tibetan yogis and magicians. They too are supposed to fly through the air, kill at a distance, master demons and ghosts, and so on. Moreover some of these eccentric Indian sectarians boast that they break all the religious taboos and social rules: that they practice human sacrifice, cannibalism, and all manner of orgies, including incestuous inter-course, and that they eat excrement, nauseating ani-mals, and devour human corpses. In other words, they proudly claim all the crimes and horrible cere-monies cited ad nauseam in the western European witch trials (Eliade, 1976, page 71).

Such evidence suggests that those who looked for witchcraft in Europe were a) looking for something that was really there, even if b) they didn't understand what they were looking for, and c) that they often found something else, which they called by the same name anyway.

In chapter 6, we will look at European witchcraft to see how it came together, what it consisted of, and why it dis-appeared. Finally in chapter 7, we will look at some of the thinking *about* witchcraft that developed after witchcraft itself had vanished, and see how those theories, speculations, and outright fantasies all became part of the mythology and ideology of the modern Witchcraft movement.

6
Witchcraft for Real:
Was There, or Wasn't There?

Rationalist theories of witchcraft dominate academic study of the subject today. The question of whether or not any actual witches existed is seldom addressed as a serious issue. The skeptical assumption, of course, is that they did not—in other words, there never was any such thing as a real witch. Some scholars, however, are skeptical of skepticism itself, and try to take the findings of folklorists and anthropologists into account. They begin by comparing the witchcraft allegations with other beliefs and practices that were known to exist in Europe at the time. One historian whose work takes that approach is Dr. Jeffrey Burton Russell, a scholar specializing in the history of ideas.

Russell researched the subject extensively for his landmark book *Witchcraft in the Middle Ages*. The evidence he assembled indicates that about 30 percent of the accusations against witches were connected with magic or sorcery, 25 percent with pre-Christian folk fertility traditions, and 25 percent with previous or existing heresies.

> If one goes on to admit, as all historians do, that sorcery existed and was practiced in Europe as it has been in most societies, and that heresies were

believed and practiced, and if one admits, as all historians familiar with the evidence do, that magical folk-beliefs and customs persisted in various forms through the Middle Ages, one must conclude that about 80% of the charges are associated with phenomena having existence independent of theological embroidery....Almost all appeared before the Inquisition intervened in witchcraft proper. Without denying that...many of the witches condemned were innocent, one is obliged to regard witchcraft as a reality (Russell, 1972, page 22).

Rationalist scholars "know" that the major components of medieval witchcraft are all unreal: Magic is a fantasy, orgies are a fantasy, and the devil is a fantasy; therefore, witchcraft itself was a fantasy—by definition. Interestingly, modern Witches accept the rationalist's *conclusion* that the medieval witch was innocent of crime, but reject the rationalist's *premise* that she was innocent of witchcraft to begin with. To the contrary, say scholars like Eliade and Russell, we can believe that medieval witchcraft was real because we already know the reality of the behavior it was accused of.

Of course, that doesn't mean witchcraft was real in the same way the Inquisition thought it was. It is clear that the Inquisition's concept of witchcraft was a stereotype, created around a standardized set of accusations that were applied in their entirety, as a template, in a variety of different situations. In addition, the growth and development of that stereotype can be charted over time. When you couple those facts with the reality that many of the details in the Inquisition's stereotype came from confessions extorted by torture, it is evident that the Church influenced the *idea* of witchcraft as much as witchcraft itself did.

Witchcraft Components and Antecedents

It is not easy to separate the reality of witchcraft (whatever it was) from speculation, superstition, and outright social hysteria, but Jeffrey Burton Russell makes a credible and convincing attempt. According to Russell's analysis, medieval witchcraft was composed of elements drawn from five sources (Russell, 1972, page 23). It blended portions of

1. folk fertility religion

2. low magic and sorcery

3. spiritism and demonology

4. heresy, mostly of the gnostic type

Those four, in turn, were interpreted and defined by

5. Christian theology

It is easy to see that the first three of those elements predate the advent of Christ. All three have their roots in beliefs and practices that are ancient and universal. It is also easy to see that the last two elements reflect the collision between those beliefs and practices and the rising influence of Christianity.

Fertility religion, sorcery, and demonology all developed independently. Although they crossed paths often, each had a history of its own. In the cosmopolitan atmosphere of the Roman Empire, all of them made the pilgrimage to Rome, and all were in place when Rome fell and the Dark Ages began. Finally, they were all pushed toward the fringes of society together under pressure from Christianity.

Yet historians agree that there was almost no organized persecution of magicians, sorcerers, or pagans during the early Middle Ages. In fact, there is a notable decline of persecution around the ninth and tenth centuries, which are otherwise the darkest of the Dark Ages.

By that time, paganism was no longer a serious threat. The Catholic Church had co-opted popular pagan piety by means of so-called "baptized paganism." The Church simply took over pagan forms and symbols and attached Christian labels to them: Legends and myths of pagan gods were attached to Christian saints; pagan holy ground was used for churches and monasteries; pagan fests and holy days marking the cycle of Nature were renamed and integrated into the Church's liturgical year. Jeffrey Burton Russell speaks of "the infinite resourcefulness with which the Church sought to destroy paganism by ingestion."

Thus, practicing paganism had dwindled to insignificance even without persecution. It was no longer socially potent. It was theologically denounced, almost as an echo of the Church's past battles, but was de facto ignored as long as it kept to itself. The various forms of occultism that were often part of paganism were also largely ignored. In fact, there wasn't a single official execution for sorcery during the Church's first millennium.

Those early attitudes are exemplified by a famous anonymous document of the tenth century called the *Canon Episcopi*. The *Canon* denied that magical phenomena are objectively real, and it ascribed them to "phantasms imposed upon the minds of infidels by the malignant spirit." In short, the *Canon* held that witches and sorcerers lived in a world of delusion created by the devil; they could not affect the real world. Obviously, such people constituted no real threat, and were more to be pitied and scorned than feared. Significantly, the *Canon* invoked no physical punishment for such behavior, requiring only that those who, in their delusion, practiced the devil's arts should be "foully disgraced from their parishes."

At this time (during the so-called "Dark Ages"), the Church was preoccupied with the internal crises of power and organization that accompanied its rapid expansion. Sorcerers were much more likely to run afoul of local officials by creating social upset than they were to be pursued for spiritual error by ecclesiastical authorities. The Church didn't have time to harass the remnants of a beaten and scattered opposition.

Enter Gnosticism

But in that context of Christianity's triumph and internal distractions, a new and more virulent challenge arose—heresy. Heresy was a vigorous, active opponent of Christianity, while the remnants of paganism were passive and constrained. The old ways were a defeated enemy; the heresies were a fresh rebellion. Eventually, the two made common cause. Gnostic heresies in particular began to absorb the remnants of pagan disaffection and cultural resistance. Gnostics also absorbed some of the spiritual baggage of paganism, including its resentment of Christianity and its backwoods occultism. Debased forms of pagan sorcery, spiritism, and fertility practices became mixed with gnostic elitism, mysticism, and antinomianism (disdain of moral rules).

What emerged from that merger was a kind of mystical anarchism, armed with the practices of degenerated occultism and sexual religion. The resulting beliefs and behavior were shocking enough to provoke the full-scale intervention of the Church. An example came to official attention early in the eleventh century, when a group of heretics appeared in Aquitaine (a region of Western France) who were accused of spurning the cross and holding sex orgies. In 1022, in Orleans, members of the movement were tried for heresy before Robert the Pious, then King of France.

We know some of the beliefs attributed to this group from the records of the trial. They included rejection of matter as evil, abstention from certain foods, stress on an inner spirituality, a hidden wisdom revealed only to initiates, and baptism by the laying on of hands. This short list clearly shows the gnostic foundation of their teaching. But the indictment against them included nondoctrinal charges as well, charges that relate to even earlier practices—fertility religion, sorcery, and spirit contact.

> The Aquitaine heretics were accused of
> 1) demon invocation, 2) promiscuous sexual orgy,
> 3) infant sacrifice by burning, and 4) cannibalism of
> the sacrificed infant. Those same charges show
> up repeatedly in the witch trials of the
> centuries to come.

The nondoctrinal charges included four elements that were important in the later development of witchcraft. The Aquitaine heretics were accused of 1) demon invocation, 2) promiscuous sexual orgy, 3) infant sacrifice by burning, and 4) cannibalism of the sacrificed infant. Those same charges show up repeatedly in the witch trials of the centuries to come. They are alleged so often, in fact, that they become legal clichés. By 1300, those four accusations were routinely made in most cases of witchcraft.

All four of those behaviors have played an important part in religion worldwide. Though universal, they have never been common, and have usually been hidden (or "occult") because they are widely condemned. That fact also made them scandal-fodder for religious controversy. From ancient times, it has been standard practice to accuse religious opponents of orgies, or of human sacrifice. The early Christians were accused of such by Roman rabble-rousers—quite possibly because some *gnostic* "Christians" had created scandals by exactly such behavior. Only in medieval witchcraft, however, do we find those four particular charges brought together and joined to the dynamism of heretical movements.

The Aquitaine heretics were not witches, but in their case we find witchlike belief and behavior being added to existing heresy for the first time. Here we see the first stages of the process that created medieval witchcraft. It is essentially a process in which ancient practices with separate histories converge and come together around the phenomenon of heresy. To describe the emphasis in reverse, it is a process in which heresy, the new and dynamic resistance to Christianity, attracts and assimilates the remnants of paganism, the old and waning resistance.

Of course, not all heresies mingled with pagan elements. But those that did found that what came from their mingling was neither paganism nor heresy, but something new. That something new was then defined by Christian theology, which cast it in a distinctly diabolical light. The result was witchcraft as we know it historically. Finally, the theological concept of witchcraft took on a sinister life of its own and became the engine for the lethal hysteria of the Renaissance witch craze.

Dualism and Witchcraft

But that process was a slow one. The trial at Orleans didn't open the gates of witch mania, or begin an Inquisitorial reign of terror. The full-blown witch craze didn't begin until four centuries later, just as the Middle Ages were giving way to the Renaissance, and it didn't end until three centuries after that, as the Renaissance gave way to the Enlightenment. In the meantime, during the early Middle Ages, the various components of witchcraft continued to develop and to interact with one another. As heresy changed and grew, so did its relation to paganism. And so did the Christian response to both of them.

Heresy changed by becoming more "dualistic." Dualism is an ancient philosophy that believes the world is defined by the conflict between two opposite but equal forces—good versus evil, light versus dark, God versus an evenly matched devil, and so on. That vision of cosmic conflict is a congenial way of thinking for a belief system under siege, and heresies tended to become more dualistic as they came under attack from the Church.

For roughly a century (1140–1230) "the heresy of Catharism was the single greatest influence upon demonology and witchcraft" (Russell, 1972, page 121). The Cathars, known in France as the Albigensians, used radical dualism to turn the tables on Christianity. Just as Christianity had demonized the pagan deities, so the Cathars demonized the Christian God. According to Cathar teaching,

> The Spirit of Evil...created the material world for the purpose of entrapping spirit in matter. He imprisoned the human soul in a cage of flesh. The creator of the world, the God of the Old Testament, is the lord of matter, the prince of this world, and the Devil. All the personages of the Old Testament, and John the Baptist in the New, are demons. Christ was a pure spirit sent down by the good God into this world in order to teach man how to escape from the matter that confines him. By the practices of

Catharism, man might follow the teachings of Christ and so liberate himself; but the Catholic Church was established by the Devil in order to delude people....Since Christ was pure spirit, he did not suffer on the cross...since the Eucharist and baptism employ material substances, they too were condemned (Russell, 1972, page 123).

The Cathars, like the Orleans heretics, were not witches per se, but they influenced the formation of witchcraft through their dualistic beliefs and their attitude of rejection toward the Church.

Cathar dualism established evil as a powerful cosmic principle—in some versions equal to God. Seldom had the force of evil seemed so majestic, or so awesome in potency. Those who sought to avoid the tribulations of this world might think it expedient to propitiate the Dark Lord of this world. Those who sought the rewards of this world might think it expedient to worship him outright. Catharism generated an *atmosphere* in which the devil and his demons were seen as both powerful and accessible. In that atmosphere, witchcraft acquired new vigor and allure.

As we have seen, Cathar dualism also functioned as an instrument of rebellion against the Christian God, the Christian establishment, and Christian values. The Cathars, like gnostics in general, were mystical elitists, a tendency that was carried to extremes by the "antinomian" gnostics. The term "antinomian," from the Greek, means "opposed to law." The antinomians believed that they, the elect, had entered a new *aeon* (age or historical phase) and were therefore wholly set free from the moral laws, rules, and regulations governing the old *aeon,* which belonged to the god of this world—that is, the devil.

Blasphemy and sexual license were seen as signs of spiritual purity because they are clear ways of rejecting the standards of this world as defined by the god of this world (the devil) and his religious establishment, the Catholic Church. Antinomians believed that sin exists only because moral rules exist. The God of the Old Testament (the devil) made the rules and thereby created sin. Abolish the rules and you abolish sin. Anyone who repudiates moral law thereby acts as his own savior and liberates himself from sin. Acts such as the defilement of an altar, mockery of the sacraments, and orgiastic sex were interpreted by the antinomians as proof that, for the gnostic elite, the New Age of sinlessness and spiritual liberty had already begun. It was the most radical way possible of proclaiming a break with the old order—and of announcing one's spiritual superiority as a warrant for doing so.

Catharism obviously expressed a high level of popular alienation from Christianity, and especially from the Christian establishment. The depth and extent of that discontent is shown in the fact that the Church considered Catharism to be as serious a threat as Islam. In 1208 Pope Innocent III preached a Crusade against the Albigensians—the Cathars of southern France. Organized and waged by the nobility of northern France, the bloody war was over by 1230, and the cult was substantially suppressed. Yet Catharism had created an environment in which organized irreverence was a demonstrated possibility. In that environment, both heresy and witchcraft continued to flourish.

Theology, the Inquisition, and Witchcraft

By stirring up the Crusade against it, Catharism also aroused the machinery of repression. Though the Cathars were defeated militarily, their heresy persisted. The Inquisition, newly created for the occasion, swept up in the wake of the slaughter by searching out lingering pockets of heretical influence. Its mandate naturally tended to extend itself, and the Inquisition began to look for variations on the theme of spiritual rebellion in general. It soon enough encountered witchcraft, which tended to flourish wherever heresy was active.

But to begin with, the Inquisition was a minor threat to witches—compared with the force of popular sentiment. *Social* rather than ecclesiastical hostility was the strongest source of pressure on witchcraft for the next 150 years. Anxiety ran high in the culture, and popular hysteria was easily released against available victims, including foreigners, Jews, Gypsies, witches, and heretics. Pogroms and lynchings were common.

As official Christendom slowly began to respond to heretical movements, it put its own stamp of interpretation on them. The heretics saw themselves in one way, the Church saw them very differently. Thus began the long process of defining witchcraft—a process directed by the Inquisition and couched in the language of Christian theology, but founded on the more limited worldview of scholasticism and taking much of its content from popular culture.

"Scholasticism" was a philosophy that dominated medieval Catholic thought. It was represented by Thomas Aquinas and was based on the view of Aristotle that the universe was essentially rational and mechanistic, and that the chain of cause and effect was unbroken throughout the natural world.

But the scholastic universe had no explanation for anomaly, chaos, or miracle. In a rational world, nonrational events are unexplainable—they are "unworldly" by definition. Such events were treated as being outside the order of nature—that is, as "super-natural."

Therefore, the worldview of scholasticism implicitly contained a category called "the supernatural." The very existence of that category provided a place for miracles and spiritual experiences to reside—both godly and ungodly. The idea of "the supernatural" implied that the devil's power might be real instead of just imaginary. By the long way around, then, scholasticism supported the idea that witches and their demonic sponsors could affect objective reality.

Scholasticism was part of the "stage setting" for the witch craze. It was a worldview that accommodated the notion of witchcraft and allowed for the reality of claimed cases. It was an ideological framework that made space for the idea of witchcraft—and the fear of it—to grow. In that respect it was a distinct departure from the spiritual mood that animated the *Canon Episcopi*. It would be an exaggeration to say that scholasticism favored the growth of superstition—but not a very great exaggeration. Scholasticism opened the door for the superstitions of popular culture to become part of the Church's definition of witchcraft.

The Contribution of Popular Culture

Popular culture provided many of the details of witch belief and behavior. Animistic and folk-magical ideas were filtered through Christian theology, and in that processed form they were woven into the Inquisition's understanding of what witchcraft was.

Some of the folk beliefs that became part of witchcraft involved encounters with ghosts, apparitions, and other quasi-supernatural creatures—such as gnomes, trolls, faeries, and the night-riding "wild women." To scholastic theology, all of those tales simply depicted different ways of trafficking with demons. Once the gnomes, sprites, and spirits of popular pagan lore had been classified as demonic, they tended to collect around the figure of the witch, since she supposedly dealt with demons. The lesser spirits of folklore thus were transformed into "familiars"—the witch's "pet demon." By the end of the fourteenth century, having a "familiar" became a standard accusation in witch trials.

Another common accusation based on folk beliefs was the charge of engaging in a Satanic "pact." The "pact" supposedly traded the witch's soul to the devil for the sake of some tangible reward. The idea of a desperate compact with the powers of evil is not a Catholic invention. In fact, it is a recurring theme of folk religion worldwide. In Siberian shamanism, for example, the shaman withdraws his soul from his eyes, brains, and entrails and hands it over to previously hostile spirits in return for certain agreed-upon assistance. Often, the pacified spirits become the shaman's spiritual attendants (Lewis, I.M., 1971, page 57).

In the developing definition of witchcraft, not all "pacts" were explicit—that is, stated and agreed to. *Any* reliance on the power of demons was considered an "implicit pact." Simple magic was simply a sin, but magic that invoked demonic assistance was an "implicit pact" and therefore a heresy, since it offered the equivalent of worship to something other than God.

That complicated theological argument became part of the Inquisition's efforts to extend its jurisdiction. Since "pact" was heresy by definition, it came under the Inquisition's authority by definition. Thus Inquisitors often brought the charge of "pact" as part of a strategy to obtain control of witchcraft cases.

The official definition of witchcraft started to come into focus with the issuance of the first Inquisitor's manuals between 1230 and 1250. The manuals advised Inquisitors on the procedure for handling all aspects of the cases before them, from investigation to sentencing. They also listed questions to be asked for seeking out particular heresies. In addition to questions on conventional heresies, many handbooks included questions related to witchcraft—questions about divination, magical operations, invoking or worshiping demons, and so on.

The Inquisition was clearly alert to the increasing connection between heresy and pagan occultism—and to the emerging phenomenon of witchcraft based on that connection. But, at the level of actual events, changes were happening more rapidly than anyone could keep track of.

The defeat of the Cathars did not crush the spirit of their heresy. On the contrary, the Crusaders' military victory simply dispersed the Cathar spirit and the Cathar ideology to a number of near and distant sanctuaries, where they began to mingle with the local holdouts against Christianity.

> The first papal Inquisitor in Germany, Konrad of Marburg, did not take long to produce a crop of witches more diabolical than any that had before been seen. That Konrad did not invent the heresies out of whole cloth is made evident by their alleged doctrines, which are partly Catharist and partly antinomian in nature....[One heretic] named Luckard, claimed that Lucifer had been unjustly cast down from heaven and would ultimately, she hoped, regain his rightful place. Here is the Catharist hidden God identified with Lucifer (Russell, 1972, page 159).

The Inquisition Takes Control

Plainly, based on that kind of Luciferian doctrine, the Inquisition was not just imagining things. Spiritual rebellion was indeed abroad in the land, expressing itself in a variety of creatively depraved ways. But the Inquisition soon made procedures for itself that gave it the power to control the results of its own investigations—a development that opened the door to fantasy and invention in defining witchcraft. The new procedures included secret accusers, no counsel for defense, no defense witnesses, denial of appeal—and torture.

The use of torture in particular gave Inquisitors the power to control the image of witchcraft they drew from their accused. In an ironically misplaced effort at humaneness, the Pope had forbidden condemnation without confession. From that point forward, confession became the single overriding objective of the entire procedure, from the opening investigation to the final turn of the thumbscrew.

> Unfortunately for theories of progress, torture derived less from the "primitive barbarism" of the so-called "Dark Ages" than from the refined law of the later Roman Empire….Torture did not create witchcraft, for witchcraft already existed, but it was responsible for fanning the flames of popular hysteria into the holocausts of the sixteenth and seventeenth centuries (Russell, 1972, page 152).

The popular image of the witch-hunting, witch-burning Inquisitor, therefore, is simply propaganda….It was the secular courts that were most active in pursuing witches and most prolific in killing them.

Not many, even of the innocent, can maintain their innocence in the face of sustained torture. The Inquisitors usually got what they wanted, and witch confessions obtained under torture are suspect, to say the least. Particularly suspect are cases in which whole segments of a community appear to be involved. That is almost always the result of prisoners being forced to implicate others in order to obtain relief from their own torments.

But even with the deck stacked so thoroughly in its favor, the Inquisition still took more than 200 years to gain control of the witchcraft phenomenon. It took that long for the Inquisitors to complete their definition of witchcraft and establish it as the controlling viewpoint for society at large.

Yet the Inquisition played an oddly inconsistent role in society's war on the witches. It created the definition of witchcraft that was the basis for the witch hysteria, and it did so using torture and coercion. But it actually exercised a restraining influence on the hysteria itself, especially during its later stages. Where the Inquisition was strong, there were few witch panics, and the ones that broke out were quickly suppressed. In 1609, for example, a local French witch craze spilled over the border into the Basque region of Spain. The Spanish Inquisition responded by issuing an "Edict of Silence," which prohibited all open discussion of witchcraft. The strategy was effective, and the craze quickly quieted down, for as one skeptical Inquisitor observed, "There were neither witches nor bewitched until they were talked and written about" (Gibbons, 1998).

The popular image of the witch-hunting, witch-burning Inquisitor, therefore, is simply propaganda. The most active persecution of witches was not driven or directed by ecclesiastical authorities, but by secular ones. It was the secular courts that were most active in pursuing witches and most prolific in killing them.

> The Inquisition...played a very small role in the persecution. From 1326–1500, few deaths occurred. Richard Kieckhefer (*European Witch Trials*) found

702 definite executions in all of Europe from 1300–1500; of these, only 137 came from inquisitorial or church courts. By the time that trials were common (early 16th century) the Inquisition focused on the proto-Protestants. When the trials peaked in the 16th and 17th century, the Inquisition was only operating in two countries: Spain and Italy, and both had extremely low death tolls (Gibbons, 1998).

A Witch-Hunting Manual

The popular image of the sinister Inquisitor in hot pursuit of some twisted fantasy of witchcraft comes primarily from a single source—the medieval witch-hunting manual known as *Malleus Maleficarum* ("hammer of witches"). The *Malleus* was the work of two active Inquisitors, and it was clearly the product of an obsessed—if not actually deranged—mentality. A strident, almost hysterical, antifeminine bias permeates the book. According to its authors, women are more drawn to witchcraft than men because they are weaker, more subject to temptation, and more stupid, sensual, and superstitious than men are.

Although the *Malleus* achieved considerable popularity within the Church, the Inquisition rejected the book for its gross legal and theological errors and later condemned its chief author for the "irregularity" of his procedures. The *Malleus* was never officially used as a guidebook by the Inquisition, but it was widely picked up and applied by the secular courts, which were leading the charge in the witch persecutions. The book had a strong influence on the popular conception of witchcraft, but by no means represented the Inquisition itself.

Heinrich Kramer, the text's demented author, was held up as a typical inquisitor. His rather stunning sexual preoccupations were presented as the Church's "official" position on witchcraft. Actually the Inquisition immediately rejected the legal procedures Kramer recommended and censured the inquisitor himself just a few years after the *Malleus* was published. Secular courts, not inquisitorial ones, resorted to the *Malleus* (Gibbons, 1998).

The *Malleus* was written in 1486, near the beginning of the witch craze per se. The full-blown hysteria, which was characterized by accusations of a vast underground conspiracy of witches, sensational trials, and widespread witch executions, peaked between 1550 and 1650.

On first impression, it seems strange to find the worst of the witch mania climaxing during the Renaissance, which is otherwise reputed as an age of enlightenment, toleration, and intellectual freedom. But there are good reasons to find it there rather than earlier. Medieval society was not really conducive either to witchcraft or to public hysteria over it. It was the *breakup* of that society, and the social *breakdown* accompanying it, that opened the door of opportunity both to witchcraft itself, and to the anxieties that fueled the fear of it.

Social Change and Alienation

Starting around 1300, the stable universe of the Middle Ages began to unravel. Politically, the notion of a united Christian society was being shattered by the emergence of the nation–states and the inevitable hostilities between them. The Holy Roman Empire began to shrink in significance and power. The papacy itself became subject to pressure from political interests; by the end of the century, a schism had damaged its credibility even further.

People were losing their bearings. All their anchors were coming loose at once. They were disoriented by a series of terrible catastrophes that wracked Europe, including wars, famines, and devastating epidemics (both literal and figurative) that forced a restructuring of economic and social institutions on all levels.

The literal epidemic was the plague of the Black Death, which may have killed as much as a third of Europe's population. In reaction to that terrifying threat, there were also epidemics of hysteria and populist frenzy; better-known examples include the flagellants, who publicly whipped themselves into a mystical trance, and the St. Vitus dancers, who publicly danced themselves into total exhaustion. And for the meringue on the century's misery pie, there were a host of political upheavals and dislocations. Peasant revolts challenging the aristocracy were suppressed with bloody brutality, and the Hundred Years' War brought the full horror and devastation of war to large parts of Europe on an apparently permanent basis.

Most unsettling of all, people were losing their faith in a Church that had been unable to predict, prevent, or even repair those disasters. To make matters worse, the Church winked at corruption, endorsed injustice, and baptized social evils at the same time that it "embraced the life of medieval man so fully that heresy often seemed to be the only way to cast off the smothering embrace of spiritual totalitarianism" (Montgomery, 1973, page 62).

Because of such frustrations and upheavals, people became alienated from the Church *and* the society it supported; thus they were ripe for movements of cultural dissent, including heresy and witchcraft. The tension between the two poles of orthodox defensiveness and heretical disaffection increased sharply. Then, into that explosive situation came a technological spark—the printing press.

Gutenberg invented movable type in 1454. In 1427, just 27 years earlier, Inquisitors and learned monks had begun to turn out theoretical treatises devoted exclusively to witchcraft. While witchcraft had previously been considered one aspect of heresy, now it became the center of scholarly attention—an intellectual trend that Gutenberg's invention caught on the rise and boosted into orbit. The witch craze can justifiably be seen as the world's first media flap.

> The fact that the printing press could now dissemi-
> nate the works of the witch theorists in a quantity
> hitherto undreamed of added enormously to the
> growth of the witch craze. The first printed book on
> witchcraft, the *Fortalicium Fidei,* was issued in 1464,
> only about ten years after Gutenberg had produced
> the first book printed with movable type. It was an
> unfortunate coincidence that printing should have
> been invented just as the fervor of the witch hunters
> was mounting, and the swift propagation of the
> witch hysteria by the press was the first evidence that
> Gutenberg had not liberated man from original sin
> (Russell, 1972, page 234).

The Classical Definition of Witchcraft

By 1486, only 32 years after printing was invented, the *Malleus Maleficarum* was published. Despite the fact that the book was rejected by the Inquisition, it achieved wide distribution and had great influence on the way witchcraft was perceived. The book's popularity was partly due to its comprehensive scope—its declared purpose was to establish the indisputable reality of witchcraft by refuting all the arguments against it. As a result, the *Malleus* put on display most of the main elements of the witchcraft stereotype as it stood after 200 years of elaboration. Some parts of the "classic" witch stereotype were curiously missing (there is no mention of orgies or familiar spirits, for instance); and other parts of the full stereotype wouldn't appear until several decades later (the now-familiar "covens" and "sabbats," for example, don't show up until the 1500s—the *Malleus* depicts witches as individuals, working alone) (Gibbons, 1999).

But despite its shortcomings and distortions, the book provides a clear outline of what witchcraft was thought to be at the end of the fifteenth century. According to the *Malleus*, witchcraft is the most abominable of all heresies and the most evil of all crimes. It has three necessary elements and four essential characteristics.

The three necessary elements are

1. the evil-intentioned witch

2. the help of the devil

3. the permission of God, who hates evil but allows it so that man may have freedom and sin may execute judgment on itself

The four essential characteristics are:

1. the renunciation of the Christian faith

2. the sacrifice of unbaptized infants to Satan

3. the devotion of body and soul to evil

4. sexual relationships with Satan or seducing demons (*incubi* and *succubi*), or both

In addition, witches were said to engage in a wide range of characteristic activities. They render obscene homage to the devil as he appears to them in various grotesque forms. Jeffrey Burton Russell summarizes the allegations:

> They use incantations, effect apparent changes in their shapes by diabolical illusion, practice various forms of maleficium (hostile magic), are transvected through the air from place to place by the power of demons, and use the Christian sacraments in their vile rites. They cook and eat children, either their own or those of others; and they use the children's flesh and bones to obtain a salve or ointment which they then employ in their magical operations (Russell, 1972, page 233).

As the fifteenth century ended and the sixteenth began, both the fear and the persecution of witches started to gather momentum. The height of the witch craze, with its lethal panics, mass trials, and multiple executions, happened in the hundred years between 1550 and 1650; many historians attribute the increase to the new disruptions and anxieties caused by the wars of the Reformation. Indeed, recent studies have confirmed that the worst panics took place in those areas where Catholics and Protestants were actively battling each other for religious and political control (Gibbons, 1998).

Renaissance: Climax and Unraveling

The beginning of the Renaissance watched the witch mania come into full and terrible bloom, while the end of the Renaissance saw the phenomenon dwindle and vanish with puzzling rapidity. Why?

The Renaissance was fertile soil for the witch craze because it set off another round of social upheaval and intellectual revolution. "Deprived of the old securities, people responded in a panic that at that particular time found vent in terror of witchcraft" (Russell, 1972, page 227). The influence of printing, the quintessential invention of the Renaissance, has already been pointed out—as has the impact of the Reformation, the defining religious event of the Renaissance.

Another factor favoring the development of witch mania during the Renaissance was the revival of pagan learning. With the revival of the Greek and Roman classics there came also a revival of the magical knowledge of antiquity. That revival validated witchcraft in spirit, if not in detail.

Another aspect of the pagan resurgence was a revival of Neoplatonism, which "caused a vast reawakening, first in intellectual circles, and then at large, of the magical world view. This in turn greatly augmented the intellectual respectability of belief in witchcraft, until eventually it became difficult to argue against it" (Russell, 1972, page 227). In the long debate that the Church was having with itself over whether the phenomena of witchcraft were "real" or "delusory," the pagan elements of the Renaissance cast a decisive vote in favor of their "reality."

Yet the same conditions that favored witchcraft also limited it. Witchcraft was defined by its conflict with Christianity at the end of the Middle Ages. The Renaissance stimulated witchcraft in the short run, but stifled it in the long run because the Renaissance put an end to the monolithic orthodoxy against which witchcraft had rebelled, and against which it had been defined. At the same time, the Renaissance opened up new channels of expression for the counter-Christian impulse that had motivated witchcraft to begin with.

The terms "Renaissance" and "humanism" are not necessarily terms of praise, clarity and ideality....

"Renaissance" was also the revival of ugly, idolatrous, and often obscene creeds, and "humanism" may mean just what it says: the adoration of man and his occult powers to create the world and himself....The result will be moral aberration (to a divine being all things are possible and permitted) and also intellectual aberration, the loss of proportion in things human, divine, scientific, cultural, social and political.

In this manner a strange alliance is concluded between the occult and the rationalistic (as opposed to the rational, the reasonable) (Molnar, 1974, pages 118–119).

Faust, after all, was as much a "Renaissance man" as Leonardo da Vinci. Faust was the literary version of the magus, who lusted after secret knowledge. Many Renaissance figures followed his example, including Paracelsus, Heinrich Cornelius Agrippa, and Giordano Bruno. In addition to pagan magic, the revival of pagan philosophies opened further options for non-Christian thinking.

The Empty Shell

Thus the official definition of witchcraft began to harden just as the spirit that animated witchcraft began to abandon it—to dissipate and find other outlets for expression. The outer features of witchcraft congealed and were targeted in that form, while the inner dynamic of witchcraft dispersed itself elsewhere through newly opened channels of opportunity. Witchcraft crystallized outwardly while being emptied inwardly. It became an abstract structure, sustained by collective fear and the activism of antiwitch zealots. Largely deserted by the spirit(s) that had energized it, by the end of the Renaissance witchcraft had become a "form of ungodliness without the power thereof."

✧ ✧ ✧ ✧ ✧ ✧ ✧ ✧ ✧ ✧ ✧ ✧ ✧ ✧ ✧ ✧ ✧ ✧

It seems as if the whole society all at once began
1) to feel moral, spiritual, and emotional exhaustion
after three centuries of hysteria and holocaust,
and 2) to suspect that the classic definition of
witchcraft had been rendered irrelevant by social
and intellectual changes.

✧ ✧ ✧ ✧ ✧ ✧ ✧ ✧ ✧ ✧ ✧ ✧ ✧ ✧ ✧ ✧ ✧ ✧

When the end came for the witchcraft craze, it came
quickly. It came with little advance warning, and for no
obvious reason. In the first half of the 1600s, the great war
against the witches continued to rage. The English
witchfinder Matthew Hopkins is said to have put over 200
"witches" to death between 1645 and 1647. In the latter
half of the century, however, the number of witch prosecu-
tions began to decline, and the severity of the penalties
began to diminish. By the end of the century the active pursuit of witches, with few exceptions, had dwindled to the
point of near invisibility. That general quieting of the hysteria was punctuated by three sensational trials toward the
end of the century: the "witches of Edinburgh"—Major
Weir and his sister Jane (1670); the "Paris witches" and
their poisoning conspiracy (1679); and, in America, the
"Salem witches" (1692). The Salem witchcraft trials were
the figurative last gasp of the Renaissance witch hysteria,
which had long since been over and done with in Europe,
where it began.

It seems as if the whole society all at once began 1) to feel
moral, spiritual, and emotional exhaustion after three centuries of hysteria and holocaust, and 2) to suspect that the

classic definition of witchcraft had been rendered irrelevant by social and intellectual changes.

That practical change of heart, by the way, was pioneered by the Inquisition. The Spanish Inquisition in particular led the way by encouraging official skepticism about witch accusations in the face of prevailing credulity. In 1611, the Inquisitor Alonzo Salazar de Frias arrived in Navarre to investigate an outbreak of fear, accusations, and executions of the previous year. Salazar came armed with an "Edict of Grace" that permitted him to undo penalties applied to alleged "witches" if he found their conviction unjust.

> Salazar received 1802 applicants [under the Edict of Grace], of whom 1384 were children of from twelve to fourteen years of age and, besides these, there were eighty-one who revoked confessions previously made....He found, by one means and another, that some 1600 persons had been falsely accused. At one place he found tales of a Sabbath held at the very place where his own secretaries had been harmlessly on the night named (Williams, 1941, pages 251–252).

From 1614 onwards, witchcraft practically disappeared from the formal religious courts of Spain. A similar trend was taking place in England, though less consciously and more sporadically. Other Inquisitions followed suit in due course. In 1657, the Roman Inquisition issued a series of instructions designed to curb the worst abuses of the witchcraft proceedings, namely "1) the arrest on common suspicion, and 2) the indiscriminate use of torture" (Williams, 1941, page 263). Slowly but progressively, European society began to back away from its blind paranoia and exterminating zeal. Gradually the realization seemed to spread that things had gotten badly out of hand.

Interestingly, people continued to believe that witchcraft itself was real, while becoming ever more skeptical of specific allegations. "At the beginning of the eighteenth century that admirable example of good taste, Joseph Addison, put the thing neatly enough. 'I believe in general,' he wrote, 'that there is such a thing as witchcraft; but at the same time can give no credit to any particular instance of it'" (Williams, 1941, page 301). The general idea of witchcraft remained undisturbed in the public mind, but particular cases stopped turning up and were disbelieved when they did so. Thus ended the witch craze of the Renaissance—its abstract identity remained intact, but concrete examples of it simply disappeared.

Concluding Thoughts

How "real" was the witchcraft of European history? Was the devil-worshiping witch a historical fact, or just an imaginary stereotype? The rationalists believe they have settled that question once and for all, but others think such claims are premature. The truth is that the available historical evidence is both sketchy and one-sided, which means that very little can be said that isn't subject to challenge. Rationalist theories of witchcraft express the attitude of most professional historians toward religious ideas in general; however, the dominance of the rationalist view is more of a current poll result than a position established by argument or enforced by evidence. In fact, by the standards of intellectual coherence, the historical scenario offered by Jeffrey Burton Russell makes more sense of more of the evidence, with fewer assumptions and leaps of logic, than any of its rationalist counterparts.

The main point of contention between the two viewpoints today concerns whether or not anyone actually believed in a "dualistic" devil who was the opposite of God, so as to "worship" him as witches were said to do. Rationalists dismiss such charges as mere "projections"—that is, horrifying thoughts dredged up from the subconscious of the accuser and attributed to someone else. Actually, this is the weakest point in the rationalist's case. In point of fact, dualism is a very old and well-documented religious attitude, described in detail by Greek, Roman, and Persian sources. It is plausible theologically and philosophically, and there is no good reason to assume that it didn't continue to exist in Europe right on through the Middle Ages (Russell, 2001). A skeptic who dismisses dualism outright, lives in a mental universe that is smaller than the real one—an inherently disabling aspect of his worldview.

From a strictly historical standpoint, the following can be said with a high degree of confidence (Russell, 1972):

1. A stereotype of witchcraft existed, in large part derived from ancient ideas.

2. No one ever embodied the full stereotype.

3. It is probable that some people embodied some of the stereotype.

4. Almost certainly, there was no witch cult—no organization of witches (however defined).

Beyond that bare-bones historical pronouncement, there are a number of observations to be made, both about witchcraft and the mania connected with it.

We can say with relative certainty that witchcraft was not a fantasy of the Inquisition, nor was it the product of popular hysteria, though both played their part in creating the concept of witchcraft as well as the craze that eventually surrounded it.

The Inquisition was basically correct in classifying dualistic witchcraft as a heresy. After all, one cannot venerate or even traffic with the devil (or "demons") unless one has already accepted the Christian worldview, at least as far as it says that such things exist. Overall, witchcraft (out of its gnostic connection) accepted that Christian picture of reality, but reversed its values. In that context, the real witches can only be considered as deviant believers; in other words, as "heretics."

As "heretics," witches sought not only to reject the establishment, but to shock and challenge it as well. Therefore it is plausible that some of them deliberately did things the establishment deemed to be most awful. The psychology of that process is not difficult to understand, even if its outcome seems bizarre. In medieval society, the image of the devil embodied everything the Church called evil. As that image of evil prevailed in society, those who consciously sought to reject society and its values acted out the image *because it would be understood by others.* The issue is communication—the spiritual rebel speaks out because he wants to be heard. Thus he expresses his rebellion in the spiritual language of his times. No spiritual anarchist wants to keep his insurrection in the closet. Above all, he wants to send a message to the establishment he is rebelling against, a message that carries the maximum offensive charge. Therefore he gravitates toward behavior that the establishment defines as maximally offensive. Because the Church said that worshiping the devil was the worst thing you could do, some people scrambled to do it for that reason alone.

There is another dynamic at work here as well. While some groups set out to oppose the Church from the beginning, others found themselves under attack from the Church willy-nilly. They were thrust into opposition without intending it. Either way, groups and individuals under siege from the

Catholic establishment felt the need for allies and support—spiritually and otherwise.

Since the Church said that the devil was its strongest and most dangerous opponent, those who found themselves at odds with the Church might well think of turning to him for aid and comfort. Since the Church said that witchcraft was an attack on Christian culture, those who felt oppressed by that culture could see witchcraft as a way to strike back at their oppressors. It was the final and ironic sign of the Church's cultural triumph that its enemies began to imitate its definition of evil.

In any event, it seems highly likely that some of those tried as witches were substantially guilty of at least some of the charges lodged against them. Unfortunately, it is also certain that the Church was complicit in causing a large number of people, perhaps as many as 50,000, to be falsely accused and wrongfully executed after subjecting them to torture that was demonically inventive in its cruelty. Irrational fear of irrational evil is not conducive to the making of subtle distinctions, and the witch hunters made few distinctions of any kind in their campaign of extirpation.

Surprisingly to some, the most barbaric and unjust features of the persecutions were not derived from Christianity, but from the adulteration of Christianity with sub-Christian values. We have already seen that torture was a vestige of Roman practice, and not a Christian innovation. Further,

> it must be admitted that for very long, superstition was admitted as an ally within the Church itself. Like the Emperors and the barbarian chiefs, the hateful energies of hate were enlisted on the side of Christendom. Cruelty, denounced as a sin, was welcomed and embraced as a savior (Williams, 1941, page 308).

By this means, one form of sin was pitted against another. The sin inside the Church clashed with the sin outside it, and the two of them together raised such a clangor that the biblical command to judge sin in sorrow and compassion was drowned out. Only by stepping outside the hysteria could the Church regain its balance and perspective, and realize what was happening to it.

Near the end of the witch craze, that began to happen. In 1683, a commission of inquiry in Germany noted the destruction wrought by the witch trials, and "raised the possibility that the trials were themselves the work of the Devil, who had induced the fear of witchcraft in the Christian community in order to turn it against itself and destroy it" (Russell, 1980, page 126).

Many modern Americans would like to think that our society is immune to such eruptions of mass hysteria as the witch craze because of our democratic institutions and our greater tolerance and rationality. But they are mistaken.

Seeing the Future in the Past

Christianity is an unabashedly concrete religion, even in its supernaturalism. In the Middle Ages, Christianity wrestled its supernatural opposition into concrete form as well. That form was witchcraft; it was shaped by its times, but it was also the conduit of timeless forces.

European witchcraft is unthinkable in anything like the form it took without the shaping influence of Christian myth and theology. But in a deeper sense, witchcraft springs out of hostility and violence that are at the same time as old as man and as contemporary. Now once again institutions are failing, and men are being thrust back upon their own formulations of symbolic order. Once again, lacking the framework of a coherent rational system, we are increasingly subject to propaganda, nihilism, and mindless violence. Dogmatic and unreasoning ideologists are preparing for us a new witch craze, couched now in secular, rather than transcendental terms.

It is in this universal context that European witchcraft is best understood. Medieval witchcraft was in one sense only the first stage of a long period of witch delusion; in another sense, it was a manifestation of the innate and perennial darkness of the human soul (Russell, 1972, page 289).

Many modern Americans would like to think that our society is immune to such eruptions of mass hysteria as the witch craze because of our democratic institutions and our greater tolerance and rationality. But they are mistaken. In fact, they themselves may be the best proof of their own mistake, since many of them are prepared to demonize Christianity and "scapegoat" Christians without recognizing the implications of their own behavior. No cultural tradition, social system, or ideology can prevent the outbreak of collective fear, blame, hatred, and persecution under the right—or wrong—conditions.

The history of witchcraft, perhaps, does not altogether encourage a belief in democratic opinion.

Nor in aristocratic opinion. It is the history of a fashion, and it has yet to be shown that either democracy or aristocracy are proof against fashion. As the Middle Ages hurried to their feverish and calamitous close, fashion rode them like a fury (Williams, 1941, page 309).

Seeing the witchcraft craze as the fruit of intellectual fashion helps us understand its place in history. The commonsense skepticism of the *Canon Episcopi* declared witchcraft to be a spiritual delusion, and belief in witches to be a disreputable superstition. Scholasticism turned that viewpoint inside out—belief in the reality of witchcraft became a high and serious duty for Christian intellectuals, while those who doubted it were marginalized at best and stigmatized at worst. Then the Enlightenment brought in yet another worldview, which reversed those intellectual polarities one more time. "Witchcraft declined because a new worldview made it a superstition. It declined because it was as intellectually disreputable to defend witchcraft under the new system as it had been to attack it under the old" (Russell, 1980, page 124).

The history of European witchcraft can also be seen in terms of the coming together and breaking up of its individual components. Prior to the Middle Ages, witchcraft did not exist as such, because it was still in pieces. Its components had not yet abandoned their separate histories and been fully joined. After the Renaissance, the process reversed itself, and witchcraft ceased to exist as such because it *went* to pieces. Its components disjoined and resumed their separate histories once again. Gnosticism dispersed itself into a spectrum of heresies, magic and sorcery continued on their own terms, and spiritism discovered a prophet in Emmanuel

Swedenborg, who would build a church in its name—and his own.

Those strands were woven together by circumstance to form witchcraft; they unraveled again when those circumstances changed. All of those strands have continued to exist on their own, and all have continued to generate their own historical trails, right down to the present day.

7

From Witchcraft to Wicca: 1700–2000

✢ ✢ ✢

Historical witchcraft had unraveled almost completely by the early 1700s. It is basically not heard from again, "save in legend, literature, and jest," as Jeffrey Burton Russell put it (Russell, 1980, page 122). By the end of the Renaissance, an intellectual and religious revolution had made scholasticism (see previous chapter) passé and turned its cherished assumptions into superstitions. The philosopher Descartes (1596–1650) thoroughly rejected the traditions of medieval philosophy, asserting that the world was run according to universal, scientific, mechanical laws of nature that rendered the work of angels and demons irrelevant. The religious revolution followed closely behind the intellectual one and led to similar conclusions. The God who presided over the scientific, mechanical cosmos ruled it by His universal laws of nature, which He would not readily allow demons to evade or suspend. Unexplained events that scholasticism would have classified as divine or demonic were now assumed to have a natural explanation—or to simply be false reports. The new mood and outlook in religion basically saw witchcraft as being beside the point.

Things That Go Bump in the Light: From the Enlightenment to Romanticism

The 1700s were the century of the "Enlightenment"—the triumph of rationalism, skepticism, and scientism. Those three vogues conspired to demystify the universe, but they could not eradicate irrationality. By rejecting the supernatural, skepticism became a veil of denial. Beneath it, spiritual aberration grew in the dark, without hindrance or attention. Thus the century of light was also a century of shadows. The Enlightenment was the century of Descartes, Newton, and Voltaire, but it was also the century of Mesmer, Cagliostro, and Casanova.* The widespread enthusiasm for alchemy, astrology, and kabbalah (Jewish occult mysticism) showed that a current of mystical irrationalism ran under the surface of skeptical self-assurance.

The humanism of the Enlightenment cast spiritual shadows in other ways as well.

> By and large the opinion of the Age of Reason was that the universe revolved around man. At any rate man was the perceptible center of things, and an extremely important part of creation. Therefore all his acts, his passions, his minutest doings must be invested with an awesome significance, as the dramatic activities of the lord of the world. This reasoning was all very well, but it placed on the individual an enormous burden in exchange for his privileged position at the center of things. Man was left to himself. He had only his own kind to turn to (Webb, 1974, page 10).

---

* *Franz Mesmer* (1734–1815) was a German physician who widely popularized a form of hypnosis as treatment for physical and mental illnesses (the term "mesmerize" is derived from his name). *Count Alessandro di Cagliostro* (1743-1795) was an Italian adventurer who became famous as a magician and alchemist. *Giovanni Giacomo Casanova* (1725–1798), Italian ecclesiastic, writer, soldier, spy, and diplomatist, in addition to gaining huge notoriety as a seducer of women, was also denounced as a magician, after earlier being expelled from seminary.

The Enlightenment's overweening spiritual pride and desire for self-sufficiency eventually produced its opposite, and our culture experienced an attack of existential anxiety that we know today as the "Romantic Movement." The Romantics correctly perceived that rationalism is hostile to human significance and human concerns. In reaction, they exalted the nonrational and the antirational, the primal, the intuitive, and the ecstatic. As Colin Wilson points out, "The romantics were driven by the spirit of magic...[and] the romantic revival brought a magical revival with it" (Wilson, 1971, pages 233, 235).

From Romanticism to the Occult Revival

The Romantic and the occultic are natural allies. Both are reactions against, and rejections of, "normal" reality, but for different reasons. The occultist reaches for the ecstasy of god-hood out of spiritual ambition; the Romantic reaches for ecstatic intensity out of spiritual desperation.

> Goethe's Faust turns to magic because he is sick of his human limitations, and he wants to explore those moments of godlike intensity that Saint-Martin wrote about. Nineteenth-century man found himself high and dry in a materialistic and boring world. In the Middle Ages, devils were a reality that everybody accepted without question. Now the shadows were gone; the common daylight made everything hard and clear. And the romantics looked back nostalgically to the age of demons and incubi, altogether more stimulating to the imagination than railways and paddle steamers. The universal complaint was boredom (Wilson, 1971, page 329).

Romanticism defined the *mood* of a whole generation, and it helped to set the stage for the occult revival of the late 1800s.

Mary Shelley, wife of the poet Percy Shelley, wove Romanticism and scientism together in *Frankenstein* (subtitled *The Modern Prometheus*). In her famous story, rationalistic science blends with mystical occultism (alchemy) to produce the monster, who represents Nature manipulated without moral (or other) guidelines.

Romanticism also created new ways of expressing our fallen tendency to rebellion and opposition. The figure of the intellectual and *artiste*—the "inspired outsider"—manning the barricades of revolution out of his passionate love for Truth (or Justice, or the People, and so on) has become a permanent cultural cliché. That same kind of Romantic imagery also permeates the Neopagan movement. Neopagans not only romanticize nature, they romanticize Neopaganism as well.

In fact, the connection between Romanticism and Neopaganism is even more direct. The romantic–occultic mood among nineteenth-century scholars and intellectuals led some of them to introduce ideas that have become an integral part of Neopagan myth and ideology.

In 1828, University of Berlin professor Karl Jarcke proposed the idea that the witchcraft of European history was actually a degenerated form of pre-Christian paganism. Jarcke wasn't trying to validate witchcraft—he was trying to discredit it. Jarcke was a Catholic, and his theory was an argumentative strategy to counter critics of the Church who saw the witch craze as an outburst of Catholic prejudice and perversity. In Jarcke's scenario, the ancient pagan religion

> had lingered among the common people, had been condemned by Christians as Satanism, and in the course of the Middle Ages had responded by adapting to the Christian stereotype and becoming devil-worshippers in earnest. As a result, proposed

Jarcke, even ordinary people began to turn away from it in disgust, and denounce it to the authorities, who proceeded to extirpate it. In this manner, the young academic brilliantly outflanked the liberals; his explanation of the witch-trials equally accepted the non-existence of witchcraft itself, while exonerating the authorities who had persecuted witches as members of an evil and anti-social cult (Hutton, 1999, page 136).

But as ingenious as Jarcke's strategy was, there was one problem—it was a pure flight of fancy, with nothing whatever to back it up. His theory was not intended to explain any actual evidence (of which he had none), but to explain away somebody else's theory. Nevertheless, his ideas achieved some currency, in part because competing theories were equally unsupported by facts.

The Work of Jules Michelet

In time, the anti-Catholic and anticlerical party responded with its own rhetorical strategy, put forth by "one of the nineteenth century's most famous liberal historians, the Frenchman, Jules Michelet" (Hutton, 1999, page 137). Michelet was an academic maverick whose works varied widely in quality. On the one hand, he could be a patient and thorough archivist, producing a multivolume history of France that is still a valued historical resource. On the other hand, he was also in the habit of churning out lurid and sensational "potboilers" to make the most amount of money in the shortest amount of time with the least amount of work, so as to support his more systematic labors. (His book on witchcraft definitely fell into the "potboiler" category, having been dashed off in a mere two months.) Furthermore, his academic colleagues had already censured him for his lack of objectivity, as he invariably colored his historical arguments with his own political attitudes. He brought a tone of passionate advocacy to every subject he dealt with, and what fueled his passion was his hatred of the medieval Church and all of the miseries he felt Christianity had inflicted on Europe (especially on France) in the form of the absolute monarchy and the parasitic aristocracy that went with it.

✦ ✦ ✦ ✦ ✦ ✦ ✦ ✦ ✦ ✦ ✦ ✦ ✦ ✦ ✦ ✦ ✦

Michelet's…idea that medieval witchcraft was a pagan survival fighting for liberty by resisting the oppressive influence of Christianity has been central to modern Witchcraft's view of its own identity.

✦ ✦ ✦ ✦ ✦ ✦ ✦ ✦ ✦ ✦ ✦ ✦ ✦ ✦ ✦ ✦ ✦

Michelet believed that "Christianity itself now had to give way to a new faith suited to a new age" (Hutton, 1999, page 138), and he toyed with the idea that the replacement religion should have a feminine focus, centered on the function of motherhood. It is no surprise, then, that Michelet turned his 1862 treatment of witchcraft *(La Sorcière)* into a sustained attack on his favorite targets—the Catholic Church and the aristocracy. That much was familiar from his other work.

The real novelty in Michelet's treatment of his subject was that he accepted the picture of witchcraft drawn by Jarcke and other Catholic apologists, but reversed the values attached to it. Yes, said Michelet, witchcraft *was* a surviving pagan religion of fertility and Nature-worship, but far from being an antisocial cult, it alone "had kept the spirit of liberty alive all through the 'thousand long, dreary, terrible years' of the Middle Ages." Michelet also went "further than any writer before or since, to proclaim that the Renaissance had been produced when the wisdom preserved by the witches broke surface again to infuse members of the culural elite" (Hutton, 1999, page 139). Basically, Michelet argued that witchcraft was a widespread religious, social, and political *protest* movement, created by medieval peasants who used surviving folk-fertility beliefs to mock and defy their oppressors—namely, the Church and the feudal aristocracy.

Michelet's approach to his subject was the very essence of Romanticism. The Romantic temperament regarded passion itself as a badge of truth and a foundation for wisdom and insight. To Romanticism, the purest vision springs from the purest passion, and the purest passion of all is the fire of Promethean rebellion. Michelet projected his personal sense of rebellious, Romantic virtue onto the witches with a blissful indifference to facts. His research for the portion of his book that dealt with medieval history was

> more or less non-existent, and it represents an extended poetic reverie, being at times actually composed in blank verse. The seventeenth-century chapters were based on a small number of pamphlets, which Michelet reinterpreted to suit his own hatred of Catholicism. As the book went on sale, he noted in his journal: "I have assumed a new position which my best friends have not as yet clearly adopted, that of proclaiming the provisional death of Christianity" (Hutton, 1999, page 138).

La Sorcière became a bestseller right away (thereby fulfilling Michelet's immediate purpose for the book) and has continued to stimulate the interest of readers right up to the present day. It was first published almost a century and a half ago and has never been out of print since that time. Michelet's own academic peers, however, virtually ignored the book—"apparently," as Ronald Hutton says, "because they recognized that it was not really history" (Hutton, 1999, page 140).

For obvious reasons, Michelet's work on witchcraft has no credibility among professional historians today, but it has exercised an extraordinary influence in other ways.

> [His] argument that witchcraft was a form of protest was adapted later by the Marxists; his argument that it was based on a fertility cult was adopted by anthropologists at the turn of the century, influencing Sir James Frazer's *Golden Bough*,...Margaret Murray's *Witch-Cult in Western Europe,* and T.S. Eliot's *The Waste Land* (Russell, 1980, page 133).

Because of its continuing popular influence, along with its (indirect) intellectual influence, Michelet's book has been part of the preparation for the twentieth century rise of Neopaganism. Furthermore, his idea that medieval witchcraft was a pagan survival fighting for liberty by resisting the oppressive influence of Christianity has been central to modern Witchcraft's view of its own identity, as we have already noted.

From Romanticism to the Occult Revival

Michelet was the perfect product of Romanticism, and appeared just as Romanticism reached its height and began its steep decline. After Michelet, as the nineteenth century's middle decades faded into its final ones, so faded the hopes and passions of the Romantic dream. The revolutions that had wracked Europe at the height of the Romantic period did indeed transform both its politics and its society—but they did not end injustice, oppression, and exploitation, as had been hoped and (implicitly) promised. Indeed, in some respects things seemed to get even worse. The Crimean War in Eastern Europe, the Civil War in the U.S.A., and the Franco–Prussian war in Europe were shocking in their ugly brutality, especially to a public that was being informed in newly graphic ways by a newly emerging popular media. A more cynical and calculating mood settled into the collective mentality.

Yet, even as Romanticism was dying, it was also setting up conditions for the dramatic spiritual and literary outburst that we know as the Occult Revival of the late nineteenth century. Many of those who were active in the Occult Revival were heavily influenced by the outlook and attitudes of Romanticism in their younger days.

> The vogue of occultism was created by a French sem-inarian, Alphonse-Louis Constant, born in 1810 and known by his *nom de plume*, Eliphas Levi. As a matter of fact, the term "occultism" was coined by this would-be priest and was used for the first time in English by the Theosophist A.D. Sinnet in 1881 (Eliade, 1976, page 49).

"Levi" was in his youth during the pivotal decades of Romanticism—the 1830s and 1840s. He died in 1875, having brought the spirit of Romanticism up to date by translating it into magic. He wrote several books between 1856 and 1861, of which Mircea Eliade remarks that they "met with a success difficult to understand today, for they are a mass of pretentious jumble" (Eliade, 1976, page 49).

The real reason that occultism became an avant-garde vogue in Europe and America at the end of the century is that it was seen as an alternative to, and a challenger of, the mainstream culture in general, and Christianity in particular. The Occult Revival simply took the animus against Christianity that Romanticism held (and Michelet showed) and expressed it in a more contemporary form.

> From Baudelaire...to André Breton and his disciples, these artists utilized the occult as a powerful weapon in their rebellion against the bourgeois establishment and its ideology. They reject the official contemporary religion, ethics, social mores, and aesthetics. Some of them are not only anti-clerical, like most of the French intelligentsia, but anti-Christian; they refuse, in fact, all the Judeo-Christian values as well as the Greco-Roman and Renaissance ideals. They have become interested in the Gnostic and other secret groups, not only for their precious occult lore, but also because such groups have been persecuted by the Church (Eliade, 1976, pages 52–53).

That is the same emotional–spiritual dynamic that helped bring the components of medieval witchcraft together to begin with. By the end of the nineteenth century, the explicitly anti-Christian part of that dynamic had begun to get a sense of its own identity, and to see itself in the context of spiritual history. It began to understand that its conflict with Christianity had a past and a future as well as a present.

In the meantime, the closing decades of the nineteenth century saw a wave of occult enthusiasm that spanned the globe. Theosophy, rooted in Asian occultism, became the rage in Europe and America. The Order of the Golden Dawn was founded in England, claiming descent from the Rosicrucians. Spiritism experienced a revival that originated in America and rapidly spread to Europe, even generating periodicals devoted to the subject. The interest in mediums and spirit contact also inspired efforts to investigate them "scientifically." The Dialectical Society was formed in London in 1869, and the Society for Psychical Research at Cambridge in 1882.

As the twentieth century dawned, Oriental versions of magic and religion preoccupied public attention. In 1893, Swami Vivekananda had opened the door for that trend with his eloquent espousal of Hinduism to a worldwide audience at Chicago's "Parliament of Religions." In India, Sir John Woodruff (writing as "Arthur Avalon") impressed the scholarly world and titillated British intellectuals by translating secret Tantric scriptures into English, thereby exposing the esoteric, pre-Hindu religion to Western eyes for the first time.

But the clearest example of orientalized occultism was Helena Blavatsky's "Theosophical Society," a complex mixture of Hinduism, Buddhism, Spiritism, and a bizarre masterrace mythology. Blavatsky's invented cult enjoyed a considerable vogue among sophisticated Westerners during the early 1900s, and Theosophy's sensational claims and exotic beliefs dominated the occult scene during the years prior to World War I.

Nevertheless, unheralded, occult spirituality was branching out in other directions as well. In a process that took half a century or so to unfold, one of those branches eventually produced modern Witchcraft and the Neopagan revival. Many colorful characters took part in that process, but four of them stand out: Charles Godfrey Leland, Margaret Murray, Robert Graves, and Gerald Gardner.

Charles Godfrey Leland: Herald of Diana

Charles Godfrey Leland (1824–1903) was an American folklorist, occultist, adventurer, and all-around soldier of fortune. He grew to maturity during the high tide of Romanticism, and took an active part in the French Revolution of 1848 while he was a student at the Sorbonne in Paris. Leland later traveled widely throughout Europe and wrote 55 books on a variety of subjects. When he was 64 years old and living in Italy, he met a peasant woman called "Maddalena," who supposedly initiated him into the "witch-lore of the Romagna." The information he thus obtained became the basis for his best-known and most influential work: *Aradia, or the Gospel of the Witches* (1899).

Aradia presents the picture of an organized cult of goddess-worship centered around the figure of Diana, the ancient Roman goddess of the moon, forests, and childbirth. According to Leland, this "old religion" was still strong enough among the peasants of the Romagna district to dominate whole villages. The "witch" belief system as Leland described it was both ancient and elaborate:

> The basic belief of this religion was that the first and most powerful deity was feminine—the goddess Diana. "Diana was the first created before all creation; in her were all things; out of herself, the first darkness, she divided herself; into darkness and light she was divided. Lucifer, her brother and son, herself and her other half, was the light."...The legend goes on to say that Diana had by her brother Lucifer, "who had fallen," a daughter whom she named Aradia. Pitying the poor and oppressed at the hands of their masters, she sent Aradia upon earth to be the first witch and to teach witchcraft to those who would learn, thus setting up a secret cult in opposition to Christianity (Valiente, 1989, page 22).

Aradia created no great stir when it was first published. Occultists of the day were preoccupied with the exoticisms of Theosophy, and the academic world paid little attention to Leland's alleged discovery. Today, scholars regard the book as a hybrid creation at best—a blending of Leland's own beliefs with some genuine folk–occult survivals he had managed to uncover. Historian Elliot Rose says that

> the whole work reads...as if one of its authors was consciously seeking to establish that the witch-cult was a cult of this particular nature, and grafted material calculated to prove it onto an existing straightforward book of incantations (Rose, 1962, page 218).

Leland himself was honest enough to acknowledge he had taken ideas from Jules Michelet and used them to interpret what Maddalena was telling him. Maddalena quickly discerned what Leland was looking for and began to shape her information to his liking. In the preface to his book, Leland went so far as to admit that Maddalena had "perfectly learned...just what I want and how to extract it from those of her kind" (Russell, 1980, page 149).

The accuracy of Leland's tale has been challenged since he first told it. That is not surprising, since he never offered proof of it, or even evidence—which should have been plentiful if his story was true. Leland never presented Maddalena for scholarly examination or produced the handwritten portions of the "oral tradition" she was supposed to have passed on to him. Leland's "research" methods were woefully deficient by modern standards (though normal enough for his own times), and he let himself willingly be led by his informant. She was, after all, not an altruistic archivist, seeking to preserve her ancient lore for the benefit of future generations—she was a professional fortune-teller, skilled at "reading" her clients. And she didn't open up to Leland because of her passion for historical truth. She wanted something in return for the information she was giving him, namely his help in emigrating to America (an ambition she fulfilled a few years later). Maddalena almost certainly re-interpreted the genuine folklore she knew in order to make it more appealing to her client, who had clear and specific ideas about what he was looking for.

Even Doreen Valiente's brief and sympathetic description of Leland's work (above) suggests a scholarly invention. *Aradia* draws on a knowledge of gnosticism, paganism, and mythology for much of its content. To that mixture it adds an awkward parody of the biblical creation story and a literate attack on Christianity. That combination is quite likely to occur in the mind of a nineteenth-century man of letters, but it is not at all likely to occur as a historical artifact.

Nevertheless, Leland's work has been appropriated—some of it word for word—by the Neopagan movement. Leland was the first to use the term "the Old Religion." Some of the spells and rituals used by contemporary Witches are simply passages lifted from *Aradia* virtually unchanged (Adler, 1986, page 57). *Aradia* also appeals to Neopagans for another reason: While the "feminist" focus of Leland's fantasy was an oddity in his own time, it is made to order for ours, which seeks a politically correct religion to complement its cultural attitudes and support its political enthusiasms.

Margaret Murray: Zeal and Faulty Scholarship

Margaret Murray (1863–1963) was an anthropologist and an Egyptologist, not a historian of the Middle Ages. But she developed an interest in witchcraft as an academic hobby and as a sideline to her personal interest in British folklore. By her account she was staying at Glastonbury, the legendary site of King Arthur's burial, when someone (whom she never identified) suggested to her that what the Church called "witchcraft" was really a leftover, pre-Christian fertility religion that had once pervaded Europe. Murray was apparently unaware that the suggestion was directly descended from Jules Michelet and other dubious sources. To her, it was a revelation that sent her into an intensive study of the Inquisition's trial records.

After much investigation, Murray argued that "witchcraft" was the Inquisition's term for an older religion that worshiped nature's fertility and abundance and had nothing to do with opposing Christianity. As Murray described the cult, it was based on ancient notions of sexual polarity as the driving force behind all of nature. The male–female, "yang–yin," positive–negative interaction at all levels provides the energetic tension that keeps nature going. Natural religion acts out that relationship in its seasonal rituals. The "witch cult" therefore acted out the endless sexual cycle of birth, growth, death, and rebirth that is the rhythm of Life and Nature.

Murray believed that the original deity behind natural religion was a bipolar, "bisexual" figure that showed up as either male or female, depending on the demands of the situation.

> After reexamining the trial documents of the Inquisition, she argued that Witchcraft could be traced to "pre-Christian times and appears to be the ancient religion of Western Europe" centered on a deity which was incarnate in a man, a woman or an animal. One of its forms was the two-faced, horned god known to the Romans as Janus or Dianus. Murray wrote that the feminine form of the name—Diana—was found throughout Western Europe as the leader of witches. Because of this, Murray called the religion the Dianic Cult, although she wrote that

the god rarely appeared in female form and a male deity had apparently superseded a female one (Adler, 1979, page 47).

Murray accepted the factual findings of the medieval and Renaissance witch trials but re-interpreted their meaning. The inquisitors recorded that the devil would appear at the witch rituals in the form of a goat or other animal. Murray wrote that this "devil" was really just a human high priest in ritual costume. His adornment included the horns and shaggy animal skins that represent carnal potency. That was "one of the pointers given to Dr. Murray by her unknown informant at Glastonbury. It proved to be the key that unlocked the door of the whole mystery. The Christians called him the Devil and the witches seem eventually to have accepted this term also" (Valiente, 1989, page 25).

Margaret Murray believed she had discovered the secret spiritual meaning behind European religious history. And so did others—her theories created an enormous stir when they first appeared, chiefly because of her credentials and her reputation. In fact, she wrote the article on "Witchcraft" that the *Encyclopedia Brittanica* used from 1929 through 1968.

Wrong but Influential

Today, scholars are agreed that Margaret Murray was more than just wrong—she was completely and embarrassingly wrong on nearly all of her basic premises. In two later books *(The God of the Witches* and *The Divine King in England)* she extended her thesis even further, claiming that the witch religion of the god who dies and is reborn not only survived, but actually dominated British royalty to the point that many English kings were ritually murdered according to the rites of the cult.

Murray's increasingly extreme opinions were matched by her increasingly sloppy scholarship. Elliot Rose, an unsympathetic Anglican scholar, characterized Murray's work as "vapid balderdash." Mircea Eliade, a kinder, gentler critic, said that "neither the documents with which she chose to illustrate her hypothesis nor the method of her interpretation are convincing" (Eliade, 1976, page 58).

Jeffrey Burton Russell sums up Murray's sins in a litany of scholarly blunders:

> Murray read back into the entire history of witchcraft, wholly without justification from the sources, witch practices that were peculiar to certain times and places, such as the coven, a late development peculiar to Scotland, and the sabbat, which she makes the center of her fertility cult but which is not mentioned in any of the sources before the fifteenth century.
>
> Indeed, Murray's use of sources in general is appalling. Not only did she force evidence to fit her theory, but she ignored vast bodies of materials, particularly for the Middle Ages, that were readily available to her and that, ironically, in some instances even would have fortified her position....The worst result of Murray's work has been the strength it lent to charlatans and occultists....Murray's theories support their contentions, they think, and they have consequently added a superstructure to her nonsense (Russell, 1972, pages 36-37).

Yet Murray's theories did have enormous influence, and they continued to have it long after the theories themselves had been rejected by scholars. Ronald Hutton comments that for many years they "had the curious status of an orthodoxy which was believed by everybody except for those who happened to be experts on the subject" (Hutton, 1991, page 304).

✤ ✤ ✤ ✤ ✤ ✤ ✤ ✤ ✤ ✤ ✤ ✤ ✤ ✤ ✤ ✤ ✤ ✤

Murray's…theories set off a wave of enthusiasm for things ancient, native, and pagan that is still with us and still gathering strength.

✤ ✤ ✤ ✤ ✤ ✤ ✤ ✤ ✤ ✤ ✤ ✤ ✤ ✤ ✤ ✤ ✤ ✤

Despite its shortcomings, Murray's work captured the public's imagination because it seized on one historical truth that was being ignored by both sides in the ongoing debate between the rationalists and antirationalists: namely, that paganism had been suppressed but not eradicated by Christianity; that "pagan folk beliefs…did not die out with the introduction of Christianity but rather remained and constituted the fundamental substratum of witchcraft" (Russell, 1972, page 37).

Murray's work, despite its grotesque distortions of fact, was an important preparation for the later rise of Neopaganism. Her theories set off a wave of enthusiasm for things ancient, native, and pagan that is still with us and still gathering strength. Murray's fantasies, like Michelet's and Leland's, have been blended into Neopagan mythology in generous measure. She has contributed ideas and terminology, as well as actual practices, to the modern Witchcraft movement. Her scholarship may have been bogus, but its results have been very real. Margaret Murray did not singlehandedly start the Neopagan revival, but she almost singlehandedly set the stage for its arrival.

Robert Graves: Servant of the Mistress Muse

Robert Graves (1895–1985) was an English poet, essayist, and novelist. He is the author of *Good-bye to All That; I, Claudius;* and *King Jesus;* as well as a large number of lesser-known works. Graves's influence on the formation of modern Witchcraft comes from his 1948 publication, *The White Goddess,* subtitled *A Historical Grammar of Poetic Myth.*

The White Goddess is a strange book—rambling and diffuse, both erudite and naive, both brilliant and muddle-headed. But if the book itself is strange, the way it was written is even stranger. In 1944, Graves was living in Devonshire when he was seized by

> "a sudden overwhelming obsession" which compelled him to suspend work on the historical novel he had set out to write, in favor of discovering the inner meaning of a mysterious old Welsh poem called *The Battle of the Trees.* In three weeks, he tells us, he had written a 70,000 word book, called at first *The Roebuck in the Thicket,* but which eventually became *The White Goddess.* His mind worked so furiously, he says, under the influence of this inspiration, that his pen could scarcely keep pace with it (Valiente, 1989, pages 28-29).

As Graves's subtitle indicates, his book is basically about the sources of myth and poetic inspiration. It is not a work of history or anthropology, but a self-conscious literary *tour de force.* Nevertheless, Graves did rely on his considerable (if eccentric) learning to piece together a picture of an ancient, pre-Christian goddess-religion that gave birth to the original language of poetic myth. Thus, for Graves, the quest for the muse of poetic inspiration led directly to the primal fertility goddesses of pagan Europe and the often orgiastic religion of fertility worship centered around them.

As Graves describes that religion, it resembles a variation on the themes put forth by Margaret Murray. Graves believed that poetry was originally created to depict the cycles of Nature by casting them in the form of a dramatic story of the god–king who is born and flourishes with the waxing summer sun, who struggles with fall's waning sun, then dies in winter's dark and chill, finally to be reborn with the renewal of springtime.

The goddess was both worshiped and desired by the god–king. She was Nature, she was Abundance and Fertility, she was the Earth. She was the mother, the wife, and the one who received him in death, all at the same time. Thus Graves portrayed her in "triple form"—a sequence of three developmental phases that paralleled the three phases of the waxing, full, and waning moon (which was also her symbol). "She was the young maiden of the new moon, the glorious lady of the full moon, and the wise old crone of the waning moon" (Valiente, 1989, page 28).

Graves's emphasis on the lunar connection led him to speculate that the number 13 was special to witches because there are 13 lunar months in a solar year, with one day left over. Thus there are normally 13 full moons per year, and 13 full-moon "Esbats," or ritual celebrations.

According to Graves, the original, universal goddess religion was overthrown and suppressed by an emerging patriarchal culture that was violent, warlike, and hostile to Nature. The last 4000 years of human history, therefore, represent a steady spiritual decline from that original, pre-patriarchal golden age.

In his concluding chapter, titled *The Return of the Goddess,* Graves pronounced the failure and irrelevance of what he called "Father-god worship"—in which he included

Christianity (Graves, 1948, page 484). He earnestly believed the time was coming when humanity would be ripe for the goddess's return. But until then, the outlook is grim. Graves is not an optimist in the short term:

> I see no change for the better until everything gets far worse. Only after a period of complete political and religious disorganization can the suppressed desire of the Western races, which is for some practical form of Goddess-worship, with her love not limited to maternal benevolence…find satisfaction at last.
>
> But the longer her hour is postponed, and therefore the more exhausted by man's irreligious improvidence the natural resources of the soil and sea become, the less merciful will her fivefold mask be, and the narrower the scope of action that she grants to whichever demi-god she chooses to take as her temporary consort in godhood. Let us placate her in advance (Graves, 1948, pages 484-486).

Graves's version of history and anthropology is not taken seriously by historians or anthropologists. His theories are a fanciful rearrangement of his own eccentric erudition, and they express his own spiritual yearnings more than they describe any historical realities.

Smoothing the Path for Gerald Gardner

And yet…Graves's theories have had remarkable impact. Like Michelet, Leland, and Murray before him, Graves combined literary invention, occult enthusiasm, defective (even appalling) scholarship, and explicit antagonism to Christianity to produce a work that has made major and detailed contributions to modern Witchcraft. The four of them together have created a school of historical revisionism that has taken hold at a grassroots level—despite repeated official refutation. Together, they are a primary source for the ideas that define Neopaganism.

Leland built on the Romantics, and on *Michelet*, in portraying witchcraft as a surviving form of goddess-worship that was preserved and transmitted in detail. He contributed the "Old Religion" terminology, a feminist emphasis, and a protest against Christianity, as well as specific ritual content in the spells he described.

Murray emphasized the idea that the "Old Religion" was really an ancient fertility religion. She denied that witchcraft arose in opposition to Christianity, saying instead that it was a pagan survival that Christianity had picked a fight with. But she plainly expressed her own rejection and dislike of Christianity in saying so. Murray also established the terminology of the "Sabbat" and the "Esbat." She contributed the concept that the witch cult was organized into "covens" of 13 people, consisting of 12 witches and their leader, or priest.

Graves added a powerful feminine focus (or "gynocentrism") to those other ideas of the "Old Religion." In addition to a generalized antipatriarchal bias, Graves contributed the specific concept of a "pre-patriarchal golden age"—a time of peace, harmony, and goddess-worship. He also provided modern Witchcraft's lunar emphasis and the "triple form" imagery of the goddess. Graves stressed the spiritual power of the feminine and proposed that the medieval witch covens were led by women.

Gerald Gardner: Father of Modern Witchcraft

But the man who pulled all the pieces together and invented modern "Witchcraft" was Gerald B. Gardner

(1884–1964), an Englishman of unconventional outlook and notably odd behavior. Drawing from both literary sources and personal experiences, Gardner assembled the concept of witchcraft that has dominated the Neopagan revival.

Gardner was widely traveled and spent much of his adult life in the Far East. He was a rubber planter in Ceylon and a tea planter in Malaysia. Later he became a British customs officer and lived for a time in India, where he studied, among other things, tantric Hinduism. Gardner remained a British civil servant until he retired and returned to England in 1936.

Gardner's lengthy sojourn in Asia gave him ample opportunity to indulge his fascination with the eccentric, the exotic, and the esoteric. He apparently became a nudist early in life (Adler, 1979, page 61), and he plunged with relish into the bizarre and offbeat aspects of whatever culture he found himself living in.

> Prior to his involvement with Wicca, he had become a member of the Sufi order as well as a Co-Mason. He was also familiar with Hinduism (particularly Kali worship) as a result of his residence in India and Malaysia with the British civil service [Kali is the Hindu goddess of death and destruction]. In addition, he corresponded with Charles Godfrey Leland, author of *Aradia, or the Gospel of the Witches* (Alba, 1989, page 29).

Gardner also knew Margaret Murray—in fact, she wrote an introduction to his first book. He was an initiate of the Ordo Templi Orientis (O.T.O.) and an acquaintance of the notorious English black magician Aleister Crowley, who called himself "the Great Beast 666." In general, it is evident that Gardner had a deep familiarity with many systems of occultism and religion. Under the circumstances, it is hardly surprising that his story of how he "rediscovered" witchcraft should have come under suspicion.

By Gardner's account, he ran across a surviving coven of the "Old Religion" almost by accident. After returning to England, Gardner naturally continued his occult interests and associations. He became involved with the Fellowship of Crotona, founded by the daughter of Theosophist Annie Besant. Among the circle of occultists and eccentrics that revolved around the Fellowship, Gardner encountered some people he found to be different from the others, but more interesting. Among them was "old Dorothy" Clutterbuck, a wealthy woman of the neighborhood.

According to Gardner, "old Dorothy" turned out to be the leader of a secretive, surviving coven of the "Old Religion," and in 1939, she initiated him into what she called "Wicca." Gardner could not write openly about the craft because the "witchcraft laws" then in effect would have subjected him to legal penalties. Consequently, he disguised his work as fiction and published a "novel" in 1949, titled *High Magic's Aid*, under the pen name "Scire." It was presented as "a historical novel about the Craft and contained two initiation rituals, but there was no reference to the Goddess" (Adler, 1979, page 62).

The witchcraft laws were finally repealed in 1951, primarily due to the political efforts of the Spiritualist societies. Free at last to acknowledge his real affiliations, Gardner published two books under his own name: *Witchcraft Today* (1954) and *The Meaning of Witchcraft* (1959).

> Gardner's version of the Craft was very different from that described by Murray. To him, Witchcraft was a peaceful, happy nature religion. Witches met in covens, led by a priestess. They worshiped two principal deities, the god of forests and what lies beyond, and the great Triple Goddess of fertility and

rebirth. They met in the nude in a nine-foot circle and raised power from their bodies through dancing and chanting and meditative techniques. They focused primarily on the Goddess; they celebrated the eight ancient Pagan festivals of Europe and sought to attune themselves to nature (Adler, 1979, page 62).

Gardner's style of Witchcraft has dominated the subsequent growth of the movement. The spread and evolution of "Gardnerian Wicca" is a long and complicated tale. I will not attempt to tell it here, especially as it is well-told elsewhere (see, for example, Margot Adler's *Drawing Down the Moon,* Jeffrey Burton Russell's *A History of Witchcraft,* and sources cited by them). Suffice it to say in brief that Gardner was charismatically effective in recruiting converts to his point of view, and that some of them helped to spread his version of the craft beyond the British Isles, both to Europe and America.

✤ ✤ ✤ ✤ ✤ ✤ ✤ ✤ ✤ ✤ ✤ ✤ ✤ ✤ ✤ ✤ ✤ ✤

The counterculture's heady cocktail of psychedelic drugs, sexual liberty, mysticism, enlightenment, self-divinization, occultism, and anti-Christianity was tailor-made (and exquisitely timed) to encourage the explosive growth of Neopaganism.

✤ ✤ ✤ ✤ ✤ ✤ ✤ ✤ ✤ ✤ ✤ ✤ ✤ ✤ ✤ ✤ ✤ ✤

One of Gardner's early initiates was Raymond Buckland. Buckland imported Gardner's Wicca to the United States in the early 1960s by establishing a coven in New York state. Buckland's coven initiated others, who in turn began their own covens and initiated still others, and so on, and so on.

The "counterculture" of the middle and late 1960s converged perfectly with these developments to stimulate the slowly growing Wiccan movement. The counterculture's heady cocktail of psychedelic drugs, sexual liberty, mysticism, enlightenment, self-divinization, occultism, and anti-Christianity was tailor-made (and exquisitely timed) to encourage the explosive growth of Neopaganism in general, and modern Witchcraft in particular. The rest is history.

The Gardnerian Controversy

But is the *beginning* history? Is Gardner's story of his own initiation credible? Or is it a work of imagination, based on his own exotic experiences? And a second issue is inseparable from the first: Was there, in 1939 England, an existing coven of "witches" that was actually a survival of an older teaching? Or did Gardner encounter something else, which he then embroidered? Or did he encounter nothing at all—and invent the whole thing from scratch?

Among scholars, the consensus is strong that Gardner's "Wicca" is a construction and an assemblage. Some have spent considerable effort in documentary research and are able to trace a development in Gardner's ideas over a period of time. Russell describes a handwritten spell-book ("grimoire") that Gardner began putting together during the Second World War. He concludes from the content of the manuscript that

> if Gardner had been initiated into a coven in 1939, they had given him almost no information at all. His ideas of the Craft were still very inchoate. The material gradually changed as Gardner's own views shifted from the elite ceremonial magic of the Golden Dawn to a more populist magic, transforming the semi-serious intellectual rituals of the

Order into simpler rituals that could be performed by ordinary people. Gradually he reduced or eliminated the Judeo-Christian-gnostic flavor of the Golden Dawn materials and added neopagan ideas derived from Murray and Leland. Later still, he absorbed ideas from Graves, James, and other writers....At first Gardner's revision followed Murray closely and emphasized the importance of the horned god. But gradually the Goddess became more and more important, until she emerged as the chief deity. As the power of the Goddess rose, so did that assigned to the High Priestess, who replaced the High Priest as leader of the coven (Russell, 1980, pages 153–154).

Among occultists and pagans, not surprisingly, opinions are more varied. The occult writer Francis King thought that Gardner was initiated into a group that represented some sort of pagan survival, but that he found their simple rituals and low-magic spells unsatisfying. He responded by trying to "found a more elaborate and romanticized witch-cult of his own." To that end, says King, Gardner hired Aleister Crowley "at a generous fee, to write elaborate rituals for the new 'Gardnerian' witch-cult and, at about the same time, either forged, or procured to be forged, the so-called 'Book of Shadows,' allegedly a sixteenth-century witches rule-book, but betraying its modern origins in every line of its unsatisfactory pastiche of Elizabethan English" (King, 1970, pages 179–180).

Doreen Valiente, an early associate of Gardner and a longtime member of his coven, traces the sources of Gardner's Wicca to "the works of Margaret Murray, Charles Godfrey Leland, Rudyard Kipling, Aleister Crowley, the Key of Solomon and the rituals of Freemasonry." Nevertheless, she continues to believe there was a real coven for Gardner to build on, primarily because she discerns (or thinks she discerns) a basic, underlying structure "which was not from Crowley or Margaret Murray or any of the other sources mentioned" (Valiente, 1989, page 63). Valiente does not consider the possibility that Gardner himself was the source of that "structure."

It is worth noting that this dispute is different from the controversy over Neopaganism's "Charter Myth," which has to do with modern Witchcraft's alleged connection to medieval Witchcraft and ancient goddess-religions. That controversy has largely been settled academically, even though it continues to generate heat within the Neopagan community. The "Gardnerian" debate, on the other hand, concerns more recent history—specifically whether Gardner was telling the truth about what happened to him in England during the late 1930s.

Aidan Kelly: Cutting History Loose

Another development in that discussion has been the work of Aidan Kelly. Kelly's own religious pilgrimage overlaps much of Neopaganism's history on the West Coast. Kelly developed a keen but untutored interest in witchcraft and paganism as a youth beginning in 1954. As a college student in 1967, he helped a friend write a "witches' sabbath" for a class in "Creating Ritual" at San Francisco State University. By 1971, Kelly and his friends were calling themselves "witches." They named their "coven" (half in jest and self-satire) the "New Reformed Order of the Golden Dawn" (NROOGD).

From 1974 to 1980, Kelly studied "Christian Origins" in graduate school in Berkeley. In 1977, he returned to practicing Catholicism, the religion of his youth. In 1987, he quit practicing Catholicism for the second time and became active in the Craft again (Kelly, 1991, pages xi–xxi).

Using the tools of textual criticism he had acquired in graduate school, Kelly made an attempt to unravel Gerald Gardner's version of Wicca. His study, entitled *Crafting the Art of Magic* (1991) compares several versions of Gardner's *Book of Shadows* and correlates them with possible sources for their content.

In Kelly's view, 1939 was the year that Gardner "and some other English occultists (possibly connected with the Golden Dawn through Dion Fortune's Fraternity of the Inner Light) started Wicca from scratch, based on the theories of anthropologist Margaret Murray, American folklorist Charles Leland, and various writers on magic" (Clifton, 1991, page 64). Kelly's primary conclusion is that no "traditional Wicca" had survived and that no pre-1939 coven existed.

But Kelly goes beyond his conclusions about Gerald Gardner to make a point about the significance of history itself. He says that the recent origin of "Wicca"—and its status as an invention—are irrelevant and beside the point. In Kelly's view, many of the world's great religions were essentially "invented" by their founders, who were typically reluctant to admit that fact. Instead, they tried to portray their religious innovations as developments within established traditions. In that context, Kelly depicts Gardner as a creative genius who succeeded in framing the worldview for a religion of the future.

Concerning modern Witchcraft, historian Jeffrey Burton Russell has said that "lack of historicity does not necessarily deprive a religion of its insight" (Russell, 1980, page 154)—a point that Kelly's argument depends on. Nevertheless, a genuine tradition (even a brief one) gives a religion more than "insight"; it gives evidence of a *body* of teaching stable enough to be passed down from one generation to the next—which conveys a kind of authority and validity in religion that cannot be obtained in any other way.

Therefore Neopaganism's "tradition" depends on the truth of Gardner's tale, and the truthfulness of his claims is a subject that stirs up some fervor in the Neopagan community. For that reason Kelly's book sparked a heated debate. "Traditional" Gardnerians came to Gardner's defense, saying that his story is not only historically plausible, but is supported by the evidence at key points. They also questioned Kelly's research and the thesis based upon it. An extensive critique of Kelly's sources, methods, and conclusions by D. Hudson Frew appeared in *Gnosis* magazine (Frew and Korn, 1991). Frew "enthusiastically" endorsed Kelly's idea that historicity doesn't matter, but he defended the historicity of Gardner's claims anyway because he believes the evidence is there to back them up.

In a 2000 interview, Frew summarized the attitude of the Neopagan community as a whole toward the historical issue:

> [A] lot of people used to believe that Craft ritual practices descended in an unbroken chain from prehistoric days. Then the pendulum swung and Witches took the attitude of "Okay, we made it all up twenty years ago, and we're still making it up. But it doesn't matter—everything's fine." Now the pendulum is swinging back to the center and we're trying to find the middle ground. A popular concept of the antiquity of the Craft involves the romantic idea of an ancient Celtic group, often women, being persecuted by the Inquisition. But that's basically a fantasy, and lacks documentation (Vale and Sulak, 2001, page 95).

Traditional Witches and the Interfaith Interface

As we saw in chapter 4, the 1996 release of the movie *The Craft* triggered the explosive growth of pop-culture Witchcraft outside of the organized Witchcraft movement. A great deal of what the public sees as the increased public presence of modern Witchcraft is really the increased media visibility of pop-culture Witchcraft. A great deal of Witchcraft's recent image makeover is the direct result of this mid-1990s pop-culture explosion.

But traditional Witches worked for more than three decades in this country to lay the groundwork for that groundswell of enthusiasm, and the Witchcraft movement they created has also benefited from the interest and attention stirred up by the media. The organized Witchcraft groups (such as Covenant of the Goddess) became much more active in public relations, and much better prepared to respond to the public's growing curiosity about Witchcraft.

Despite reinforcing one another, the two kinds of Witchcraft represent two different routes into the mainstream. Pop-culture Witchcraft spreads a broad, shallow form of itself through sensational media presentations. Traditional Witches, on the other hand, are working to establish their religious credibility through involvement with the interfaith movement.

The Witchcraft community's ongoing involvement with interfaith work goes back to 1975, when the Covenant of the Goddess (CoG) was formed in Berkeley as "a networking group for Witches of all traditions." One of the first things CoG did as an organization was to join the local interfaith council, but their participation was sporadic for the next ten years or so. CoG's interfaith work began in earnest in 1985, when Wiccan elder Don Frew was appointed as CoG's interfaith representative. Frew walked into his first meeting of the

Berkeley Area Interfaith Council to find a room uneasily divided between traditional believers on one side (Christians, Jews, Buddhists) and "alternative" believers on the other (Scientologists, Hare Krishnas, "New Age" groups). Because he represented an alternative faith but had friends among the traditionalists, Frew was able to act as a connection between the two sides; Neopagans have been an integral part of the Berkeley council and its work ever since.

Perhaps only in Berkeley could a Witch spontaneously act as a bridge between traditional and "fringe" religions at an interfaith meeting, but the eventual effects of that interfaith connection were not local at all. In fact, they went literally around the world. Witches got involved in interfaith work for a reason, and what had begun on a small scale and at a local level eventually became organized policy—first for CoG on the West Coast, and later for other Wiccan and Neopagan groups around the country.

The purpose of interfaith work, from the Witches' point of view, was to establish Witchcraft as a religion among religions, thus increasing the acceptance and acceptability of Witchcraft in society—and thereby serving the ultimate purpose of increasing the physical safety and enlarging the social comfort zone of Witches in general. Judged by those standards, the Witches' "interfaith interface" has been remarkably successful. Today the Witchcraft movement has already achieved legal status as one religion among many, and is on the verge of achieving it socially—which is exactly what the interfaith approach was designed to accomplish.

Nevertheless, for several years after Frew became an interfaith activist, his work was still pursued on a local and largely personal basis. It was one thing to get spiritual respect and religious recognition in the context of Berkeley's spiritual zoo, where traditional Witches sometimes seemed like the "safe and sane" part of the religious fringe. However, it was quite another thing to get respect and recognition in the larger religious community, where Witches were often regarded with skepticism at best, suspicion at worst, and disdain in any case. But all of that changed in 1993.

"The Parliament of the World's Religions"

1993 was a critical year, partly out of coincidence and partly out of convergence.

By coincidence, that year was the one-hundredth anniversary of the "Parliament of the World's Religions," which had been part of the century-ending Columbian Exposition in Chicago in 1893. One of the most charismatic figures at that earlier event was a dynamic young advocate of Hinduism named Swami Vivekananda. As a traveling speaker, the swami mesmerized Western audiences; he and the Parliament have been credited with opening the Western world to Eastern religious teachings for the first time. The Parliament is also widely acknowledged as the beginning of formal inter-religious dialogue worldwide. A hundred years later, an elaborate celebration was planned that included holding a second "Parliament of the World's Religions," in honor of the first one.

As 1993 approached, word of the second Parliament spread throughout the North American Interfaith Network. CoG representatives learned of the event through their interfaith connections and made plans to attend. As it turns out, they were not alone; nationwide, three other Neopagan groups also signed up to become sponsors of the event (Circle Sanctuary in the Midwest, EarthSpirit in Boston, and the Fellowship of Isis in Chicago).

CoG originally hoped to send three representatives to the Parliament, but their members responded so warmly to the project that they ended up with a volunteer group of more than 40, many of whom traveled to Chicago at their own expense. A few of them were there to make a public presentation of their religion—to give talks, hold seminars, and so on. The rest were there for logistical support—to make copies, run errands, staff the hospitality suite, and so on. As the group headed off to Chicago, they were uncertain what they would encounter or what their reception would be. This would be their first major engagement with the world of interreligious dialogue beyond the exotic spiritual environment of Berkeley.

What they encountered in Chicago was a startling convergence of worries and hopes that placed Witches squarely in the international spotlight and placed Witchcraft squarely within the mainstream of modern religious thought—literally overnight. CoG officer Don Frew tells how overlapping themes propelled Neopaganism to center stage in the international arena.

> In the first plenary session of the 1993 Parliament, Dr. Gerald Barney, the scientist who had prepared the Global 2000 report on the environment for President Jimmy Carter, told the crowd about the imminent environmental collapse of the planet: There are *this* many people, he said. Each person requires *this* much land to produce food. There is *this* much arable land left. It's being used up at *this* rate while the population is increasing at *this* rate. Do the math and you see that the Earth begins to die in 2025.
>
> Dr. Barney, a Christian, went on to lay much of the blame for this with the major, "world" religions, especially Christianity. "What we need," he said, "are new spiritualities and new ways to re-sacralize nature, if the Earth is to survive."
>
> And there we were.
>
> From its very first session, the 1993 Parliament was focused on re-sacralizing Nature. Everyone's

attention was immediately focused on two religious groups: the Native Americans and the Neopagans.

But the Native Americans tended to keep to themselves and were seemingly reticent to share many of their traditions. In contrast, the Covenant of the Goddess had a person attending the morning press briefings every day, handing out press packets, and had a hospitality suite staffed with folks ready and willing to answer questions.

Suddenly, we Witches found ourselves the media darlings of the conference! Our "What is Wicca?" workshops had to be moved to larger rooms to accommodate the huge numbers wanting to attend. Our Full Moon ceremony in a nearby park, planned for a circle of 50, drew 500!...By the end of the nine days, the academics attending the Parliament were saying "In 1893, America was introduced to the Buddhists and Hindus; in 1993, we met the Neopagans." One media person described the Parliament as "the coming out party for the Neopagans."

From that point on, Neopagans would be included in almost every national or global interfaith event. At the 1993 Parliament, we ceased being a bunch of weirdos and became a religious minority. As Michael Thorn said after returning from Chicago, "This was the most important event in the history of the Craft since the publication of *Witchcraft Today* in 1954!" (Frew, 2003).

Convergence: Witchcraft, Interfaith, and Messianic Globalism

After the startling public relations success of the 1993 Parliament, Frew made interfaith work a priority for CoG—so much so that it is now the second largest item in CoG's budget, right after the organizational newsletter (Frew, 2002). Moreover, just as an unplanned convergence of ideas and concerns was the key to their 1993 breakthrough, the same kind of convergence has continued to drive CoG toward global activism and to increase CoG's role in the worldwide interfaith community.

✤ ✤ ✤ ✤ ✤ ✤ ✤ ✤ ✤ ✤ ✤ ✤ ✤ ✤ ✤ ✤ ✤

Because of the Neopagans' interfaith activities, modern Witchcraft has moved far toward mainstream acceptance—not only in the United States, but around the world.

✤ ✤ ✤ ✤ ✤ ✤ ✤ ✤ ✤ ✤ ✤ ✤ ✤ ✤ ✤ ✤ ✤

Within two years of the Chicago Parliament, CoG was active in another interreligious project with global aspirations—Episcopal bishop William Swing's United Religions Initiative. The Initiative was conceived in 1995 as a religious counterpart to the United Nations after Bishop Swing was commissioned to write an ecumenical liturgy for the UN's fiftieth anniversary. Feeling shamed by the religious world's failure to match the UN's "successful" half century, Swing decided it was time to bring the world's religions together on a permanent basis in some kind of organization.

The result was the United Religions Initiative. CoG members were involved in the earliest stages of creating it, and they even helped to write the Initiative's charter, which reflects the influence of Neopaganism in its opening words:

> We, people of diverse religions, spiritual expressions
> and indigenous traditions throughout the world,

hereby establish the United Religions Initiative to promote enduring, daily interfaith cooperation, to end religiously motivated violence and to create cultures of peace, justice and healing for the Earth and all living beings.

In the years since its founding, the Initiative has speeded up the convergence of religious concerns and political causes that has always typified the ecumenical movement. The Initiative has become an international forum to bring together religious and secular activists over issues that concern them both. As the Neopagans aligned themselves with that activist mentality, they moved into prominence within the organization. In the process, they also discovered their own convergence with "other paths," thereby creating a new kind of religious identity. At one of the Initiative's charter-writing conferences in 1998,

> [t]he representatives of the many Earth-based religions...got together for lunch, sitting in a very visible circle on the ground in the central courtyard of the conference. There were practitioners of Wicca, Shinto, North/Central/South American indigenous traditions, Candomble, Taoism, and Hinduism. To our surprise, the environmental scientists joined our group, saying they felt more at home with us than in the other traditions. Looking around our circle, we, and the other folks having their lunches and watching us, suddenly realized that the Earth-religions were 13% of the delegates at the conference!
>
> No longer were we seen as disparate groups. The Earth-religions had established an identity in common as a "way" of being religious—a Pagan identity, broader than the concept of Neopagan (Frew, 2003).

There are numerous opportunities for interfaith work, and CoG has moved into as many of them as their resources permit. The 1993 Parliament generated several follow-up conferences; another Parliament was held in Cape Town in 1999, and yet another is scheduled for Barcelona in 2004. Increasingly, the focus of CoG's interfaith work is on "good works" programs, mostly overseas, that advance various political and social agendas, mostly of a "progressive" and "internationalist" nature. Through its involvement with interfaith groups, CoG actively supports

- AIDS education in East Africa

- Jewish–Muslim dialogue for peace in Israel and Palestine

- a vegetarian restaurant in Vietnam that serves affordable, fresh food through volunteers to about 200 to 300 people every day

- a blood drive in Bali in response to the October 12, 2002, bombing

- energy audits in homes and churches in Tennessee and the Carolinas

- the elimination of handguns in Rio de Janeiro through the "Rio: Put That Gun Down!" program, destroying over 10,000 handguns in 2002 and getting the sale of handguns banned in Rio

- a youth camp in Sri Lanka, where 4000 young people worked together in environmental cleanup programs

- a program in Malawi to buy school uniforms for orphans

- another program in Malawi to assist AIDS orphans in their area

- on-the-ground facilitators for the World Health Organization's "Roll Back Malaria" campaign, aimed at eradicating malaria in Mozambique in five years

- a program in India that rescued 75 cattle from ritual slaughter and gave them to the poor

- a program raising money in northern California for the Humanity Club of Vietnam to provide housing and medical assistance for the poor in Vietnam

- an orphanage in Uganda caring for more than 400 children orphaned because of civil war and AIDS

- a micro-credit bank for women in Kenya

(all of the above Frew, 2003)

There are several reasons for Witches to become involved in such far-flung social activism. The obvious ones have to do with cultivating political connections and expressing open solidarity with the "progressive" or "politically correct" line of thinking. What is not so obvious is the coming together of the spiritual motives for doing such work with the secular ones, and the coming together of both with an ambitious agenda of social engineering. That combination creates a collective enterprise with aims and aspirations that can only be called "messianic"—that is, it sees itself as the only force that can save the world from self-destruction. Frew makes the blending evident as he explains why he has committed CoG to interfaith work and why he has made it a priority in his own life.

> A movement to bring the religions of the world together in peace to work for the betterment of all is, potentially, the most powerful force for positive change in existence. As a person of faith, called by

my Gods to care for and protect the Earth, how can I not be involved?

Interfaith work is, in my opinion, the best hope for the future of the Earth. Neopagans...are active at the heart of the global interfaith movement. This is our opportunity to be part of the change we wish to see (Frew, 2003).

In the meantime, regardless of what happens to the Neopagans' utopian hopes, there can be no doubt that their interfaith strategy has been an unqualified success. Because of their interfaith activities, modern Witchcraft has moved far toward mainstream acceptance—not only in the United States, but around the world. Frew explains how he came to understand the effectiveness of CoG's interfaith work:

Neopagans are now welcome in interfaith events all over the world. And it is paying off in increased understanding. In both Cape Town and half way 'round the world in Rio de Janeiro, I didn't meet a single person who didn't know what Wicca is! "Oh, yeah, the Goddess. Earth-religion. I've heard of that!" was the usual response we got. We didn't teach them this, the interfaith groups did (Frew, 2003).

Conclusion
Witchcraft, Christianity, and Cultural Change

WITCHCRAFT IS GOING MAINSTREAM. That's not a predic-
tion—it's a description of current reality. As we have seen in
this book, much of that process has already happened, and
the rest is happening before our eyes. The speed with which
this development has occurred is unprecedented. In fact,
compared to the normal pace of historical change, it has been
almost instantaneous. Even though it took the work of 30
years to prepare the way, the public's attitude toward
Witchcraft was effectively turned upside down in less than a
decade (1993–2000). It took place so fast that, if you knew
what to look for, you could actually watch it happen.

Changes that rapid and that profound are hard to cope
with, much less comprehend. Only by seeing those changes
as part of a bigger picture can we step back from them far
enough to grasp their meaning. We can begin by asking two
questions:

1. What do these changes mean for the future of modern
   Witchcraft and the Neopagan movement?

2. What do they mean for the future of our country and
   our culture?

In 1965, Pennethorne Hughes, a British authority on the history of witchcraft, declared that witchcraft itself was a vanishing superstition. It was, he said, "dying rapidly" under the influence of the popular press, popular education, and the popular materialism of general prosperity. According to Hughes, "Witchcraft as a cult belief in Europe is dead. As a degenerate form of primitive fertility belief, incorporating the earliest instructive wisdom, the practice is over" (Hughes, 1965, page 217).

What makes Hughes's wrongheadedness so ironic is that in 1965, the counterculture and Neopaganism were both just beginning to find their wings, and British Wicca was already finding fertile ground for its growth in the United States. As usual, the "experts" are the last to notice anything that falls outside the assumptions of their expertise.

Indeed, since Hughes proclaimed its demise, modern Witchcraft has known nothing but advance and achievement. It is a striking fact that the Neopagan movement, spearheaded by modern Witchcraft, has experienced an unbroken string of breakthroughs and successes over the last 35 years, legally, socially, and politically. None of this has occurred without friction, of course, and Witches have run into plenty of opposition and hostility as part of that process. Nevertheless, in the context of the ongoing "culture war," the sum of things is that Neopaganism has not been on the losing side of any major battle it has fought. The few legal skirmishes that have broken out along the way have been victories for the Witches as well.

With such a record of accomplishment under its belt, it is no surprise that Neopaganism is in a confident and expansive mood. Neopagans are very conscious of the fact that our society is changing, and they sense that those changes are opening up new opportunities for their movement to grow and develop. But the kind of explosive growth Witchcraft experienced during the 1990s brings more than opportunities—it brings problems as well.

Modern Witchcraft's Two Cultures

In the first place, it has produced, if not an identity crisis, at least a case of identity confusion in the movement. Before 1996, the Neopagan movement consisted mostly of religious Witches, who saw themselves linked together by their common separation from the "mundane" world and all of its (Christian-based) values, institutions, and activities. But as we discussed in chapters 3 and 4, the release of *The Craft* triggered the rise of pop-culture Witchcraft, almost literally overnight, and created a crop of new Witches who had no part in the mental universe that traditional Witches shared. Pop-culture Witches, for the most part, had no "initiation" or any kind of occult training; they had no connection to any teaching or tradition; they either couldn't or didn't join existing organizations; and they were fully part of the mundane world, with little sense of separation from it—aside from having a rebellious attitude toward society in general.

The division between traditional Witchcraft and pop-culture Witchcraft was almost total at the outset. The new Witches weren't getting much help from the traditionals; if they reached out to any of the existing organizations, they were likely to be turned away. The traditionals, for their part, were alarmed by the legal dangers of dealing with minors and suspicious of a flock of fad-witches who adopted the identity glibly, without preparation, commitment, or even understanding. That division then reinforced itself as the young Witch wannabes had no choice but to build their concept of Witchcraft based on what they saw on TV, or on the Internet, or just from talking with their friends.

The result has been to create two substantially different and separate cultures within the broad category of "modern Witchcraft." The "traditional" culture includes the Witches who see their craft as a survival, or revival, or reinvention of older beliefs and practices (such as those Gerald Gardner claimed to have discovered in 1939)—and they tend to think of their beliefs as "religious." The history of this culture has been traced in chapter 7, and their movement toward the mainstream today is along the route of interfaith work and interreligious cooperation. The goal of their mainstreaming efforts is to achieve acceptance as a legitimate religion in the eyes of society and the law.

"Pop-culture" Witchcraft, on the other hand, is much less tied to any specific history or tradition and is much less inclined to see itself as "religious." Having begun in 1996, pop-culture Witchcraft is less than a decade old as of this writing, and it is still being shaped by the forces that brought it into being. *New Witch* magazine (first issue, Autumn 2002) could be considered the journalistic voice of pop-culture Witchcraft, as well as its commercial bazaar. The magazine is packed with advertisements, such as those for Snapdragon Gifts ("Nothing Mundane") and Mystic Treasures Clothier ("Cloak Yourself in Mystery"), along with book reviews, articles, and editorials. Overall, *New Witch* presents an impression of Witchcraft, not so much as a "religion," but as a "lifestyle"—propped up by musings that are sometimes expressed in "religious" language.

New Witch: Idol-Making in the Modern World

A recent cover article in the magazine shows how pop-culture Witchcraft blends idolatry and magic. The article, entitled "Invoking Buffy—Discovering the Magic of Pop Icons," is a how-to manual for making idols of the mind.

The author admits that some will scoff at using TV characters for "deities," but he dismisses the skeptics ("traditional" Witches?) with his single disdainful reference to them:

> Many magickal practitioners sneer at the idea of using pop culture as a means of doing magick. But I believe that popular culture is an extremely effective magickal medium. Any pop culture icon can be made into a helpful focus of magick. Buffy the Vampire Slayer makes an especially good example (Ellmore, 2003, page 57).

The author then explains how Buffy (or any other fictional character) can be turned into a functioning "god form" for use in occult ritual. According to a theory common among Neopagans, a "god form" is created on a "higher plane" when large numbers of people pour the energy of belief into their collective idea of who or what a god or goddess is. The "god form" people create in that way takes on a reality that is bigger than the people who create it. The more people there are who believe in that "god form," and the longer they believe in it, the more powerful the "god form" becomes. Thus a pop icon like Buffy—at least for the few years of her popularity—becomes a receptacle for the mental energy of adulation from her fans; by turning the Buffy character into one's own personal "god form," one can tap into that accumulated energy and use it for magical purposes. The author then explains exactly how to do that, laying out a series of instructions for the reader to follow.

Once you buy into the author's way of looking at the world, his instructions make perfect sense. Without the benefit of that worldview however, they seem like utter nonsense—childish, let's-pretend nonsense at best, and dangerous, deluded nonsense at worst. But the article does plainly illustrate three things: 1) it shows where pop-culture Witchcraft is headed; 2) it shows the differences between pop-culture Witchcraft and the "traditional" kind—as well as their similarities; and 3) the fact that this approach finds increasing acceptance today shows how desperate the spiritual condition of our society has become.

Here are the author's step-by-step instructions (Ellmore, 2003, page 57, abridged) for making your own personal occult "deity" (in other words, mental idol) out of a pop-culture icon.

1. "*Observe your target.* You need to observe your target deity very carefully, get an idea of his or her mannerisms and attributes. In the case of Buffy, I read books about her and watched her show, taking careful notes....Devise a list of your deity's relevant characteristics...."

2. "*Create a shrine.* When working with Buffy, I made a collage of images from fanzines, Web site art and book covers. The collage showed several aspects about her that reinforced my list of attributes....I created an altar of Buffy...[and] wrote a statement of intent on the back of the collage. It went something like this: 'Buffy, through the medium of this collage, I create a link with you. I give of myself to you and in return ask that you act as my guardian when I call on you.' I also dedicated a personal object (something of value to me) that I intended to offer Buffy in return for her help...."

3. "*Bring it down to earth.* After I created my altar, I performed a ritual to Buffy to continue the work of reinforcing our connection....I lit the [collage] and my

sacrifice on fire and chanted as it burned: 'Through the power of Buffy I will focus on improving my independence and will.' I chanted this until the paper had turned into ash. By chanting I was adding energy to the focus of the spell...."

4. "*Listen to your deity.* After I burned the paper and chanted, I went inside, laid down and tranced out. This means I let go of my conscious mind and followed the energy I'd just released to the god form of Buffy. While in the trance, I felt Buffy's presence. She and I spoke about my situation and she explained how she'd keep me focused on improving it. She advised invoking her once a day to remind myself of what I was doing...."

5. "*Know when to let go.* I stopped invoking Buffy after the situation I felt I needed her help with had been resolved. Remember that any entity, pop culture or otherwise, should only be used as long as you need it. Otherwise the entity becomes a crutch and you are back where you started."

In conclusion, the author says that he worked with Buffy for as long as she was useful to him, adding, "And then I moved on to other pop culture god forms, such as Harry Potter" (Ellmore, 2003, page 58).

Idolatry, Religion, and the Two Cultures of Witchcraft

"Invoking Buffy" is a snapshot of pop-culture Witchcraft in the process of evolving downward. The article is startling in its spiritual superficiality, its casual vandalism of symbols and ideas, and its systematic indifference to anything that isn't of the self, by the self, and for the self. And the invitation to demonic presences in "trancing out" and "listening to your deity" is transparent. Yet all of those things, deplorable as they may be, are nothing more than classic qualities of fallen human nature—amplified, simplified, and speeded up for modern consumption, and conveyed by means of modern media. "Invoking Buffy" is nothing more (or less) than a graphic picture of the human condition today, reduced to cartoon simplicity.

✣ ✣ ✣ ✣ ✣ ✣ ✣ ✣ ✣ ✣ ✣ ✣ ✣ ✣ ✣ ✣ ✣

"Invoking Buffy" shows what paganism comes to when it is stripped of compromises and distractions: Make a god; use it up; throw it away.

✣ ✣ ✣ ✣ ✣ ✣ ✣ ✣ ✣ ✣ ✣ ✣ ✣ ✣ ✣ ✣ ✣

The fact that pop-culture Witchcraft is a boiled-down version of fallen human nature is one of the things it has in common with other forms of paganism, ancient as well as modern. When "Invoking Buffy" reduces spirituality to the techniques of getting and using power, it just brings the basic dilemma of paganism front and center. C.S. Lewis called pantheism "the permanent natural inclination of the human heart." Neopaganism is one version of that "permanent natural inclination," and pop-culture Witchcraft is what the inclination becomes under the influence of our stripped-down, speeded-up society. "Invoking Buffy" shows what paganism comes to when it is stripped of compromises and distractions: Make a god; use it up; throw it away.

That plainly illustrates the convergence of idolatry and occultism, but it is stretching a point to call it "religion." And therein lies the problem for the Witchcraft movement. "Traditional" Witches are committed to mainstreaming themselves as a "religion," and the emergence of pop-culture Witchcraft confuses that picture. It is one thing to seek constitutional freedoms and protections for organized behavior that is identifiably "religious." It is another thing to seek the same guarantees for a "lifestyle choice" that is sprinkled with god-talk.

The two cultures within modern Witchcraft represent different ways of approaching the mainstream, ways that are not necessarily compatible. Their diverging agendas are clearly an additional source of friction between traditional Witches and their pop-culture cousins. The gap is bridged to some extent by Web sites (such as witchvox.com) and publications (such as *New Witch*) that are read by Witches from both cultures; it is also bridged by large, semipublic Neopagan gatherings (such as PantheaCon) that are attended by both kinds of Witches. But the gap itself is real, large, and ongoing, and it is a source of continuing tension within what outsiders see as the modern Witchcraft movement.

So—is modern Witchcraft religious, or not? The question is impossible to answer in its broad form as stated, and it can be hard to answer even in individual cases. It all depends, as the saying goes—and it doesn't just depend on how you define "religion." It also depends on how the Witches define themselves, and on how they actually behave. Keeping in mind that "anyone is a Witch who calls themselves a Witch," sorting out one kind of Witch from another can be a confusing and time-consuming process. As individuals, we can decide whether a Witch is religious or not on a case-by-case basis, weighing the cases as they come up, but social and legal policies need a more efficient way of assigning labels and distinguishing religious Witchcraft from the other kind(s).

The process of defining "religion" for constitutional purposes is already underway in the federal courts, and it clearly includes at least some organized forms of modern Witchcraft in its definition. Evangelical Christians tend to bristle at the idea that Witchcraft should hold parity with Christianity as a valid expression of religion. But that issue has been effectively settled since 1986, when the Fourth Circuit Court of Appeals decided the case of *Dettmer v. Landon.* The Court declared that the mail-order "Church of Wicca" is in fact a religion, and that its adherents are entitled to constitutional rights of free exercise. While that decision has not been directly affirmed by the U.S. Supreme Court, the principles of secular pluralism on which it is based are not likely to be overturned.

Witches and Christians

The Witches I have personally had contact with have largely been "traditional," "religious" Witches—followers of what is essentially Gardnerian Wicca, along with its offshoots and derivatives. After some time spent speaking with those Witches, reading their books and magazines, browsing their Web sites, and generally trying to tune in to their viewpoint, I take their profession of "religion" at face value. Modern Witchcraft is indeed a "made-up" religion, but then so are several other modern religions. Modern Witchcraft is spiritually wrong, socially subversive, and psychologically dangerous in my judgment, but so (in my judgment) are a number of other religions—ancient as well as modern. And from the biblical standpoint, all human "religions" are really wrongheaded attempts to get to God on our own terms anyway (and thus "made up")—so in the long run the differences between them are more apparent than real. If Mormonism and Scientology can be "religions," it is hard to justify closing the category to modern Witchcraft. And if I, as a Christian, can sit down to a polite and reasoned "dialogue" with someone who believes in no God (a Buddhist) and with someone who believes in an elephant-headed god of good luck (a Hindu), why would I balk at doing the same with someone who believes that Nature is God (a Witch)?

Yet many Christians *would* balk at the prospect, and would have a hard time treating a Witch the same way they would treat, say, a Buddhist or a Mormon in ordinary social conversation, or as a next-door neighbor. One reason for that reluctance is that many Christians falsely identify modern Witchcraft with the lurid stereotypes of medieval witchcraft (see chapter 5). But simply correcting that ignorance is not enough to make the problem go away. There is a tension between Christianity and modern Witchcraft that is very real and that is *not* based on misunderstanding—even though it is often misunderstood. In fact, there is more than a "tension" between Christianity and Witchcraft—there is an outright conflict over their respective visions for personal development and social progress.

Those two visions are emphatically *not* compatible, and to the extent that one vision prospers among us, the other will languish. There is a hard kernel of spiritual conflict between Witches and Christians that will not be erased by any amount of education or overcome by any amount of goodwill. My experience in "dialogue" (both formal and informal) with Neopagans has convinced me of one thing: Real respect and appreciation can indeed be built between Witches and Christians on a personal basis, but only if both parties can acknowledge the elements of conflict between them and agree to put them temporarily on hold with the attitude of "we'll let history decide those issues," for the sake of making the relationship possible. It takes more work, mutual honesty, and goodwill than the average relationship, but it certainly can be done—assuming that both parties want to do it.

Christians are used to the idea of repentance, so we should not be abashed to acknowledge ignorance and bad behavior on the Church's part, both historically and contemporarily; the greater problem is in separating real bad behavior from hysterical rumors and false accusations. But the most difficult thing of all may be for modern Witches to acknowledge how much of their own religion is built on anti-Christian prejudice, and how much of that prejudice is built on distortion and outright falsehood.

Interestingly, the Witches who are most willing to come to terms with that part of their legacy seem to be the "traditional," "religious" Witches; in contrast, the anti-Christian attitudes of Witchcraft's Charter Myth flourish unrestrained among pop-culture, "lifestyle" Witches. There are at least three reasons for that difference: 1) Religious Witches are generally more thoughtful and more "serious" people, who care about things like factual accuracy and the credibility of their religion in the eyes of the public; they also tend to be more aware of the recent scholarship that invalidates the claims of the Charter Myth; 2) as time goes by, more people are attracted to religious Witchcraft because it appeals to them on its own terms, not just for its rejection of Christianity; and 3) as religious Witchcraft mainstreams itself, especially via interfaith involvement, getting along with Christians and Christianity becomes a familiar routine to increasing numbers of religious Witches.

Witchcraft and Anti-Christianity

In any honest conversation between Witches and Christians, both sides need to acknowledge they are opposed in fundamental ways. Christians have their own theological explanation for that conflict, but even from a historical standpoint, it is plain that modern Witchcraft's anti-Christianity is basic, both to its origins and to its own self-image. An anti-Christian attitude is inherent in the false history Gerald Gardner invented to tie his "Wicca" back to medieval witchcraft and ancient goddess-worship. In fact, an element of anti-Christianity was built into the culturally subversive nature of his whole enterprise—insofar as the culture he was subverting was Christian-based.

From the beginning, Gardner understood that one of his chief objectives was to alter the image and perception of witchcraft in the public mind. Much of what Gardner wrote and did had the specific purpose of changing people's attitudes about what historical witchcraft was. Gardner also understood that the image change he had in mind was part of a bigger picture; it could not happen in isolation. The public could not come to see medieval witchcraft the way he wanted them to see it without turning the prevailing scheme of cultural values upside down—as Gardner himself had long since done in his own mind. After all, witchcraft's evil reputation came at the hands of a religious and cultural system (Christianity) that not only defined witchcraft as "evil," but did so by a standard that defined itself as "good." You can't reverse just one pole out of a pair of polar opposites; you have to reverse the whole arrangement. If medieval witchcraft was *in fact* good, and *not* evil, then the system that *called* it evil *was* evil. There is no way to escape the logic of that relationship.

Gardner himself, of course, didn't try to escape it; nor, for that matter, did any of his predecessors. When seen from that angle, the consistency of anti-Christian bias among those who have made major contributions to modern Witchcraft is really quite remarkable. Jules Michelet made no secret of his loathing for the Catholic Church and for Christianity, and his attempt to vindicate medieval witchcraft by portraying it as a champion of freedom was really a roundabout way of attacking the Church. Charles Godfrey Leland was an explicit admirer of Michelet and not only adopted his anti-Christianity but brought it up to date by couching it in terms of the newly popular "scientific" study of religion. Margaret Murray made Christianity the bad guy in her completely bogus picture of witchcraft as a pagan survival hounded by Church authorities. Robert Graves held a smoldering resentment toward Christianity for a variety of reasons and railed at length against "Father-God worship," which he regarded as the religion of oppressors and barbarians. Gardner, as already noted, extended, refined, and intensified the anti-Christianity exhibited by all of his forerunners, portraying medieval witchcraft as an innocent victim of Christian persecution.

And the tradition continues. Modern Witchcraft first found its identity in opposition to Christianity, and there is still a strong current of hostility to everything Christian that runs through the movement. The song I referred to in the introduction, titled "Heretic Heart," is just one example. That song and others like it express an attitude that is widely embraced and openly encouraged within the Neopagan community—an attitude that not only rejects the Christian message but also blames the Christian church and demonizes Christian believers.

Another popular Neopagan song, called "Burning Times," sets the false history of the Charter Myth to music, depicting medieval witches as freedom-loving goddess-worshipers in heroic struggle against the deadening, repressive hand of Christianity. One verse refers to Christians in extremely negative terms, deriding them for worshiping a dead person and demeaning their motives—which, the song says, stem from nothing more than a lust for control over ordinary people through the Roman Catholic Church. Other anti-Christian parts of the myth appear in later verses: The Pope declared the Inquisition as a war on the women of Europe, nine million of them died in the holocaust of the "burning times," and so on—the usual litany of bogus facts and erroneous accusations. All of that is familiar enough to anyone who delves into the literature of Neopaganism—and the false history behind it has been debunked repeatedly, even by Neopagans.

And yet, while that false history is being abandoned, the songs that teach and celebrate it are not—specifically because of the emotions and attitudes they stir up. A Neopagan told me in conversation that "Burning Times" was an evocative, emotional song that had been a moving experience for many Witches during their "conversion" process. Another told of weeping uncontrollably at a recitation of ancient goddess names in one of the verses of the song. In correspondence, a Wiccan elder added, "Needless to say, I and many of my fellows agree neither with the history nor the sentiment of many of the lyrics, but cannot deny the power of the song in the creation of oppositional identity."

In any case, there is a level of conflict between Witchcraft and Christianity that has nothing to do with history. The Pagans identify that conflict very clearly (though not its implications) as they celebrate their side of it in song. The conflict is recognized in the lyrics of "Heretic Heart," referred to at the beginning of this book. A later verse in that song ridicules the very concept that obedience might be a component of holiness and, in its refrain, once more proclaims that the singer's "Heretic Heart" is his or her own final authority.

✚ ✚ ✚ ✚ ✚ ✚ ✚ ✚ ✚ ✚ ✚ ✚ ✚ ✚ ✚ ✚ ✚ ✚

The conflict proclaimed in "Heretic Heart" is the primal antagonism between the sovereignty of God and the self-assertion of the fallen human will...the same conflict that is being played out before our eyes on the stage of history.

✚ ✚ ✚ ✚ ✚ ✚ ✚ ✚ ✚ ✚ ✚ ✚ ✚ ✚ ✚ ✚ ✚ ✚

The conflict proclaimed in "Heretic Heart" is the primal antagonism between the sovereignty of God and the self-assertion of the fallen human will. It is the same conflict being played out before our eyes on the stage of history in the form of the "culture wars." To see it in that way is to set it in the largest possible context—the context of God's purposes toward fallen humanity, and the movement of human history toward the fulfillment of those purposes.

Culture Wars: Rise of the "New Religious Synthesis"

The ministry known as the Spiritual Counterfeits Project (SCP) has been a partisan in the culture wars from the beginning of its work in 1973. That is probably the best-known aspect of SCP's activity, but its underlying objective has always been to understand and chart the progress of the cultural changes set in motion by the upheavals of the 1960s. Those of us who became Christians out of the counterculture recognized that the worldview we had found so magnetic was already working its way through other levels of society, and would continue to do so unless the process was somehow interrupted. But how could we write about what we were seeing in terms that would be meaningful to the average reader? In a word, what could we *call* the emerging worldview—which we understood as a synthesis of occultism, humanism, secularism, and the "religion" of self-deification? There was no agreed-upon term for such a combination. Depending on which aspect of the subject we were dealing with, we wrote of "cosmic humanism" (Alexander, 1982), "occult philosophy" (Alexander, 1984), or "the New Age worldview" (Alexander and Burrows, 1984).

The idea of a coming transformation in our collective viewpoint is what the New Age movement was all about, of course (they called it a "paradigm shift"), and its proponents were eager to claim that the change they wanted to see was already underway. Marilyn Ferguson wrote about the "Aquarian Conspiracy" in her book of the same title (J.P. Tarcher, 1980) and the concept of a shift in worldviews became common currency for advocates and critics alike. For instance, historian Carl Raschke drew attention to a rising "new religious consciousness" in his book *The Interruption of Eternity: Modern Gnosticism and the Origins of the New Religious Consciousness* (Nelson-Hall, 1980).

✥ ✥ ✥ ✥ ✥ ✥ ✥ ✥ ✥ ✥ ✥ ✥ ✥ ✥ ✥ ✥ ✥ ✥

The distinctive—and disturbing—part of Herrick's book is his assessment that "the New Spirituality" is rapidly replacing the biblical worldview as a source of values and attitudes in Western culture.

✥ ✥ ✥ ✥ ✥ ✥ ✥ ✥ ✥ ✥ ✥ ✥ ✥ ✥ ✥ ✥ ✥ ✥

More recently, Professsor James A. Herrick's *The Making of the New Spirituality* (2003, InterVarsity Press) has offered a helpful analysis. The title of the book provides a thumbnail term for its subject, but a more focused description emerges in the text. Herrick observes that "dozens of writers and media celebrities...have helped both to shape and popularize a medley of religious ideas that I will be referring to...as the New Religious Synthesis" (Herrick, 2003, page 15). The better part of his book is devoted to describing the components of the New Religious Synthesis, its history, and its cultural presence today. Herrick's most valuable contribution may be that his breadth of vision is able to see the construction of the New Religious Synthesis as a long-term process covering centuries; he speaks of "a three-hundred-year-long public persuasive process" (Herrick, 2003, page 17).

Herrick makes four other points that are relevant to our discussion of Neopagan Witchcraft. They are 1) his observation that the New Religious Synthesis has been (and continues to be) promoted by a series of talented and persuasive public advocates; 2) his observation that the magnitude of cultural change is masked by the diversity of its manifestations; 3) his observation that the New Religious Synthesis is an active opponent and competitor of the biblical worldview that lies at the heart of Western civilization; and 4) his grim but considered judgment that the New Religious Synthesis is winning the competition.

The first three points will not come as a revelation to anyone who has studied new religious movements from an evangelical point of view. Herrick's main contribution here has been to make those points explicit, and to make them indisputable by means of documentation. The distinctive—and disturbing—part of his book is his assessment that "the New Spirituality" is rapidly replacing the biblical worldview as a source of values and attitudes in Western culture; *The Making of the New Spirituality* is ominously subtitled *The Eclipse of the Western Religious Tradition*.

Herrick speaks of "the fundamental, and fundamentally opposed components of two perspectives currently competing for the Western religious mind—the New Religious Synthesis and the Revealed Word" (Herrick, 2003, page 15). He also says that the opposition between them is total and complete, observing that "the New Synthesis reverses each major tenet of the Revealed Word" (Herrick, 2003, page 251). Even though it is referred to as a "competition," the interplay between the two opposed belief systems often seems more like a relentless process of cultural decay and decline, for which there is no remedy but renewal. Herrick speaks of "this massive transformation in Western spiritual thought" and "the dramatic shift now occurring from one spirituality to another." Then he delivers the sobering substance of his conclusion:

> So substantial has been the shaping influence of the New Religious Synthesis in contemporary religious thought that it has now displaced the Revealed Word as the religious framework of a large and growing number of Western people. This powerfully persuasive synthesis blends strands of religious thought that began to appear, or reappear, in Western religious writing around 1700. Over the past three centuries, and under the guidance of scores of gifted public advocates working in a number of genres and media, the New Religious Synthesis has now successfully colonized Western religious consciousness. The intriguing migration of these provocative ideas from the fringes of religious exotica to Western spirituality's Main Street is the story told in this book (Herrick, 2003, page 15).

The migration of these ideas from the fringes to the mainstream is precisely the larger process within which modern Witchcraft needs to be understood. In that context, Witchcraft is plainly part of the wave of enthusiasm for such things that is moving through our culture. The main questions that remain are, Where is this wave taking us, and how, as Christians, should we respond?

Back to the Future, Forward to the Past

For the religious Witches of the Neopagan Movement, that wave is propelling them beyond the acceptability they have achieved so far, to outright respectability. The second

"Parliament of Religions" in 1993 showed how closely Neopaganism is attuned to the mood and temper of our times. At the 1993 Parliament, Neopagans discovered how precisely their agenda matches the worries and yearnings of the wider religious world; the wider world in turn discovered Neopaganism as an attractive, articulate partner to help spread its message. It was a perfect fit. And for the wider secular world, Witchcraft's environmentalism, feminism, and benediction of homosexuality make it a perfect fit as well. Modern Witchcraft has a bright future as a vehicle for the "Spirit of the Age"—assuming, that is, that the "Age" itself has a future at all.

Eschatology aside, if "pantheism" is the permanent natural inclination of the fallen human mind (as C.S. Lewis said), then resurgent paganism in one form or another will certainly rise to fill the cultural void created by a weakened and retreating Christianity. That doesn't mean that Neopagan Witchcraft itself will ever be more than a minor (if influential) presence on the religious landscape. There is a limit to the number of people who will be attracted to religious Witchcraft, simply because of the discipline and systematic practice it involves—and that number is probably fairly low. "Lifestyle" Witchcraft, on the other hand, has the potential to achieve a much wider popularity, in part because it doesn't distinguish itself as sharply from the "mundane" world. And the *ideas* Neopaganism represents—the worldview it conveys—have an audience that is potentially as wide as fallen humanity's rejection of the gospel.

If we want to get an idea of what such a development might mean for our culture, there is no need to peer into the future; we can look to the past. We already know what a culture is like that is thoroughly steeped in paganism, and we know how such a culture relates to Christianity. The culture, of course, is ancient Rome—and spiritually, America today resembles Rome in its declining days far more than it resembles America itself a hundred years ago. If you think that is an exaggerated comparison, consider the following. In 1912, Franz Cumont wrote *Astrology and Religion Among the Greeks and Romans.* In it, he described the crumbling classical world in terms that are indistinguishable from the "New Religious Synthesis" that Herrick speaks of—and that Neopagans are a part of. Specifically, Cumont said that "in the declining days of antiquity, the common creed of all pagans came to be a scientific pantheism, in which the infinite power of the divinity that pervaded the universe was revealed by all the elements of nature" (Cumont, 1912, page 56).

What Cumont describes is not where we are headed, it's where we already are. The worldview he summarizes is the essence of "natural religion," and it has already become the prevailing worldview for many of our cultural and intellectual elites. In one form or another, it is certain to be the worldview of the future for most people unless God acts to reverse the process of decay and decline that is currently underway. And it will indeed take an act of God to turn things around; it seems clear at this point that no human agency or stratagem is going to do the job.

Three Reasons Why

There are at least three reasons why it will take divine intervention to stop our headlong plunge down the slippery slope of cultural decay. The first (and from a biblical standpoint, foremost) reason is that "our struggle is not against flesh and blood, but...against the world forces of this darkness, against the spiritual forces of wickedness in the heavenly places" (Ephesians 6:12). This is not to let us off the hook as Christians from having to respond and act, it is simply to say that the moral, social, and psychological symptoms of our decline are just that—symptoms of a deeper derangement—and they will not be affected by our attempts to treat them as problems to be solved. Our cultural crisis is not amenable to policy solutions.

The second reason that no human effort is going to stop our slide into terminal decadence can be summed up in one word: "convergence." The escalating power and pace of cultural change we have seen in this book is not just happening to public attitudes about Witchcraft, it is happening to public attitudes about everything—and it is happening at all levels of society. Inevitably, the various countercultural currents tend to run together, as their common cultural rebellion brings them into common cause. Like converging branches of an avalanche, separate passions and purposes combine into a social force of enormous momentum and power.

We have already looked at an example of convergence in this book: the 1993 Parliament of Religions, which showed the remarkable coming together of three separate factors: environmental fears, religious yearnings, and the ideology of Neopaganism. An even earlier case is the coming together of radical feminism with religious yearnings to create "goddess spirituality," which in turn came together with what Gerald Gardner started to help create—the Neopagan movement of today.

Another powerful converging factor today is homosexuality. Neopagans tend to be aggressive in their endorsement of homosexuality, and there is a strong homosexual contingent within modern Witchcraft. But along with wanting to change public attitudes about homosexuality, the homosexual community also harbors a strong resentment toward Christianity and bristles with hostility toward Christians— yet another point of harmony with elements that are deeply embedded within modern Witchcraft.

Indeed, anti-Christianity is becoming a converging factor in its own right; many of the movements and enthusiasms of the last 50 years have independently contained their own anti-Christian element. Cultural insurrection in a Christian-based culture inherently involves repudiating some aspects of Christianity, and any movement that takes a countercultural stance will inevitably contain some counter-Christian component. The modern environmental movement provides a particularly good example of that connection—a linkage that has also brought environmentalism into harmony with the outlook and attitude of modern Witchcraft.

The beginnings of modern environmentalism are often traced to an article that has been called "the eco-shot heard 'round the world." Lynn White Jr., a medieval historian, presented a paper at a meeting of the American Association for the Advancement of Science in December 1966. White blasted the Christian belief system for justifying the rape of nature in the name of our "God-given dominion." His paper was published the following March in *Science* magazine, titled "The Historic Roots of Our Ecologic Crisis." White argued that Christianity was not just responsible for our environmental crisis, but that it was therefore wrong and worthy of blame. He concluded by urging that Christianity should be rejected in favor of pagan or Eastern religious thinking or both—or some new version of the same. Here is some of what White actually said:

> Human ecology is deeply conditioned by beliefs about our nature and destiny—that is, by religion....Christianity, in absolute contrast to ancient paganism and Asia's religions...insisted that it is God's will that man exploit nature for his proper ends....By destroying pagan animism, Christianity made it possible to exploit nature in a mood of

indifference to the feelings of natural objects.... Christianity bears a huge burden of guilt. More science and more technology are not going to get us out of the present ecologic crisis until we find a new religion (White, 1967).

Notice that in White's view, the root sin of Christianity is that it fosters "a mood of indifference to the feelings of natural objects." Paganism, by contrast, presumably cultivates a mood of concern for "the feelings of natural objects." Ignore for a moment the question of whether "natural objects" have "feelings"; that is just White's animistic sympathy coming to the fore. More to the point, when White assumes that "mood" and "feeling" are the heart of the problem, he highlights the third reason that no human effort is going to turn our culture around: The social forces that are converging to propel our cultural transformation are emotional not rational—and they won't be affected by rational strategies.

Changing Attitudes, Changing Culture

Evangelicals are fond of saying that "beliefs have consequences"—meaning that what we believe will determine what we do. For that reason, evangelicals often concentrate on addressing beliefs on a rational level, and on trying to change a person's beliefs by rational means. It is certainly true that beliefs have consequences, but it is also true, and prior in time, that *attitudes have beliefs*—meaning that our yearnings and our anxieties, what we fear and what we desire, will determine what we believe. The cultural change we are going through today involves more than replacing one set of ideas with another. It involves replacing one set of fears and desires with another—a much more fundamental process, and a much more difficult one to recognize and respond to.

✠ ✠ ✠ ✠ ✠ ✠ ✠ ✠ ✠ ✠ ✠ ✠ ✠ ✠ ✠ ✠ ✠ ✠

What we are seeing in the United States today is a massive shift in the underlying "loves" of the people, as increasing numbers…turn away from the Christian faith and the love of God.

✠ ✠ ✠ ✠ ✠ ✠ ✠ ✠ ✠ ✠ ✠ ✠ ✠ ✠ ✠ ✠ ✠ ✠

Saint Augustine understood those deeper dimensions of culture change. After all, he oversaw one of the most momentous culture changes in history: the transition from the dying pagan culture of the late Roman world to the emerging Christian culture of post-imperial Europe. In his landmark book *The City of God*, Augustine draws his contrast between the City of God and its opposite number, the Earthly City, precisely in terms of their contrasting fears and desires. In Augustine's own words,

> Two loves have constituted two cities—the earthly is formed by love of self even to contempt of God, the heavenly by love of God, even to the contempt of self. For the one glories in herself, the other in the Lord.…In the one, the lust for power prevails, both in her own rulers and in the nations she subdues; in the other, all serve each other in charity, governors by taking thought for all and subjects by obeying (*City of God*, XIV. 28).

In short, Augustine sees any human community (generic "City") as an organic whole, almost as a living entity. What gives any "City" its character is the sum force of its people's hopes and worries, their ambitions and their anxieties—in a word, their "loves." To Augustine, so-called "politics" is a symptom; it is one of several ways that people act out impulses that lie far deeper in themselves. In the same way, the beliefs that people adopt and the ideas that shape their societies are also symptoms of more basic inclinations.

What we are seeing in the United States today is a massive shift in the underlying "loves" of the people, as increasing numbers (including many nominal "Christians") turn away from the Christian faith and the love of God—and toward the pagan pursuit of power, pleasure, and the love of Self. The result has been growing weakness in the church—especially in its cultural presence—and growing strength in its cultural opposition. There is an inverse relationship between the cultural presence and strength of Christianity and that of its pagan competition; as one increases, the other diminishes—and vice versa.

That is hardly a novel observation; what's novel is to see the process running in a new direction. Early Christian apologists made the point that the spiritual darkness of occult and obscene religions that flourished in ancient Rome had been pushed by the light of the gospel to the fringes of society. One of the talking points of Christianity in all periods of history is that it has kept that darkness at its fringes. Modern Christian apologists have warned that the reverse could also occur, and the decline of Christianity's influence in our times means that the fringes are withdrawing inward, bringing the darkness that lies behind them to the center of society. Os Guinness compared contemporary Christianity to a campfire in the night that is burning low, allowing animals with their "encircling eyes" to approach behind the shrinking perimeter of light. In *The Dust of Death,* Guinness said, "As we have witnessed the erosion and breakdown of the Christian culture of the West, so we have seen the vacuum filled by an upsurge of ideas that would have been unthinkable when the fires of the Christian culture were high" (Guinness, 1994, page 276).

Secular critics of Christianity dismiss such warnings as alarmist propaganda. Secular scholars, however, have documented the connection. In 1979, respected sociologists William Sims Bainbridge and Rodney Stark set out to study the rising wave of cultish religion and occult thinking in our society. They assumed at the outset that conservative Christianity was part of the pattern of irrationality they were trying to analyze. They discovered instead that Christian belief was a specific *antidote* to irrationality. By their own admission, the conclusion that Bainbridge and Stark came to startled even themselves:

> "Born agains" are much less likely than others to accept radical cults and pseudo-scientific beliefs... [while] the group with no religious affiliation is receptive to these unscientific notions. *Those who hope that a decline in traditional religion would inaugurate a new Age of Reason ought to think again....* Our questionnaire research suggests that strong religion prevents occultism. Therefore we would expect to find that interest in deviant cults and in the paranormal was greatest where the churches are weakest—in the Pacific region. In fact, this is the case....
>
> Apparently when Christianity loses its grip on large numbers of people, deviant religious alternatives arise and get hold of some of the unchurched.... *Therefore, a further decline in the influence of conventional religion may not inaugurate a scientific Age of Reason, but might instead open the floodgates for a bizarre new Age of Superstition* (Bainbridge and Stark, 1980, pages 26–30, emphasis added).

Bainbridge and Stark's assessment was rendered some 25 years ago; today, the only modification we could make to their formula would be to change "*might* open the floodgates" to "*has* opened the floodgates." Clearly, the "bizarre new Age of Superstition" they spoke of has already arrived. And it arrived exactly the way they said it would—namely, in the wake of waning Christian influence in our culture. That's as close to a secular "prophecy" as you are likely to get.

Neopaganism and the "Spirit of the Age"

Our culture change is driven by a process of convergence. As the cultural trends and social movements of the "New Religious Synthesis" overlap and run together, they are discovering what Augustine already knew—that what draws and binds them together is not their allegiance to a common agenda, but rather their common participation in a mood or attitude. Their common attitude is one of rejection and refusal toward the main culture, and especially toward its Christian-based concept of moral and spiritual limits.

That "gut-level" energy of culture change is one of the things that is fueling our "culture wars," in the form of social and political conflicts over such things as abortion, homosexuality, and cloning. All of those conflicts arise out of an indignant refusal to accept any limits at all on the right of the self to do whatever it wants in pursuit of its own self-interest. That is the mood and temper of our times; it is the Spirit of the Age, the "Zeitgeist." Today it is approaching critical mass through the convergence of cultural trends, fads, and fashions. The change we are seeing around us represents a revolt by the world system, by worldly values, and by worldly people against the constraints of Christian culture, and Neopagan Witchcraft is just one part of that general insurrection. James Herrick spends almost 300 pages cataloging the varied movements, trends, and schools of thought that go to make up the "New Religious Synthesis," and all of them are expressions, in one way or another, of that same Spirit of the Age.

But Neopaganism is not just one among a welter of equals in that picture. It stands out from the crowd, both as an example of our changing culture and as a factor in producing it. Modern Witchcraft is perfectly timed and tailored to be a vehicle for the Spirit of the Age, giving it a more central position and a more important influence than some of the others in the synthesis we are seeing.

Neopaganism provides a good example of what's happening today because it explicitly embodies the "gut-level" energy of culture change (or, as we might call it, the "Augustinian level" of culture change). In attempting to define itself, modern Witchcraft stresses that its real identity is found at the level of outlook and attitude. It also instructs its own followers at that level, and it appeals to outsiders at that level in order to spread its viewpoint.

Remember the defining principle laid down by the Covenant of the Goddess in 1975 (quoted in chapter 1): "Our reality is intuitive. We know when we encounter someone who we feel is worshipping in the same way, who follows the same religion we do..." Witches are unwilling to define themselves in objective terms because the identity they share is not objective, but a matter of attitude. The common threads of Neopaganism are less in the details of beliefs and practices than they are in a sense of agreement on outlook, attitude, mood, and perspective. Modern Witches are saying, in effect, that they know what spiritual and cultural currents are flowing and are able to tell when someone is following the same ones they are.

Modern Witches understand that their identity is "intuitive," and that it is based on mood and attitude. They also understand that the most effective way to spread that identity (that is, to "re-paganize" society), is not to spread the identity itself, but to spread the mood and attitude it is based on. I have already observed (in chapter 1) that "the contagious excitement of cultural insurrection is modern Witchcraft's functional substitute for missionary zeal." Neopagans know that if the attitude spreads, the ideology will follow.

Narrative and Neopaganism

What is the best way to spread the mood and attitude? It isn't by preaching and exhortation. It is by telling stories. Storytelling, after all, is the oldest form of instruction we know of. The traditional knowledge of ancient peoples was preserved in story form—dramatic narratives that were committed to memory and recited on special occasions by priests who acted as the "tribal encyclopedia."

Writing destroyed that culture of oral tradition—and the order of society that went along with it. Technology has transformed our civilization many times over since then, but what hasn't changed is our use of stories to communicate values and viewpoints. Today, as in prehistoric times, dramatic narratives are still the most effective tool of communication—and of manipulation. There is no better way of getting others to feel the way you do—or of getting them to feel in a way that supports your agenda—than by telling them stories.

Academic scholars have recognized the role that dramatic narrative plays in giving shape and substance to Neopagan religion. Graham Harvey of King Alfred's College in the U.K. studied how imaginative literature is used in Neopaganism, noting that "while no single text is read by all Pagans, the construction and narration of Pagan identity commonly entails reading...especially fantasy literature." His landmark article titled "Fantasy in the Study of Religion" reached the following notable conclusion:

> Paganism is a spirituality centred on celebration of and engagement with Nature. Like many (perhaps most) religions, its experience is *more adequately expressed in imaginative stories than in dogmatic assertions.* Theatrical rituals and creative stories are closer to its heart than plain descriptions or narratives purporting to say "what witches do." Thus *Paganism is better understood and certainly better taught using these forms* (Harvey, 2000, emphasis added).

Neopagans clearly comprehend this concept. If they didn't, the reverberating impact of *The Craft* and *Buffy* is enough to make the point self-evident to almost anyone, and the point is this: Storytelling preaches the message more effectively than preaching does. People get the point of a story more directly, and they get it in a more personal way, because a story moves them at the level of their fears and desires, their "loves"—which, as Augustine understood, is the level from which they act. When Joss Whedon says of *Buffy,* "I wanted people to internalize it, and make up fantasies where they were in the story, to take it home with them, for it to exist beyond the TV show," he is only making conscious and deliberate what has always been true of storytelling at its most effective.

While Whedon is not a Pagan, his clarity about what he is up to suggests another way of looking at the progress and presence of Neopaganism in our culture—to see it not as the spread of an intellectual ideology, but as the spread of an existential infection (in Augustinian terms, the spreading corruption of our "loves"). The carriers of that infection have been stories told by others to our children while we were busy preaching to the world. From that angle, the "competition" Herrick speaks of—between the New Religious Synthesis and the Revealed Word perspective—is really a contest between competing stories about the origin and destiny of mankind.

Why describe it this way? Because the truth is that Christianity, like Paganism, is also "better understood and...better taught" using dramatic narratives. For the ultimate example of that, look no further than the Gospels themselves; the very foundation of Christianity rests upon four separate tellings of the same dramatic tale: a tale of temptation and trial, of suffering and sacrifice, of a tragedy that turns into triumph. That is how the Christian faith has always been conveyed; indeed, it is how God has always chosen to reveal Himself, both in history and in Scripture—the Bible itself is a story, from beginning to end.

Culture War and the Battle of the Narratives

James Herrick says that the New Religious Synthesis is winning the competition of worldviews, displacing the Revealed Word perspective as the source of values and attitudes for our cultural elite. The material we have surveyed in this book suggests that the same holds true at the popular level as well, where the culture war shows up not as a contest of worldviews, but as a battle of the narratives.

The biblical–Christian story is the familiar one of creation, temptation and betrayal, judgment and fall, sacrifice and redemption, return and restoration. The competing story, much like the New Religious Synthesis itself, is not one narrative but many, all of them having a similar thrust. At bottom it is the story of "the striving human will seeking desperately to launch itself into minor godhood in an evolving cosmos" (Herrick, 2003, page 279). The basic story line is well described in the work of the late Joseph Campbell, whose 1988 PBS video series *The Power of Myth* brought his ideas to millions of viewers. As Campbell famously pointed out, the story of the struggle for enlightenment is essentially the story of a hero, one "with a thousand faces," the particular face depending on the culture that gives him a name and a history. In our secularized, sophisticated culture today, the "hero" of occult enlightenment wears every one of his thousand faces, and then some.

Teens...are the people who need to "get" the tradition of Christian culture in order for it to survive, and right now, they're not getting it.

In the context of Christianity's cultural dominance, that diversity itself becomes part of the "New Spirituality's" challenge. In order to achieve its objective, the New Spirituality does not need to *re*place the Christian story with its own as the ruling narrative of our culture. All it needs is to *dis*place the Christian story from its privileged position by making it just one story among many, one version of the truth and nothing more, with Christ as just one more of the occult hero's many masks. If the proponents of the New Religious Synthesis can accomplish that much in the minds of the public, they may be able to interfere with the transmission of Christian culture from one generation to the next; if that transmission fails, the results will be more far-reaching than the fall of Rome.

It has been said that no great civilization is more than one generation away from barbarism, no matter how secure its cultural dominance may seem to be. If a civilization's underlying values are not passed from one generation to the next, they will not be re-acquired by the generation after that. They are, effectively..."history." That is the crisis our culture is facing at this historical moment. It is a crisis that is being created by the convergence of several factors we have looked at in this book: the self-contained isolation of teen culture; the inherent vulnerability of teens to manipulation; the domination of our culture (and especially teen culture) by the visual media; and the domination of the visual media by stories (and storytellers) that support the New Religious Synthesis.

For many teens (apart from the ones in strongly committed Christian families), the substance of Christian civilization is not being passed on, because the Christian story is not being coherently transmitted in their culture—and even where it is accessible, it gets lost in the babble at best. These are the people who need to "get" the tradition of Christian culture in order for it to survive, and right now, they're not getting it. The message that does come through loud and clear in teen culture, interestingly, is the message of pop-culture Witchcraft. For the Spirit of the Age, it seems, the channels are clear.

Today's teens and young adults are making their bid to be the generation that beats a retreat back across the bridge from civilization to barbarism by turning away from the tradition that is their legacy. There is no way to know at this point whether their retreat can be turned around, or whether it will turn into a rout—a lemming-like rush back to "the permanent natural inclination of the human heart" in C.S. Lewis's memorable phrase. If it does, then Christians would do well to heed the warning of the Dirge for a New Dark Age: "The twilight is ending; night is descending; and Angels of Light come dancing in the dark."

A Final Word
from the Author
What Now?

✛ ✛ ✛

AMERICAN CULTURE STANDS at a point of crisis, brought here by historical forces beyond our ability to foresee or forestall. The question within the crisis is whether the Christian-based traditions of Western culture will be successfully passed down from this generation to the next, or whether the process will be fatally interrupted. It is not at all a sure thing that the transmission will succeed. It is possible that the link will be broken, and the traditions that have shaped 1500 years of Western history will just sink into the sands of America's secular desert—preserved only in the teachings of eccentric and marginalized sects of Christianity.

But the forces that have brought us to this crossroads have not simply dumped us here with the admonition to choose our future. We have arrived at this destination with a direction and with momentum (historically speaking), and they are still carrying us forward—in effect, doing the choosing for us. That is one reason I suggested in the concluding chapter that no merely human effort is going to slow our descent into decadence or stop us from turning our backs on our own history. It will take an act of God to turn things around.

That doesn't mean human beings can sit on the sidelines and watch God perform. Biblically speaking, when God takes a hand in history, He typically does so by acting through His own people. There will be plenty for Christians to do if God decides to intervene. For that matter, there will be plenty for Christians to do if God decides not to intervene. The basic duty of Christians in facing the hostility and resistance of "the world" remains essentially the same in all times and places: to personally *be* a flag of the City of God planted in the heart of the Earthly City—wherever you may happen to be—and to *be* an outpost of God's gospel, a sign of His standing offer of mercy and a warning of His impending judgment. That responsibility doesn't change, no matter what conditions we find ourselves in. The plain duty set before us is summed up in Christ's instruction that in any and all circumstances, we are simply to "bear witness" to Him (see Matthew 10:18).

How Might Renewal Come About?

But in our current circumstances, we find ourselves facing the two additional problems I have already touched on: the challenge of cultural decadence and the crisis of cultural transmission. Both of those issues present themselves with a certain degree of urgency, and one of the first things Christians can (and should) do today is simply to ask *God* to do something—to intervene in the downward spiral we are caught in before we crash and burn altogether. Readers who are serious about coming to grips with our cultural crisis should therefore consider resorting to the classic triad for effectively invoking the intervention of God: repentance, fasting, and prayer.

The explicit expectation behind those prayers is that God would act so as to renew ("revive") His people, and through them produce a more general renewal in society as a whole. The logical (and biblical) assumption is that if God's Spirit is strongly present in His people, then the Spirit's influence will radiate outward in society, producing effects that mirror God's justice, God's compassion, and God's righteousness. Thus, the hope of social renewal is that God will grant us a stronger dose of His Spirit, which will thereby bring us back into alignment with something resembling sanity—spiritually and otherwise.

There is only one problem with that scenario—it presupposes a society that is already primed and prepped to accept the influence of God's Spirit. The familiar examples of such social renewal come from Old Testament Israel, a nation soaked in the consciousness of God, or else they come from the America of a hundred-plus years ago—a society that was likewise dominated by the concepts and images of the Christian Bible. The categories for receiving God's influence already existed in the public mind, and needed only to be brought to life.

But that is no longer the case, and such a society no longer exists for us. One result of the changes we have examined in this book has been to eliminate those pre-formed biblical categories from our collective consciousness. Biblical ways of thinking are no longer common currency—people no longer speak the dialect (as it were), and they don't understand what you are saying when you talk to them in biblical terms. Collectively, we have "hardened" our hearts and minds to the biblical message.

Therefore, even if our prayers are answered and God graces us with His Spirit, it is by no means certain that the outcome will be renewal. If the pressure of God's presence can't freely communicate itself to the general public, it is more likely to produce a social explosion than create social harmony. If our culture has compromised with the Spirit of the Age to the point that God's Spirit meets with more resistance than acceptance, the result will not be renewal, but polarization. When God appears among people who are predisposed to reject Him, the result will be conflict rather than concord. That's essentially what happened at Jesus' first coming, and the active presence of God in our midst today could easily provoke a similar kind of spiritual and social turmoil. The "New Religious Synthesis" has made great social and public relations gains in recent years, and its proponents are not prepared to see those gain reversed without resistance.

How Can We Prepare for Interaction?

It is impossible to know at this juncture whether our culture can be brought back from the brink of (self-)destruction or not. But we don't need that knowledge in order to prepare for the next stage of our spiritual warfare. Whether the culture collapses completely or struggles back to its feet, Christians will be called upon to represent the gospel in relation to resurgent paganism of all kinds. Therefore we should expect to be in contact with Neopagans and expect to have opportunities for apologetic and evangelistic interaction— and we should prepare ourselves accordingly.

In that context, "prepare ourselves" means "educate ourselves." To begin with, that means taking Neopaganism seriously, both as a religion and as a social phenomenon. It also means taking Neopagans seriously as people, not just as "the opposition" or as potential converts. Read up on the subject. Take the time to look into the resources listed in appendix B. Follow up on some of the resources they provide. Browse the Pagan Internet. Type in "Witchcraft," "Wicca," or "Neopaganism" on Google or Yahoo, and they will give you more links than you will care to follow. Or type in witchvox.com or cog.org (the Web site of the Covenant of the Goddess) on the Internet and go directly to the nexus for pop-culture witchcraft or traditional Witchcraft respectively. And pay attention to what you find there. Take notes. Collect information. Begin to accumulate a knowledge and experience base of your own.

When it comes to "dialogue" with Neopagans, five minutes of experience is worth a bookful of advice. Because of the extreme diversity among modern Witches, it is difficult to offer conversational pointers that will apply in more than a limited number of cases. Nevertheless, some observations from my own experience in talking with Neopagans may be helpful.

First and foremost: Assume nothing and be prepared for anything. Bring no stereotypes to the encounter. Determine to find out first hand about the Witch you are dealing with. Most Witches who are open to talking to outsiders about Witchcraft are open to an honest inquiry about what they believe. But be prepared for anything. From any given Witch you may encounter a bristling hostility toward Christians that will foreclose any further discussion. Or you may encounter a bias against Christianity that is grounded in historical falsehood, and is thus subject to historical correction. Or you may encounter someone who is willing to engage in an extended philosophical discussion about natural versus revealed religion. In one way, Witches are much like anyone else—they will give respect if they are given respect. If you can approach the conversation without being fearful, hostile, dismissive, condescending, or disdainful, it will further open doors of communication.

Witches tend to be very touchy about "evangelism," apparently believing that Christians have little genuine interest in them except as potential converts. Showing a little genuine interest in them as representatives of an alternate culture will go far to dismantle that misunderstanding. My own approach has been to stress that I have no interest in whether they choose to accept the gospel or not; my interest is in seeing to it that the message of the gospel is clearly presented and clearly understood, free from distortion and misunderstanding. Once they have understood what the gospel is and what the good news proclaims, they can respond to it however they want—believe it, reject it, or take it under advisement. That is consistent with the free will God gave them, and I can accord them no less.

The good news about talking to Neopagans is that if you can maneuver past the rhetorical landmines and barriers to communication, they can be quite open to the full, industrial-strength supernaturalism of the gospel message. The bad news is that there is a lot of maneuvering to do—and a lot of distortions to dispel—before your communication can reach that level. What's needed is for enough Neopagans to encounter enough knowledgeable, articulate Christians to discredit the stereotypes and misunderstandings they have of Christianity. As Witchcraft goes mainstream, the opportunities multiply for such encounters to happen. Christians should be preparing now to play their role effectively when those occasions occur.

—Brooks Alexander
July 2004

Appendixes

✤ ✤ ✤

Bibliography

Appendix A
Witchcraft in the Military
"Our Time Has Finally Come"—
A Case Study in Cultural Change

FORT HOOD IS AMERICA'S LARGEST military base. It is sprawled across 340 square miles of sun-baked limestone and scrub brush in the Texas hill country north of Austin. It is also home to 42,000 soldiers of the First (Armored) Cavalry Division and the Fourth (Mechanized) Infantry Division—dedicated, highly trained, no-nonsense warriors who are the top tier of America's military forces. In the nearby town of Killeen, the civilian population is politically and culturally conservative, with religious sympathies that are strongly Christian and evangelical.

To all appearances, Fort Hood is the last place you would expect to be a hotbed of exotic religious experimentation. But in 1999, Fort Hood became the focus of an international media "flap" when word got out that Witchcraft ceremonies were being performed on the base, apparently with the blessing of the base commanders.

Actually, the Wiccan rituals had been going on at Fort Hood for the previous three years—without publicity, without incident, and without anyone really noticing. And as it turned out, Fort Hood wasn't the only military base where this was happening. In fact, it wasn't even the first. That distinction goes to the Army post at Kaiserslautern, Germany, where Wiccan services were being held as early as 1992. So there was, strictly speaking, no "news" at Fort Hood—in the sense there were no new facts to report, and no cover-up of old facts to expose. But when an enterprising local reporter turned the known facts into a story, the story turned into an issue, and the issue turned into a national controversy.

The controversy in turn became an object lesson in cultural warfare for the Christian community. Unfortunately, the lesson for us was a rather uncomfortable one. As the controversy grew, Christians and other cultural conservatives began to wake up to the fact that the critical battles on the issue had already been fought—and lost—years ago, before most people even knew what was happening. By the time the dispute went public and a public reaction developed, it was literally all over but the shouting.

In addition, opponents of the army's policy often spoke in ignorance and haste. Knowing little or nothing of the Neo-pagan movement, they rushed to make charges and offer characterizations that turned out to be false—often flagrantly so—thereby undermining their own credibility. For a few months that summer, the missteps and misstatements of the "new witch hunters" became comic fodder for the columnists and commentators of the cultural left. Gradually it became clear that those who opposed the army's Witches had no real legal basis for their objections. Eventually, the opposition to military Witchcraft dissolved in disarray and confusion. Some opponents abandoned their positions publicly; most simply quit talking about the issue.

The Anatomy of a Flap

But at the outset, the story was surprisingly slow to attract widespread attention. On May 11, 1999, the *Austin*

American–Statesman published an article by reporter Kim Sue Lia Perkes about the officially sanctioned Wiccan ceremonies that had been going on at the base for nearly three years. The centerpiece of that article was Perkes's description of her attendance at a Wiccan ritual celebrating the spring equinox, complete with photos showing the soldier Witches "dancing the circle" and "jumping the fire." The text of her article also set forth the Neopagans' view of themselves as "a reconstruction of nature worship from tribal Europe and other parts of the world." Almost as an aside, Perkes remarked that officials at the base seemed reluctant to discuss the matter, and also noted that there had been protests from a local Baptist church.

Strangely, the article had no immediate media "bounce." No other American media outlets picked the story up and repeated it right away—although both the *Times of London* and the *London Daily Telegraph* published "filler" articles on the Witches of the American Army ("Onward Pagan Soldiers," read one headline). The story finally went national in the U.S., ever so briefly, on May 15 when Fox News Channel's Bill O'Reilly used the Fort Hood Witches as his "most ridiculous item of the day," quipping that there was "no truth to the rumor that the Army is developing a Bradley Fighting Broomstick."

Apparently based on that media mention, Representative Bob Barr of Georgia raised both the stakes and the national profile of the controversy three days later. On May 18, he issued a press release announcing he had written to the Secretary of the Army and Fort Hood's commanding officer, insisting they cease allowing Witchcraft practices at the base. Barr charged that sanctioning Witchcraft as a religion was destructive to "good order and discipline" and warned against starting down that slippery slope: "Will armored divisions be forced to travel with sacrificial animals for

Satanic rituals? Will Rastafarians demand the inclusion of ritualistic marijuana cigarettes in their rations?" he asked in his letter and press release.

Meanwhile, back in Barr's home district, the *Atlanta Journal–Constitution* reported that Georgia's Witches were publicly protesting his pronouncements. Barr responded to their protest with a hometown public event of his own:

> At a May 29 "town meeting" filled largely with supportive constituents, Barr declared that elected leaders should decide which religions could be practiced in the military (Silk, 1999, page 1).

Barr's activism stirred up familiar partisans on both sides of the culture war. The *Washington Post* gave major "bounce" to the story with a June 8 article that contrasted Barr's uptight attitude (and the hostility of local Christians) with the relaxed and tolerant outlook of the Army and its Witches. The *Post*'s story even invoked the "diversity is strength" mantra, leaving no doubt which side of the argument wore the mantle of political correctitude:

> Barr is threatening hearings and legislation, but, so far, the Army brass at Fort Hood is shrugging. *In the new equal-opportunity military, where diversity is strength,* minority religions are not merely tolerated but welcomed....Far from clashing cultures, the wiccans and the military coexist cheerfully. To the Army, the wiccans are part of a proud American tradition, proof that "people with different religious beliefs are all working together successfully."...To the wiccans, the military is an adopted home, far more tolerant than the world outside (Rosin, 1999, emphasis added).

The Rhetoric Heats Up

After the *Washington Post* joined the debate, developments began to unfold more rapidly.

> The saga's next chapter—possibly occasioned by the report in the June 8 *Washington Post*—began with a June 9 announcement by conservative activist Paul Weyrich that his Free Congress Foundation and 12 other conservative groups were calling for Christians to stop joining or re-enlisting in the Army until it prohibited witchcraft rituals on posts.
>
> "What is it going to take, you believers in God?" he cried in an op-ed piece distributed by Knight-Ridder and published in Austin, Fort Worth, Omaha, and Salt Lake. "Do we just accept what is happening as normal? Or do we believers finally say we've had it? We are not going to let pagans claim an equal footing with God. Institutions that go that route are institutions that will just have to function without young people" (Silk, 1999, page 2).

Weyrich's call to boycott the military proved immediately controversial among conservatives. Several of the groups that were part of his alliance publicly backed away from the idea—including the Christian Coalition and the American Freedom Institute. It was suggested that the boycott call reflected "Weyrich's own post-impeachment view that religious conservatives should separate themselves from corrupted American institutions" (Silk, 1999, page 2). Whatever its intent, it was not a strategy designed to attract broad support. Strict cultural separation has always been a minority option, even among American fundamentalists.

Most of the major denominations declined to participate in the anti-Wiccan crusade. So did most politicians—sensing, perhaps, that it was not a politically winning issue. One exception was South Carolina senator Strom Thurmond, who lodged a protest with Pentagon officials and threatened to introduce legislation banning Witchcraft from the armed forces. Another exception was Presidential candidate George W. Bush. As he was then governor of Texas, Bush's hometown paper had broken the story, and he could hardly profess ignorance of an issue that had raised a minor publicity storm in his own backyard. The subject came up during his June 24, 1999, appearance on ABC's *Good Morning America*. Bush said, "I don't think witchcraft is a religion, and I wish the military would take another look at this and decide against it." He has not commented further on the subject since becoming President.

Media pundits and opinionizers (the so-called "chattering classes") had a great time poking fun at "the real witch hunters" during 1999's "silly season"—the traditionally slow news period of summertime, when minor matters often receive exaggerated media attention. Reporters traveled to Killeen looking for local Christians to indulge in ignorant, bigoted behavior that could be held up to ridicule and disdain.

They were not disappointed. Beginning with the *Washington Post* report, anti-Wiccan Christians rose to the bait, apparently lured by the prospect of major media coverage for their ministry and their message. An article in *The Texas Monthly* ("Witch Hunt," by John Ratliff) was typical. The author opens his article with a rhetorical question: "Who's scarier: the circle of Wiccans leaping bonfires at Fort Hood or the Republican congressman and the Baptist preacher who want them thrown off the base?" He then answers his own question with a verbal portrait of the Baptist preacher that depicts him as part dumb hayseed and part Grand Inquisitor—a freakish combination of Forrest Gump and Torquemada:

"They're devils!" cries the Reverend...whacking his
meaty palm against a Bible densely annotated with
blue ballpoint scrawlings. "They're wicked! And
they're letting them dance around a fire out there!"...

"I don't judge these people; my Book does," [he]
says, quoting Exodus 22:18: "Thou shalt not suffer
a witch to live."...His message is plain, at least when
it comes to what he says is the Bible's prescribed punishment for unrepentant witches: "They should be
warned, and then if they come out in the open with
their evil, they should be done away with," he says.
Although stressing that he has no intention of vio-
lating man's law to enforce God's, he makes a point
of mentioning public stoning as the designated
means of execution for witches. Toward the end of
our discussion he apologizes for his fervor. "I hope
you didn't think I was hateful," he chuckles. "I get a
little excited" (Ratliff, 1999, pages 1, 3).

End of the Affair

After a sustained period of that kind of coverage, public
opinion was lining up solidly behind the Witches, while the
movement against them was torn by disagreements and was
running out of steam. At the end of June, the Neopagans
held a "Full Moon Circle" and rally in Washington DC to
support the Fort Hood Witches and protest Barr's anti-Witch
agenda. The event was poorly attended by the media—at
seven o'clock in the evening, it was out of sync with the
normal news and deadline cycles. Ironically, one of the few
national news outlets to cover the event was the Christian
Broadcasting Network (CBN). Their report was aired on *The
700 Club* June 30, and it effectively signaled the end of the
organized national resistance to Witchcraft in the military.

(Barr tried in July to amend the defense appropriations bill to ban Witchcraft in the armed forces, but was unsuccessful.)

✣   ✣   ✣   ✣   ✣   ✣   ✣   ✣   ✣   ✣   ✣   ✣   ✣   ✣   ✣   ✣   ✣

[As to the claim that] elected officials should decide which religions pass muster and which do not…Christians need to consider what that kind of arbitrary power might come to mean in a culture that is turning less friendly to Christianity every day.

✣   ✣   ✣   ✣   ✣   ✣   ✣   ✣   ✣   ✣   ✣   ✣   ✣   ✣   ✣   ✣   ✣

CBN's report was evenly balanced, in that it gave equal time to comments from Andrea Sheldon of the Traditional Values Coalition and John Machate of the Military Pagan Network. Sheldon stressed the cultural danger that religious Witchcraft represents: "They are inviting Satan into our military. Whether people like it or not, this country was founded on Judeo–Christian principles....This Witchcraft is an anti-religion, and it is denigrating and it does undercut the military" (CBN, 1999). She also repeated Weyrich's call for a boycott of the armed forces.

Machate presented the dispute as a matter of religious liberty and constitutional law: "The Constitution doesn't say only Christianity is valid. If you start taking away one religion, you're going to start picking at the other religions" (CBN, 1999).

But the most significant comment in the report came from CBN's founder and chief commentator, Pat Robertson himself, who left no doubt where he personally stood on the issue.

After the story concluded, Robertson, as is his wont, delivered his own assessment: "I'm not worried about a little coven of witches running around.... Rather than suppress us all, we might give them their freedom."

To which Machate, in a prepared statement, replied: "Religious tolerance is the price of religious freedom for all. We were pleased that the Christian Broadcasting Network attended our press event. Their story was fair and balanced. We thank Reverend Robertson for his support of religious freedom" (Silk, 1999, page 4).

Robertson was far too glib in his dismissal of the Neopagan movement. There is considerably more going on here than "a little coven of witches running around." But he was undoubtedly right to back away from this issue—and from Barr's claim that elected officials should decide which religions pass muster and which do not. Christians need to consider what that kind of arbitrary power might come to mean in a culture that is turning less friendly to Christianity every day. Robertson does seem to understand that dimension of the problem at any rate.

Why the Military?

Witchcraft and the military seem like strange bedfellows. If asked to name a place in society where Neopaganism might find a cozy home, most people would not think first of the army. The military, after all, has traditionally been seen as a socially "conservative" institution, while Witchcraft clearly represents a departure from society's traditional norms and forms. But that appearance of incongruity is misleading because it is based on superficial contrasts.

Students of history will know better. Armies have often been agents of cultural change, completely apart from anyone's attitudes or intentions. The armies of Alexander the Great marched to the limits of the known world—and beyond—in search of conquest and plunder. And when they came home, they brought with them not only the physical spoils of war but cultural plunder as well, in the form of foreign philosophies and religions. In doing so, they started a process that has characterized Western empires ever since—severing cultural products (such as religions) from their cultural setting and turning them into detached options for people with completely different cultural assumptions (or none at all). After Alexander died (323 B.C.), the process he started eventually led to two centuries of religious borrowing and blending ("syncretism") that we know today as "the Hellenistic Age."

Rome repeated the same pattern, sending her armies, her highways, her merchants, and her bureaucrats out to far-flung lands in every direction, from Britain to Western Asia. And again, the traffic on Roman roads ran in both directions—the traffic in gods as well as the traffic in goods. The imperial capital became a magnet for religions, creeds, and superstitions from all over the world, and by the time of Nero (A.D. 54-68), the historian Tacitus was scandalized by the influx of alien faiths. With the new religion of Christianity specifically in mind, Tacitus complained that the city of Rome itself had become a place "where all kinds of shameful and sordid activities are attracted and catch on" (Tacitus, *Annals* 15:44). Rome was the undisputed center of cultural gravity for the ancient world, and everything detachable was drawn there—often carried by returning legionaries.

In our own day, the Beat movement of the late 1950s (predecessor to the hippies and the Eastern religious boom of the 1960s) was fed by American soldiers returning from the occupation of Japan with an enthusiasm for Zen Buddhism—and an aversion to conformity. The pattern does not vary, no matter the era or the society in view. Expeditionary armies acquire, harbor, and bring home alien and destabilizing influences. Even the soldiers who never leave home become more open to the exotic, as the unfamiliar becomes familiar through the recounted experiences of their comrades. By virtue of such practical worldliness, the military may have offered a more agreeable atmosphere for Witches and Neopagans than society at large.

By the early 1980s, that kind of tolerant attitude was evident in a handbook used by the military Chaplains' Corps. The *Chaplains' Handbook* uncritically repeated the claim that Neopaganism is a descendant of ancient paganism by way of medieval witchcraft—a claim now largely abandoned by the Neopagan movement (see chapter 4). Nevertheless, that claim from the *Chaplains' Handbook* was cited by the Federal Appeals Court as a basis for its 1986 decision in the case of *Dettmer v. Landon,* which declared Witchcraft to be a constitutionally recognized "religion," with the same rights and protections that other religions enjoy.

But for the military, the *Dettmer* ruling simply made official what was already happening unofficially. The *Chaplains' Handbook* included Neopaganism in its pages because the Army already included Neopagans in its ranks. By 1992, there were enough of them to form a support group (the Military Pagan Network) to lend them aid and comfort and to provide pagan contacts on and near military bases around the world.

The military has already shown itself to be one of the factors driving our cultural transformation, as indeed it has been throughout history. It is likely to continue its role as an agent of cultural change as America continues to extend its military presence around the world.

Lessons, Learned and Otherwise

The 1999 controversy over military Witchcraft seems like a trifling matter in the larger scheme of things, and in many ways it was. It was purely a media episode, a war of words that became a summertime diversion for writers and readers alike, with little real-world impact. After all was said and done, a lot was said and nothing at all was done. At the end of the day, all of the rhetoric fired back and forth produced absolutely no changes in anything—except for the public's attitude toward the Witches and their critics. And that changed substantially.

For Christians and other cultural conservatives, the Fort Hood Witchcraft flap was a public relations debacle. The anti-Witch crusaders entered the fray with great fanfare and left it looking foolish. Indeed, their campaign failed so completely that every item on their agenda was rejected. Worst of all, the crusaders themselves were widely perceived to be intemperate and uninformed. By the time the affair finally played itself out in the fall, it had vigorously reinforced every negative stereotype of Christianity available. It also conveyed the impression that when Christians create a public stir over something, their concerns are likely to have little merit, and less relevance, to the rest of society.

It was also a public relations triumph for modern Witchcraft. In effect, the episode put an exclamation point on a decade filled with changes in the way that Witchcraft is seen and understood. It both symbolized and speeded up the process of transformation that was already taking place.

The military Witches are aware of that cultural transformation—and very aware of their place within it. At Fort Hood, Marcie Palmer, high priestess of the base's Neopagan group (and a decorated military policewoman), made the point to some of her Wiccan students at a Wednesday night class: " 'We are at the end of one age and the beginning of another,' said Palmer.... 'Our time has finally come' " (Rosin, 1999).

Appendix B
"Getting Ready":
Suggested Reading
A Brief Annotated Bibliography

THE CULTURAL SHIFT WE ARE UNDERGOING (also known as the "culture war") means that Christians will be called upon to explain and exemplify the gospel in new situations, to a new kind of audience, using new communication tools and skills. It also means that an active new "mission field" is not only here among us, it will shortly come looking for you. The day is coming, and probably sooner than you think, when you or someone you know will meet a Witch or some other variety of Neopagan in a social or professional situation. When that day comes, you will want to be prepared ahead of time with enough information to respond knowledgeably and navigate the encounter with confidence and skill.

The books and articles annotated below are not intended to provide a comprehensive reading list or convey the substance of scholarship on ancient paganism, historical witchcraft, or modern Witchcraft and Neopaganism. They are intended to provide a summary of basic information on those subjects through sources that are (at least for those with Internet access) easy to find, easy to read, and easy to understand. They will introduce you to essential facts and main ideas on the topic in a form that is both accessible and digestible.

Witchcraft's "Charter Myth"

Allen, Charlotte, 2001; "The Scholars and the Goddess"

The Atlantic Monthly *(January 2001); volume 287, no. 1; pages 18-22 (online version: www.theatlantic.com/cgi-bin/o/issues/2001/01/allen.htm).*

This article is an extended debunking of Neopaganism's "Charter Myth" (see chapter 5). And "debunking " is the right word—literally. The tagline beneath the title reads, "Historically speaking, the 'ancient' rituals of the Goddess movement are almost certainly bunk."

Allen lays out the basic story line of the myth as it is described by the popular Wiccan writer Starhawk. Starhawk's version contains all of the standard elements— the idyllic, prehistorical, matriarchal, Mother-Goddess-worshiping society, which was overthrown by violent, warlike, patriarchal, Father-God-worshiping barbarians; the coming of Christianity as a hostile force; and the extermi-nating fury of the Inquisition, which allegedly killed some nine million people in Europe over a span of three centuries. Allen also notes the wider influence this mythology has had in "a broad swath of the intellectual and literary fabric of the past hundred years." The ideas in the myth show up in a number of literary and intellectual sources, including Robert Graves, D.H. Lawrence, T.S. Eliot, and William Butler Yeats, as well as James Frazer's *Golden Bough* and Jungian psychology.

But, Allen says, "In all probability, not a single element of the Wiccan story is true." The remainder of her article is a summary discussion of the actual evidence pertaining to each aspect of the myth. She cites Philip Davis and Ronald Hutton as scholars who have shown Wicca to be a modern creation. She also traces the origins of the frequently cited figure of "9 million victims" of the witch hunts and throws cold water on the overheated claims of savage persecution and institutional victimhood. But she devotes the most substantial part of her article to one aspect of the myth that is important to "feminist Witches" in particular—the concept of ancient goddess-worship.

The idea that ancient societies were matriarchal and goddess-oriented has a long, if not particularly distinguished, history—and Allen surveys it expertly. Today, however, the idea has been given mainstream credibility by the work of Marija Gimbutas, the Lithuanian-born archaeologist at UCLA whose excavations in Turkey led her to claim that the theory was supported by the evidence she uncovered. Allen discusses those discoveries—and the sometimes scornful criticism of other scholars in the field, who generally regard Gimbutas's theory as fanciful, misguided, and ideologically driven.

Historical Witchcraft

Gibbons, Jennifer, 1998; "Recent Developments in the Study of the Great European Witch-Hunt"

The Pomegranate: Journal of Pagan Studies, *issue #5; Lammas, 1998 (online version: www.cog.org/witch_hunt.html).*

In her essay *A Time For Truth*, Margot Adler calls upon Wiccans and Neopagans "to look honestly at their history." Jennifer Gibbons is a Wiccan who has answered that call. An academically trained historian (with an M.A. in medieval history) who also happens to be a practicing Witch, Gibbons was acutely aware of the misinformation and outright historical falsehood that Neopagans accept (and promote) as part of their own self-definition. She was also aware, as an academic, that modern Witches would never be taken seriously in that world as long as they believed and taught the literal truth of their historically false mythology.

"Recent Developments in the Study of the Great European Witch-Hunt" is Gibbons's appeal for the Neopagan community to quit clinging to its increasingly untenable mythology and shed its outdated ideas about medieval witchcraft. One of the points Gibbons makes in her article is that Neopagan stereotypes of Christians and Christianity are not supported by the evidence and need to be jettisoned as well. Gibbons skillfully deconstructs the stereotype of the fanatical Inquisitor who obsessively pursues some lurid fantasy of demons, perverted sex, and witchcraft—pointing out, for example, that the witch hysteria was actually much milder where the Inquisition's rule was strong, but raged where it was weak. Gibbons forcefully makes the point that the Neopagan habit of blaming the Church as the driving force behind the "burning times" goes hand in hand with the equally false image of medieval witchcraft that prevails in the Neopagan community—and equally needs to be corrected.

Russell, Jeffrey Burton, 1980; A History of Witchcraft

(London: Thames and Hudson).

Jeffrey Burton Russell is a historian known for his ability to explain complex subjects in clear and simple language; his book on witchcraft shows how he got that reputation. Russell's research into witchcraft is just one part of his larger interests in 1) the Middle Ages and 2) the history of human thinking about evil, the devil, and the demonic. He has written a series of highly praised books on both subjects, but his fields of knowledge overlap uniquely in his study of Witchcraft.

His book *Witchcraft in the Middle Ages* (1972) is highly recommended for readers who have an appetite for the meat of real historical scholarship presented in an eminently readable form, but his *History of Witchcraft* is a gem of historical writing that makes the full scope of his expertise on the subject accessible to almost anyone. The book is a one-stop resource for reliable information on, and insightful analysis of, magic and sorcery worldwide, the roots and growth of historical witchcraft, the rise and decline of the witch hysteria, the end of general belief in witchcraft after 1700, and the rise and development of modern Witchcraft and the Neopagan movement in the twentieth century. If I had to name one work that covers as many aspects of the subject as possible, as comprehensively and accurately as possible, this would be the one. *A History of Witchcraft* is simply the best single source of reliable information on its subject, bar none.

Modern Witchcraft and Neopaganism

Adler, Margot, 1986; Drawing Down the Moon: Witches, Druids, Goddess-Worshippers and Other Pagans in America Today, *2nd ed.*

(Boston, MA: Beacon Press).

Drawing Down the Moon is a truly indispensable resource for anyone who expects (or wants) to be in contact or dialogue with Neopagans. Adler provides a detailed history of the origins and development of the modern Neopagan movement, with an emphasis on its Witchcraft component. In addition to that historical survey, the book also offers a necessary guide to the various branches and varieties of Neopaganism. The old cliché that "you can't tell the players without a program" applies in spades to the modern Witchcraft movement. Adler provides that program, explaining, for example, the difference between "Heredi- tary," "Traditional," "Gardnerian," "Alexandrian," "Geor- gian," and "Dianic" Witchcraft, and describing various forms of "Pagan Reconstructionism" (attempts to re-create the ancient pre-Christian religions of Europe and elsewhere). Those distinctions are as subtle and obscure to most non- Pagans as the differences between Christian denominations are to the average non-Christian, but when a family of Wic- cans moves into your neighborhood and becomes your literal neighbors, it is information you are going to want to have.

Adler is a self-declared follower of "the Craft," so her book is in large degree a promotional piece on behalf of the move- ment, and it should be read with that in mind. At the same time, she is honest enough to criticize (some of) the move- ment's failings and excesses, and she is able to offer an insider's commentary on aspects of Neopaganism that outsiders are unlikely to understand on their own—such as the place of magic and ritual, the influence of feminism, the place of envi- ronmentalism, and most importantly, the general angle on life that constitutes the Pagan worldview. If you dialogue— in your own mind—with the ideas that Adler puts forth, you will begin to understand how Neopagans think, and how that thinking shows up in what they say and do. Reading this book will not make you an "expert" on Neopaganism, but it will enable you to converse intelligently with those who are—and with Neopagans themselves.

Pike, Sarah M., 2001; Earthly Bodies, Magical Selves: Contemporary Pagans and the Search for Community

(Berkeley, CA: University of California Press).

What is it like to *be* a Witch, or Neopagan? What is it like to belong to that "community"? What do Witches actually *do* in the practice of their religion? This book gives readers as good a look inside the Neopagan subculture as outsiders are likely to get. Sarah Pike is an academic researcher who became a "participant–observer" of Neopaganism for a period of five years. This gave her remarkable access to the Neopagan community, and to the state of mind (and spirit) within it. That level of involvement also presupposes that she is actively sympathetic to the movement and presents a positive view of it. Indeed, Pike herself says, "I do not claim to be a Neopagan or to represent this religion as an insider might, but I have been transformed by my experiences in Neopagan communities, and this transformation is surely reflected in the way I tell their stories"(page xvi). Such transparent biases are easy to identify and filter out.

To Pike, the most dynamic expression of Neopaganism, and the core of the religion, is to be found in its "festivals"— organized community gatherings that are part ritual, part camp meeting, part carnival, and part party. This is a central feature of the movement that most outsiders miss entirely, since the average non-Neopagan is unlikely to even hear of such events, much less actually attend them. Pike believes the festivals are where Neopaganism strengthens and refreshes itself, and where it grows and changes. That is because the festivals and other large gatherings are the focus of the "self-transformation" process that Pike believes to be at the core of Neopagan religion—a process that uses both magic and sexuality as tools to achieve its objective.

Pike also devotes a chapter to discussing how Witches and Neopagans react to the often hostile attitudes of the "mundane" world (chapter 3: "The Great Evil That Is in Your Backyard—Festival Neighbors and Satanism Rumors"). For Christians, this may be the most interesting part of the book, as it gives a clear depiction of how we are seen through Wiccan eyes—an unflattering portrait, to be sure, based partly on ignorance, partly on distortion, and partly on Christian misbehavior. It is important to distinguish between those components of Neopagan hostility to Christianity if we are to overcome the considerable barriers to communicating with this community.

Vale, V., and Sulak, John, 2001; Modern Paganism: An Investigation of Contemporary Pagan Practices

(San Francisco, RE/Search Publications [www.researchpubs. com]).

This is a resource for Christians who are serious about communicating with Neopagans, whether in dialogue, evangelism, or ordinary social interaction. This unusual and fascinating book is one of a series published by RE/Search Publications in San Francisco. RE/Search is a small independent publishing house that specializes in documenting a variety of fringe cultural phenomena (such as Punk Rock, Sado-Masochism, bodily modification, Neopaganism, and so on). The distinctive feature of RE/Search books is that they concentrate on primary source material, featuring interviews with the actual participants, with very little interpretive work written by outsiders. Indeed, this is what makes *Modern Paganism* such a valuable resource *to* outsiders. This 212-page book contains 41 interviews with 48 Witches and Neopagans, plus a highly useful "Pagan Glossary." The interviewees represent a range of different Neopagan "traditions" and "types" (Druids, Gardnerians, Norse Pagans, Queer Pagans, eco-pagans, techno-pagans, and so on), talking at length about a variety of subjects that concern them. Together, they give the reader a unique look at typical Neopagan attitudes, taken straight from the source. If you want to understand how Neopagans think—and what they think about—this is the book you want to read. (Note: Some of the interviews in this book discuss socially and sexually deviant behavior, and some of the photo illustrations contain some nudity. Read with discretion and discernment.)

Bibliography

Adler, Margot, 1986; *Drawing Down the Moon: Witches, Druids, Goddess-Worshippers and Other Pagans in America Today,* 2nd ed. (Boston, MA: Beacon Press).

_____, 2000; "A Time for Truth" *Beliefnet,* August 2000. [www.belief.net/story/40/story_4007_1.html]

Alba, De-Anna, 1989; "The Goddess Emerging" *Gnosis,* Fall 1989.

Alexander, Brooks, 1982; "The Rise of Cosmic Humanism" *SCP Journal,* vol. 5:1, 1982.

_____, 1984; "Occult Philosophy and Mystical Experience" *SCP Journal,* vol. 6:1; Winter 1984.

Alexander, Brooks, and Burrows, Robert, 1984; "New Age and Biblical Worldviews" *SCP Newsletter,* vol. 10, no. 5; Winter 1984-5.

Badman, Derik A., 2002; "Academic Buffy Bibliography" *Slayage: The Online Journal of Buffy Studies,* no. 7; December 2002. [http://slayage.tv/essays/slayage7/Badman.htm]

Bainbridge, William Sims, and Stark, Rodney, 1980; "Superstitions, Old and New" *The Skeptical Inquirer;* Summer 1980.

Barker, Jason, 1998 I; "Youth and the Occult" *Watchman Expositor,* vol. 15, no. 6; 1998. [online version: www.watchman.org/occult/teen witch.htm]

Barker, Jason, 1998 II; "Youth-Oriented TV and the Occult" *Watchman Expositor,* vol. 15, no. 6; 1998. [online version: www.watchman.org/occult/youthandoccult.htm]

Berger, Helen, 1999; *A Community of Witches—Contemporary Neopaganism and Witchcraft in the United States* (Columbia: University of South Carolina Press).

"Bewitched" (Web page). [www.cwrl.utexas.edu/7Ewomen/mysteries/siesing/final/witchy_women/untitled/bewitching.html]

Binford, Sally; "Are Goddesses and Matriarchy Merely Figments of Feminist Imagination?"; in Spretnak, ed., 1982 (see full entry below).

Branwen's Cauldron (Web site). [www.branwenscauldron.com/ new_ books.html]

Brooke, Tal, 1990; "Lowering the Stairway to Heaven into the Abyss" *SCP Journal*, vol. 9:3; 1990.

CBN, 1999; "CBN News Report," aired on *The 700 Club*, June 30, 1999.

Clark, Lynn Schofield, 2003; *From Angels to Aliens—Teenagers, the Media and the Supernatural* (Oxford: Oxford University Press).

Clifton, Charles S., 1991; "How the Craft Was Crafted" *Gnosis*, Fall 1991.

Cohn, Norman, 1977; *Europe's Inner Demons: an Enquiry Inspired by the Great Witch-Hunt* (New York: Penguin USA).

Cumont, Franz, 1912; *Astrology and Religion Among the Greeks and Romans* (Mineola, NY: Dover Publications).

Davis, Erik, 1993: "Techgnosis, Magic, Memory, and the Angels of Information" *The South Atlantic Quarterly*, vol. 92, no. 4; Fall 1993.

_____, 1995: "Technopagans: May The Astral Plane Be Reborn In Cyberspace" *Wired*, no. 3.07; July 1995. [online version: www.wired.com/wired/archive/3.07/technopagans.html]

Devin, Pat, 1998; "An Interview with Pat Devin" Web site of Cyberwitch.com [www.cyberwitch.com/wychwood/Library/interviewWith PatDevin.htm].

Dugan, Ellen, 2003; *Elements of Witchcraft: Natural Magick for Teens* (St. Paul, MN: Llewellyn Publishers).

Edwards, Catherine, 1999; "Wicca Casts Spell on Teenage Girls" *Insight*, October 25, 1999.

Eliade, Mircea, 1958; *Patterns in Comparative Religion* (London: Sheed and Ward; reprint ed. 1963; NY: Meridian Books).

_____, 1976; *Occultism, Witchcraft and Cultural Fashions—Essays in Comparative Religion* (Chicago: University of Chicago Press).

Eller, Cynthia, 1993; *Living in the Lap of the Goddess: The Feminist Spirituality Movement in America* (Boston: Beacon Press).

Ellmore, Taylor, 2003; "Invoking Buffy—Discovering the Magic of Pop Icons" *New Witch*, issue #4, Summer 2004.

Frew, D. Hudson, and Korn, Anna, 1991; "Or Was It?" *Gnosis*, Fall 1991.

Frew, Don, 2002; interview with author.

_____, 2003; "The Covenant of the Goddess & the Interfaith Movement: Transforming Our Community, Changing the World." [CoG Web site: www.cog.org/interfaith/index.html]

Genge, N.E., 2000; *The Book of Shadows: The Unofficial "Charmed" Companion* (New York: Three Rivers Press).

Gibbons, Jennifer, 1998; "Recent Developments in the Study of the Great European Witch-Hunt" *The Pomegranate: Journal of Pagan Studies,* issue #5; Lammas, 1998. [online version: www.cog.org/witch_hunt.html]

_____, 1999; personal correspondence with author.

"Goth," 1998; "Goth," Alt.Culture Web site. [www.altculture.com/aen tries/g/goth.html]

Graves, Robert, 1948 (amended and enlarged ed., 1966); *The White Goddess* (NY: Farrar, Straus and Giroux).

Guinness, Os, 1994 (original ed., 1973); *The Dust of Death: The Sixties Counterculture and How It Changed America Forever* (Wheaton, IL: Crossway Books).

Harvey, Graham, 2000; "Fantasy in the Study of Religions: Paganism as Observed and Enhanced by Terry Pratchett" *DISKUS* vol. 6 (2000). [online version: www.uni-marburg.de/religionswissenschaft/journal/diskus]

Harvey, Linda P., 2002; "Heresy in the Hood II: Witchcraft among Children and Teens in America" Web site of Leadership U. [www.leaderu.com/theology/teenwitchcraft.html]

Hawkins, Craig S., 1990; "The Modern World of Witchcraft, Part One" *Christian Research Journal,* Winter/Spring 1990.

_____, (1990) "The Modern World of Witchcraft, Part Two" *Christian Research Journal,* Summer 1990.

_____, 1996; *Witchcraft—Exploring the World of Wicca* (Grand Rapids, MI: Baker Books).

Herrick, James A., 2003; *The Making of the New Spirituality: The Eclipse of the Western Religious Tradition* (Downers Grove, IL: InterVarsity Press).

Horne, Fiona, 2003; *Witchin: A Handbook for Teen Witches* (Rockport, MA: Thorson's Publishing).

Hughes, Pennethorne, 1965; *Witchcraft* (Baltimore: Penguin Books).

Hutton, Ronald, 1991; *The Pagan Religion of the Ancient British Isles* (Cambridge, MA: Blackwell).

_____, 1999; *The Triumph of the Moon—A History of Modern Pagan Witchcraft* (Oxford: Oxford University Press).

Isaacs, Barbara, 1997; "Most Teens Don't Cross the Line, Say Students," *Lexington Herald-Leader,* April 13, 1997.

Kelly, Aidan A., 1991; *Crafting the Art of Magic, Book I: A History of Modern Witchcraft, 1939-1964* (St. Paul, MN: Llewellyn Publications).

King, Francis, 1970; *The Rites of Modern Occult Magic* (NY: Macmillan).

Leland, Charles Godfrey, 1974; *Aradia, or the Gospel of the Witches* (London: David Nutt; reprint ed. New York: Samuel Weiser).

Lewis, I.M., 1971; *Ecstatic Religion: An Anthropological Study of Spirit Possession and Shamanism* (Baltimore: Penguin Books).

Lewis, James R., 1999; *Witchcraft Today: An Encyclopedia of Wiccan and Neopagan Traditions* (Santa Barbara, CA: ABC-CLIO).

Lippy, Charles, 1994; *Being Religious, American Style: A History of Popular Religiosity in the United States* (Westport, CT: Greenwood Press).

Loveland, Anne C., 1997; *American Evangelicals and the U.S. Military, 1942-1993* (Baton Rouge: Louisiana State University Press).

Manoy, Lauren, 2002; *Where to Park Your Broomstick: A Teen's Guide to Witchcraft* (New York: Simon & Schuster/Fireside).

Martello, Leo, 1973; *Witchcraft: The Old Religion* (Secaucus, NJ: University Books).

McGuire, Seanan, 2002; "Witchcraft on 'Buffy'" *New Witch*, #1, Autumn 2002.

Miller, Laura, 2003; "The Man Behind the Slayer" *Salon*, May 20, 2003. [online version: http://archive.salon.com/ent/tv/int/2003/05/20/whedon/]

Molnar, Thomas, 1974; "The Gnostic Tradition and Renaissance Occultism" *The Journal of Christian Reconstruction*, Winter 1974.

Montgomery, John Warwick, 1973; *Principalities and Powers* (Minneapolis, MN: Bethany Fellowship).

Mulrine, Anna, 1999; "So you want to be a teenage witch? How-to books may be just for fun—or not" *U.S. News and World Report*, March 1, 1999.

Murray, Margaret, 1921; *The Witch Cult in Western Europe* (Oxford: Oxford University Press).

_____, 1933; *The God of the Witches* (London: Sampson, Low, Marston & Co., Ltd.).

_____, 1954; *The Divine King in England* (London: Faber & Faber, Ltd.).

Nightmare, M. Macha, 2001; *Witchcraft and the Web: Weaving Pagan Traditions Online* (Toronto: ECW Press).

Nigosian, Solomon Alexander, 1978; *Occultism in the Old Testament* (Philadelphia and Ardmore, PA: Dorrance and Company).

Nisbet, Matt, 1998; "Why Are We Pushing Witch Craft on Girls?" *The Skeptical Inquirer Electronic Digest;* October 28, 1998.

Nugent, Christopher, 1983; *Masks of Satan* (London: Sheed and Ward).

Pagans on Campus (Web site). [www.apocalypse.org/pub/u/hilda/collpgn.html]

Pike, Sarah M., 2001; *Earthly Bodies, Magical Selves: Contemporary Pagans and the Search for Community* (Berkeley, CA: University of California Press).

R., Skippy, 2002; "The Door Theologian of the Year" *The Door;* Sept.-Oct., 2002, #183. [http://thedoormagazine.com/archives/buffy.html]

Radio U, 1999; Columbus (Ohio) interview on Bash morning show, August 12, 1999.

Rain, Gwinevere, 2002; *Spellcraft for Teens: A Magickal Guide to Writing and Casting Spells* (St. Paul, MN: Llewellyn Publishers).

Ratliff, John, 1999; "Witch Hunt" *Texas Monthly;* October 1999.

Ravenwolf, Silver, 1998; *Teen Witch: Wicca for a New Generation* (St. Paul, MN: Llewellyn Publications).

Reisberg, Leo, 2000; "Campus Witches May Wear Black, But Don't Look For Hats or Broomsticks" *Chronicle of Higher Education, Internet edition;* October 20, 2000. [http://chronicle.com/free/v47/i08/08a04901.htm]

Robinson, Tasha, 2001; "Joss Whedon" *The Onion;* Sept. 5, 2001. [www.theonionavclub.com/avclub3731/avfeature_3731.html]

Rose, Elliot, 1962; *A Razor for a Goat—A Discussion of Certain Problems in the History of Witchcraft and Diabolism* (Toronto: University of Toronto Press).

Rosin, Hanna, 1999; "Religious Base" *Washington Post;* June 8, 1999.

Russell, Jeffrey Burton, 1972; *Witchcraft in the Middle Ages* (Ithaca, NY: Cornell University Press).

_____, 1980; *A History of Witchcraft* (London: Thames and Hudson).

Silk, Mark, 1999; "Something Wiccan This Way Comes" *Religion in the News;* vol. 2, no. 2; Summer 1999 (The Leonard E. Greenberg Center for the Study of Religion in Public Life, Trinity College, Hartford, CT).

Spretnak, Charlene, ed., 1982; *The Politics of Women's Spirituality* (Garden City, NJ: Anchor/Doubleday).

Summers, Montague, 1926; *History of Witchcraft and Demonology* (London: Kegan Paul).

_____, 1926; *Geography of Witchcraft* (London: Kegan Paul).

_____, 1937; *Popular History of Witchcraft* (London: Kegan Paul).

Topel, Fred, 2004; "Talking about the Buffy Series Finale" About Network. [http://actionadventure.about.com/cs/weeklystories/a/aa041903.htm ?terms=Joss+Whedon]

Vale, V. and Sulak, John, 2001; *Modern Paganism: An Investigation of Contemporary Pagan Practices* (San Francisco, RE/Search Publications).

Valiente, Doreen, 1973; *An ABC of Witchcraft Past and Present* (NY: St. Martin's Press).

_____, 1989; *The Rebirth of Witchcraft* (Custer, WA: Phoenix Publishing).

Walker, Wren, 1998; "Were We 'Charmed'?" Witchvox.com; October 13, 1998. [www.witchvox.com/media/charmed.html]

Webb, James, 1974; *The Occult Underground* (La Salle, IL: Open Court).

_____, 1976; *The Occult Establishment* (La Salle, IL: Open Court).

Wereszynski, Kathleen, 2002; "Wicca Casts Spell Over College Students" Fox News Network, December 10, 2002.

Wheatley, Dennis, 1935; *The Devil Rides Out* (London: Hutchinson).

_____, 1943; *To the Devil—A Daughter* (London: Hutchinson).

_____, 1960; *The Satanist* (London: Hutchinson).

_____, 1971; *The Devil and All His Works* (London: Hutchinson).

White, Jr., Lynn, 1967; "The Historic Roots of Our Ecologic Crisis" *Science* (March 1967; 155: 1203-7).

Williams, Charles, 1941; *Witchcraft* (London: Faber and Faber; reprint ed., 1959; New York: World Publishing/Meridian Books).

Wilson, Colin, 1971; *The Occult* (New York: Random House).

Winslade, J. Lawton, 2001; "Teen Witches, Wiccans, and 'Wanna-Blessed-Be's': Pop-Culture Magic in Buffy the Vampire Slayer" *Slayage: The Online International Journal of Buffy Studies 1* (2001). [www.slayage.tv/essays/slayage1/winslade.htm]

Wood, Jamie, 2001; *The Teen Spell Book: Magick for Young Witches* (Berkeley, CA: Celestial Arts).

Wood, Peter, 2001; "Strange Gods—Neopaganism on Campus" *National Review Online*, September 5, 2001. [www.nationalreview.com/comment/comment-wood090501.shtml]

Cultural Background from Harvest House Publishers

Becoming Gods

Richard Abanes

As man is, God once was;
As God is, man may become.
—Lorenzo Snow (1814–1901), former LDS president

Did You Know Mormons Hope to Eventually Become Gods?

This and other Latter-day Saint doctrines can lead to misunderstanding and conflict when you interact with Mormon friends, neighbors, and co-workers. If you find yourself confused by their religion—a religion that has increasingly come to resemble mainstream Christianity—you're not alone.

Richard Abanes' thorough yet accessible approach helps you understand not only what today's Mormons believe, but also how they think about and defend their faith. The award-winning journalist offers the results of his research into many key teachings and beliefs, such as—

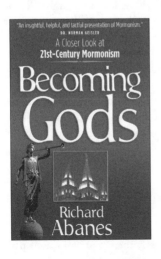

- who God is, who Jesus is, and what it means for us to participate in their divine nature

- why Joseph Smith and his visions have such a central place in the hearts of Mormons

- what role the Book of Mormon and other authoritative writings play in LDS beliefs

- how Mormons are now dealing with evangelicals' criticisms of their faith

- how you can graciously live out God's love in your interactions with members of The Church of Jesus Christ of Latter-day Saints.

"An insightful, helpful, and tactful presentation of Mormonism."
—Dr. Norman Geisler

Books You Can Believe In®
HARVEST HOUSE PUBLISHERS

Cultural Background from Harvest House Publishers

The Battle for Truth

DAVID NOEBEL

*"This is, in my opinion, one of the finest books to
come off the press in this century."*
—D. James Kennedy, Ph.D.

*"Today's [Christians] are not being destroyed because secular
humanism is superior but because they are not exposed to the biblical
alternative, which makes much more sense. This book provides that
alternative in an interesting and convincing manner."*
—Dr. Tim LaHaye

The battle that rages for our hearts and minds is nothing less than a battle for truth. The Christian worldview is under attack from a variety of directions. Competing worldviews have infiltrated every area of modern society—education, politics, business, the media—and exercised a powerful influence on the way we think and behave. In such a battle, there is no room for ignorance. We cannot effectively combat an adversary we don't understand.

In this engaging book you'll find an easy-to-read summary of the worldviews that challenge traditional Christian values, as well as the resources you need to develop a better understanding of the biblical perspective on such subjects as economics, ethics, sociology, and psychology. *The Battle for Truth* is an important resource for every Christian who wants to make a greater impact for Jesus Christ in today's world.

Ways to Engage Our Culture from Harvest House Publishers

Fearless Faith

JOHN FISCHER

My prayer is not that you take them out of the world but that you protect them from the evil one.
—Jesus (John 17:15)

Living Beyond the Walls of "Safe" Christianity

FEARLESS FAITH

JOHN FISCHER

Author of *Real Christians Don't Dance*

It's not always easy to be a Christian these days. We live in a culture that frequently challenges the very foundations of our faith. Our natural response is to flee from the criticisms and the negative influences that surround us, creating our own safe Christian environment in an unsafe world. But as John Fischer reminds us, that's not what Jesus intended.

We are not called to form a Christian subculture to protect ourselves from being offended or challenged, but to fearlessly engage our culture at every level with the hope and promise of the gospel. In this provocative book, Fischer reminds us that we are to be *in the world*—part of the dialogue—and making a contribution to every area of our lives from a perspective of faith.

Fearless Faith will help those who desire to impact their world...

- understand the true meaning of being "in the world, but not of the world"
- find the courage to bring God's light to life's darkest corners
- learn to recognize the many ways that God is already at work in the world
- change their world by becoming constructively involved in it

Ways to Engage Our Culture from Harvest House Publishers

Finding God Where You Least Expect Him

JOHN FISCHER

Where Has God Gone?

Wouldn't it be great to be able to see God not just high and lifted up, but here on earth in the flawed, the poor, or the unfinished qualities of our lives? To

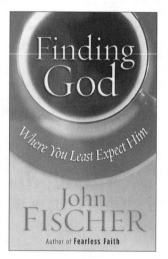

really see Him in the average, everyday activities we take for granted? Imagine being able to find God—and all the wisdom, strength, and solace of his presence—where we least expect him.

John Fischer has taken his gift of words and put them down in a thoughtful, encouraging way that will help you discover more of God in the world around you. You will see how you can

- find a holy God in an unholy world
- be changed from the inside out
- relate to the humanity of Christ
- hear God in unlikely places
- worship in each new moment

This is where real faith begins: seeing God down...around...in...out...through ...beyond...before...after...between...and in the middle of...everything.